M A R Y ' S   R E C I P E   B O X

Mary's Recipe Box

CULINARY

SOUVENIRS

FROM AROUND

THE WORLD

by Mary Gubser

5 JUIL 1964
FRANCE

CONSULATE OF THE HASHEMITE

23 MAR
1967

★ NEW YORK ★

COUNCIL OAK BOOKS, TULSA

Council Oak Books, Tulsa, OK 74120

First edition
00 99 98 97 96   7 6 5 4 3 2 1

Book and cover design by Carol Haralson
Cover illustrations by Pat Briggs

ISBN No. 1-57178-015-7

Library of Congress Cataloging-in-Publication Data

Gubser, Mary.
    Mary's recipe box : culinary souvenirs from around the world / by Mary
Gubser. -- 1st ed.
                    p.   cm.
        Includes index.
        ISBN 1-57178-015-7

        1. Cookery, International.   2. Gubser family.   I.Title.
TX725.A1G755   1996
641.59--dc20   96-9002
                                                          CIP

FOR NICK, PETER
AND MICHAEL

Itinerary

The Bewitching Egg

SUMMER IN THE COUNTRY

Salads

POINTS OF DESTINATION

Entrees

BEEF

VOYAGES BY SEA

Fish and Seafood

Vegetables

WHOLESOME ADVENTURES

Grains

SAVORING THE MEMORY

Desserts

When my three sons approached the dining table for a meal, the first requisite was removing shoes. Boys kick! Kicking is a natural instinct and not one that a parent can really control. Without shoes, the kicks are softer, creating a minimum of fussing from combatants and fewer reprimands from parents. We did not demand that the boys clean their plates for this is an unjust disciplinary action inherited from the old world that could turn a lovely meal into disaster.

With three healthy, active sons and a busy husband to feed, cooking became one of my main priorities. Their health depended on what I offered for breakfast, lunch and dinner. I approached cooking seriously, dabbled a little in the field of nutritional studies (where prevailing opinions have certainly swirled in circles the past fifty-five years) and worked at cooking well balanced meals. With all this preparation, I had no intention of spoiling a meal by constantly subverting surreptitious kicks and chiding the boys to clean their plates. I wished to create a memorable, satisfying meal with conversation at the boys' level as well as our own, a meal meant to be a delightful family time, just as I was fortunate enough to enjoy as a girl.

I received three small cookbooks as wedding presents. (I still have one — a *Good Housekeeping* now in tatters and held together with a rubber band.) With advice from my mother and mother-in-law and a fairly logical twenty-one-year-old mind able generally to follow a recipe, I began melding food together into menus and figuring out how to whip all that stuff on the table hot. I learned what a family enjoyed. I became adventuresome and tried new ideas, then listened to various verdicts and opinions, such as, "What is that?" At times I simply whisked everything off the table and brought out the jar of peanut butter, crackers, cheese, plenty of milk and dessert. As the boys became older, I occasionally heard one slyly comment, "This tastes like peanut butter."

New experiences accrued with dinner and cocktail parties, special holiday meals, cooking outside, and picnics aboard the Queen Mary. The latter was a houseboat built as our sons entered their teens where for eleven summers we floated each weekend, surrounded by skiing boats, feeding and sleeping twenty to thirty parents and teenagers from a kitchen just large enough for me. What fun to try a myriad of ideas, some of which have remained as permanent cards in my files. Fad foods faded in and out. They were fun to try and mostly forget. As the boys grew older and World War II ended, traveling became an integral part of our family life and this, too, widened my knowledge. I learned of foods that I knew little about, foods often not available in the Midwest.

When our eldest son was seventeen, he decided to take time off between high school and college, to go around the world with a pack on his back. He had saved money from raising pigs on our small farm. We matched the amount, gave our consent and off he journeyed on five dollars a day. When he returned a year later I put the final touch on my curry dinner, page 128. He taught me to love yogurt, for in his travels this was cheap food that he could load with free sugar. Another son at seventeen obtained a job with a French pipeline crew in southern France and became fascinated watching the French workmen wash their luncheon glasses in wine. He taught me how to cook asparagus in a French manner, hot with a vinaigrette dressing. The third son hitchhiked from Sweden to Greece bringing me a variety of food ideas, for this son would eventually go into the food business. When our eldest son took a degree in Oxford, we joined him to enjoy a Tale of Two Cities, London and Paris, experiencing the charms and cuisine of both English and French private homes — from English trifle to rabbit pâté. Fortunately my husband was willing to wander off the beaten track not only in the United States, but also in Canada, Mexico and around the world. Even in Soviet Russia we found fascinating foods and people. Often we were the only foreigners, and there my love for fine caviar was satisfied.

A three-week journey through southern Florida with my sister, Kay Loring, restaurant columnist for the *Chicago Tribune*, was one of my most superb and enlightening experiences. We literally ate our way from Palm Beach to Key West, across the Tamiami Trail and up the western coast to Tampa diverting to interior restaurants such as Chalet Suzanne where syrup for pancakes is served in a bud vase. We ate diligently, interviewed chefs and owners, watched kitchen preparations, tried an incredible variety of foods while my sister wrote stories about our adventures for two weeks. Then one night we quit, ate a bowl of cereal, slept well, and started in again, happily joined by my husband and youngest son for the final meals. The *Chicago Tribune* printed a series of thirteen narratives that I still treasure — "Have Appetite, Will Travel, Kay Loring in Florida." How much weight did I gain? Five pounds; not bad!

I've loved working with both elegant and delightfully simple foods, but also have had great fun with wild experiences such as Scottish haggis — not too bad if drowned in aged Scotch whiskey! I tried all the "innards," heart, brains, kidneys, sweetbreads, using mostly French concepts, for they waste nothing. I've watched men cooking in a restaurant kitchen in the country of Georgia, women making breads in the blistering heat of Egypt, a young hippie preparing sourdough pancakes in Alaska. I've admired the magnificent kitchen of famous chef Paul Bocuse in Lyons, France, and exchanged books with him. I've baked johnnycake with real Indian corn in a charming kitchen in Rhode Island, learned the secret of Indian fry bread in the Navajo Nation capitol, Window Rock, Arizona, enjoyed sniffing a tremendous lamb stew simmering for 125 Hutterites in their communal kitchen in Montana, relished an elegant luncheon with J. Paul Getty at his castle in Guilford, England, sipped coffee and nibbled on hot biscuits with an Amish family in Pennsylvania accompanied by a nineteen-year-old grandson, and been enthusiastically hugged by a huge female Armenian cook in a hillside restaurant overlooking the city of Yerevan, Armenia.

Through all these challenging years of experiences, I read, researched foods both modern and ancient, enjoyed lessons with the famous, and loved it all. Constantly I have fought for a reasonably healthy diet, accepting with "a grain of salt" the denunciation of many foods. When the opportunity arrived, I began teaching, writing, demonstrating, working in television, and finally — the icing on the cake — my youngest son Michael opened a restaurant-bakery which he named Mary's Bread Basket for my first book. Following this success, three more Mary's Bread Basket restaurants have been created.

Much has happened during the fifty-two years of my marriage, so join me in reading adventure stories and trying recipes my family and friends have enjoyed, those I have taught and researched. There will be my own escapades, those of my sons, and those of my six grandchildren. This look at the contents of my "recipe box" is also a nostalgic look at the past, for I've literally enjoyed two lives — first with my family, and then in a profession. Cooking has given me many pleasures, pleasures I have been fortunate to share with other people whose lives have touched mine.

To create a cookbook and family travelogue from a lifetime of favorite recipes and the memories they evoke has given me the opportunity to reminisce, modernize old recipes, incorporate many from my classes and invent new ideas. Such a personal cookbook could only be accomplished with the assistance of my family and very special friends. This story begins with my marriage in 1937 when all I knew how to cook was hot fluffy rice, and continues to the present. Finally, I have the opportunity to write a grateful thanks to these wonderful people for helping to fashion my work.

To my youngest son, Michael, who has an unusually fine sense of flavors, for his thoughtful suggestions and to both Michael and his wife, Laura, for proofreading that helped mold the manuscript together.

To Dora Malone for her patient support in testing and tasting.

To special people for specific recipes: Annie Gubser, Janet Loring, Pat Biggs, Ana Maria Jones, Judy Bell, Rosalie Talbott, Jonnie Johnson, Lynn Davis, Josette Spehl, Frank Hightower, Jo Spencer, Karen Weber, Denise Minard, Jeanne Earlougher, Beth Hemm.

To those who are always willing to taste, compare and return again: Ethel Kulhanek, Lois Brown, Marge Cooper, Dottie Wood, Margaret Davis, Midge Shanks, Margie Earl, Martha Cole, Emily Jane Etherton, Rosie Child, Mary Helen Stanley, Clara Walrod, Mary Jane Kaho, Ruth Holton, Maxine Nickel, Mary Ringland, Nancy and Raymond Feldman.

It was only with the advice and support of a devoted family and superb friends that my recipe box and head full of memories developed into this book, and I thank them all.

Appetizers

Spain, Italy and Lebanon, their shorelines on the warm Mediterranean, are blessed with olives, herbs and lemons. Through many years they have developed an incredible variety of subtle and delicious appetizers, yet each is quite different. Spain is redolent with history, revolutions, art, olives and oranges. Italy is filled with treasures and superb food, and Lebanon is steeped with ancient history, though it has recently suffered political chaos. All three I've enjoyed during their most engaging periods of modern history.

A drive across southern Spain can be almost monotonous with seemingly millions of olive trees but walking into a bar for *tapas* is very exciting. Most people enjoy their glasses of wine and *tapas*, which means "covered," while standing — perhaps the better to move from one lively conversation to another. Centuries ago, bartenders placed small rounds of bread atop glasses of wine to keep out flying insects. Little dishes of food eventually began to be served with the bread. Everywhere, in *tapas* bars and in hotels, there are always lush, meaty green olives and beautifully toasted almonds. There is often a choice of baked eggs and chorizo sausage, a variety of cod dishes, fish of all kinds, salads and even "potato chips"! In a country where lunch may be served at two or three in the afternoon and dinner as late as midnight, *tapas* quell or enhance the appetite — and sometimes make a complete meal as they did for a friend and me on the Costa del Sol. What fun to dip into a variety of divine dishes, several of which we could not identify.

In Rome it was suggested we drive a few kilometers outside the city to a country restaurant just to enjoy the hors d'oeuvres. My husband and I approached the rustic, rambling house surrounded by trees and were immediately relieved of our car and escorted inside. After all the formalities had been quietly observed, we requested the hors d'oeuvres. To our amazement we were conducted to a large room filled with tables overflowing with flowers and herbs and gazed at tiers of trays holding 100 appetizers. I was totally bewildered to be engulfed by so many beautiful bits of foods, all of which I would enjoy tasting. My favorite, zucchini flowers stuffed with a soufflé of cheese and quickly deep fried, melted in my mouth. With waiters hovering, anxious to explain their lovely cuisine, we did make a small dent, relishing each bite.

Before our first visit to Beirut, we were invited to dinner at a Lebanese-American home in a small city south of Tulsa where the living room reminded me of that country Italian restaurant. But here several ornately arranged tables were covered not with Italian appetizers but with a multitude of Middle Eastern hors d'oeuvres. And we were surrounded by one of the happiest families I've had the pleasure of meeting — a perfect beginning for our adventure into a world of flavors theretofore unknown to us. A favorite was *baba ghannouj* (eggplant) and steak tartare but all were beautifully seasoned with sesame seed paste, cinnamon, basil, parsley and lovely fresh olive oil. The next time I reveled in such flavors was in magnificent Beirut, where my son Peter found his bride and her wonderful Armenian family. When Peter received his master's degree, he honored us with a cocktail party at the Alumni Club on the campus of the American University of Beirut so we could meet his friends and professors. Three long tables arranged in a U shape were decorated lavishly with colorful flowers and a multitude of Lebanese appetizers. There was even sliced lamb on an upright spit with a tall, handsome chef wielding a long, sharp knife to slice off bits of lemon-scented meat. Before guests arrived I poked around leisurely and found many dishes we had enjoyed during our introduction to Lebanese cuisine in Oklahoma. The most delightful event of the beautiful evening was meeting lovely, dark-eyed Annie. Although she and Peter were just dating, my instinct told me that she was going to be a part of our lives.

Later we walked through the gold *souk* filled with tiny shops glittering with jewelry. In each one we entered a small boy immediately dashed out and returned within seconds swinging a tray of tiny cups filled with strong hot coffee. Finally we entered a large store specializing in copper, brass and jewelry. After an effusive greeting and a few purchases, the owner approached my husband with the greatest bargain in Beirut. He had just received, from a princess, an elaborate emerald necklace, earrings, bracelet and ring, all for a very special price. As my husband shrugged, he offered the possibility of just the ring or perhaps the earrings which could be purchased separately. My husband loved the presentation but declined. That evening we dined on the top floor of our hotel, the Phoenicia, watching the United States aircraft carrier *Enterprise* outlined with lights where it lay anchored in the bay. As we were dining on American steaks flown in that day, I saw the owner of the copper and brass store gaily escorting a modishly dressed, tall, dark beauty to a special table. He must have sold the entire emerald package!

Often in a Beirut restaurant we were presented with a small bowl of *hummus tahini*. I began to wonder if this was the national dish. If so, they could not have chosen a better one, though I doubt our daughter-in-law Annie Gubser would agree, for her passion was stopping in a bakery to order what I would call a quick Lebanese pizza —

pita bread sprinkled with *zataar* (a combination of herbs, mostly thyme) and olive oil, then run quickly into a huge oven, rolled and thrust into a piece of protective paper. One ate it walking down the street. There seemed to be tiny bakeries every other block. When Annie asked me to make a special bread for New Year's, I requested yeast so she dashed into one of these bakeries and came out with a huge blob of fresh yeast wrapped in paper – price five cents.

It really is a toss-up which dip I love the best — *hummus tahini* or *baba ghannouj*. Both are most flavorful and delightfully nutritious, as one concentrates on eggplant and the other on garbanzo beans. Both include t*ahini*, sesame seed paste, that may be purchased in specialty and import shops or health food stores. Often the oil has gathered at the top; stir very well. Refrigerate and it will keep much like peanut butter.

HUMMUS TAHINI (CHICK PEA DIP)

2 to 3 cloves of garlic

2 cups canned chick peas (garbanzos)

Half of the liquid from the can of chick peas

$^1\!/_2$ teaspoon salt

7 tablespoons tahini (sesame seed paste)

$^1\!/_3$ cup lemon juice

Olive oil

Chopped parsley

Pita bread

Peel the garlic and whirl in a food processor fitted with the steel blade. Add the chick peas, liquid from the can, salt, tahini and lemon juice. Whirl until the mixture is smooth. Stop once and scrape down the sides with a rubber spatula and pulse again. Transfer to a shallow decorative dish, making a swirl with the end of a wooden spoon. Fill the swirl with olive oil and sprinkle the parsley over all. Serve with pita bread torn in pieces on a side dish. This will make about 3 cups of chick pea dip.

BABA GHANNOUJ (EGGPLANT DIP)

2 large eggplants

2 large cloves, garlic, peeled 1 teaspoon salt

4 tablespoons tahini (sesame seed paste)

Juice of 2 lemons

Olive oil

Chopped parsley

Pita bread

Char the eggplant in a hot oven, placed on a baking sheet, turning to blacken the skin all around the vegetables. Or stick an eggplant on a long fork and char over the flame of a gas burner. Keep turning until the skin is black. When the skin has blackened, place the vegetables in cool water and peel. Transfer the eggplants to a large bowl. Put the garlic cloves through a press and combine with the salt, mashing together and add the tahini and lemon juice stirring very well. Mash the eggplant to a fairly smooth consistency. (Do not use a food processor, for there must be some texture.) Blend in the garlic-tahini sauce. Taste for salt and lemon and adjust. Pour the dip into an attractive shallow serving bowl and swirl olive oil around the top. Sprinkle with chopped parsley. This amount will be sufficient for 25 to 30 people for a cocktail party. Serve with pita bread sliced or torn into pieces for dipping.

One of my nostalgic memories of pre-civil war Beirut is of a small nut shop. In the center of the room was a huge round copper bin with compartments, each with a glass front displaying huge pistachios, almonds hazelnuts, cashews, pine nuts — even walnuts, but not pecans. The copper bin was heated so all the nuts were cozy and warm. Every cocktail bar, restaurant, private home — all served small bowls of nuts, carrots and potato chips. I love mixed nuts served warmed. It's fun just to watch guests flip through picking out their favorites — a pastime of my youngest grandchildren.

TOASTED NUTS

Purchase untoasted, unsalted mixed nuts in a health food store and then toast them in your own oven. Heat the oven to 300°, place the nuts on a baking sheet and toast until just turning color. Stir occasionally and watch carefully so they do not overcook or burn.

The adventures of my sons have led to a number of food discoveries for me. One involved not the southern Mediterranean, but the American South, where people delight in entertaining. Mississippians are experts in giving lavish barbecues and cocktail parties that always feature genuine mint juleps. Southern hospitality is epitomized by "Aunt Kate" who picked up two of my sons on a barge when they canoed the length of the Mississippi River, took them home, washed their clothes through three cycles and let them gorge on fresh vegetables, then put them back on the river. This is Aunt Kate's dip.

VICKSBURG CLAM DIP

3 cups minced onions

2 cups minced green peppers

¾ cup butter

2 pounds American or Velveeta cheese

7 six-ounce cans minced clams, drained

1 cup tomato ketchup

3 tablespoons Worcestershire sauce

4 tablespoons dry sherry

1 teaspoon cayenne pepper

Large corn chips

In a large skillet sauté the onions and green peppers in the butter until soft. Cut the cheese in cubes and add to the skillet, stirring until melted. Blend in the clams, ketchup, Worcestershire sauce and sherry. When the mixture just begins to bubble, stir in the cayenne pepper very well. Taste and adjust — it should have a good peppery flavor. Serve in a heated chafing dish with large corn chips. The recipe makes a goodly amount, easily sufficient for 30 people. The clam dip may be doubled and can be prepared and frozen for future use.

One versatile food as welcome as hospitality is cheese. Pastry-encrusted cheese makes a luscious appetizer to be offered in small portions Serve in elegant simplicity on a tray or board for ease in slicing. A larger cheese may be used, and if so the pastry can easily be doubled.

CAMEMBERT OR BRIE EN CROÛTE

½ cups sifted all purpose flour

⅛ teaspoon salt

2 ounces cream cheese

¼ cup unsalted butter

1 Camembert or Brie cheese, 4½ ounces

1 teaspoon lemon juice

1 egg yolk beaten with 2 teaspoons water

Sift flour and salt together. Place the cream cheese and butter in a mixing bowl and add the flour mixture. Cut the butter and cream cheese into the flour with a pastry blender until mixture resembles coarse crumbs. Shape into a ball. If preferred, combine the flour, salt, cheese and butter in a food processor fitted with the steel blade. Pulse until the mixture forms a ball. Remove, shape into a firm ball and cover with plastic wrap. Refrigerate 4 hours or overnight.

Unwrap the Camembert, make cross marks on top with a fork and sprinkle with the lemon juice, rubbing it in gently with a finger. Place in a small bowl, cover and refrigerate 3 to 4 hours. Remove pastry from refrigerator. Flour a board or pastry cloth and a rolling pin liberally. Roll pastry, cutting out and 8-inch circle and transfer to a baking sheet. Place the cheese in the center of the pastry circle. Pick up edges of pastry and pleat around the cheese, pulling together at the top. With remaining pastry, cut out leaves with a small pastry wheel, 2 to 3 inches long. With the tip of a sharp knife, etch veins in each leaf. Place the three leaves atop the pastry with stems at the center and pinch together. The leaves should drape over the sides. Cover loosely and refrigerate overnight. Preheat oven to 425°. Bake the cheese 20 minutes or until it is a light golden color. Place on serving tray and let cool about 10 to 15 minutes before slicing. Serves 4 to 6.

Cheese also stars in miniature pizzas, which make intriguing small appetizers that may be partially prepared in advance, then finished and baked when guests arrive. They are perfect with cocktails, except that they seem to disappear with one round of serving. The croustades can be made several days in advance and frozen. The recipe makes 24 mini-pizzas with perhaps a bit of cheese left.

MINIATURE PIZZAS

Soft butter

1 loaf unsliced white, whole wheat or oatmeal bread

Cherry or Italian plum tomatoes

2 tablespoons Dijon-type mustard

6 ounces Gruyere cheese, thinly sliced

1 to 2 teaspoons mixed Italian herbs*

Freshly ground black pepper

3 ounces Gruyere cheese, grated

Olive oil

Brush 24 muffin cups (2½ inches) thoroughly with soft butter. Slice the loaf of bread into 24 thin slices, about ¼ inch thick. With a biscuit cutter, 2¾ to 3 inches, cut one round out of each slice of bread. (Use remainder of bread to make bread crumbs, croutons for salads or feed to the birds). Fit each slice into a muffin cup and press down lightly. They should flare up the sides a tiny bit. Toast in a preheated 350° oven about 10 minutes or just until a light golden color. (No more for they must bake again.) Remove from muffin tins to cook and place on a baking sheet. Or the croustades may be covered carefully and frozen.

Preheat oven to 400°. Wash, dry and slice tomatoes. Drain on paper toweling to get rid of excess moisture. With a spoon or brush, coat the inside of each croustade with the mustard. Place a thin slice of cheese on the bottom. Top the cheese with a slice of tomato. Sprinkle with Italian herbs, a bit of pepper and grated cheese. Just before baking, sprinkle each with a few drops of oil. Bake about 5 to 8 minutes or just until the cheese is bubbling. Do not overcook as the croustades will have burned edges. Serve while warm.

*Italian herbs: Several spice companies sell jars of mixed Italian herbs in the supermarket. If not available, combine one teaspoon each of the following herbs: oregano, marjoram, thyme, savory, basil, rosemary and ½ teaspoon sage. Mix well and store in a covered jar.

FETA CHEESE IN A CHAFING DISH

Melt 2 tablespoons butter in a small chafing dish (6 to 8 inches wide) and coarsely crumble ½ pound of feta cheese into the butter. Insert a half lemon in a muslin cap and place on the tray holding the chafing dish. As the feta becomes hot, squeeze lemon juice over the cheese.

With a teaspoon serve the hot cheese on crackers or lavosch (Armenian cracker bread). A most charming appetizer to lay out in front of guests on a coffee table.

BAKED BRIE

Especially suited for a Brie that is not quite ripe, for the result is a quick and delicious warm cheese. The following ingredients will be needed: 1 whole medium or small Brie, butter, sliced almonds and brandy. Preheat oven to 325°. Place one tablespoon of butter on a baking sheet with the Brie on top. Dot the Brie with bits of butter, sprinkle with sliced almonds and then lightly with brandy. Place in the oven to heat about 10 minutes or until soft inside but not runny. Timing should be extended if the Brie is cold. If the Brie becomes too soft it is difficult to slice. Serve while warm with delicate white crackers.

GOAT CHEESE SPREAD

Allow the following ingredients to reach room temperature: 4 ounces cream cheese, 4 ounces goat cheese and ½ cup butter or margarine. Try yogurt or tofu in place of the cream cheese - not quite so rich and certainly most healthful. Mix together in a bowl thoroughly. Spread the mixture on small slices of pumpernickel or mixed grain bread or rye crackers. Serve as an open sandwich when using the bread or closed with two thin slices of bread.

BELGIAN ENDIVE WITH CHEESE

Wash and dry Belgian endive leaves. Pipe soft cream cheese filled with herbs down the center of each leaf. A variety of soft cream cheeses flavored with different ingredients are easily available. Or when the very first asparagus arrives that is tiny and slender, wash, pour boiling water over the vegetable and drain immediately. Run cool tap water over the vegetable and drain. Place a single spear in the center of an endive leaf and cover lightly with alfalfa spouts. Arrange in a spoke fashion with a flower at the ends. Lovely to see and guests appreciate the light calorie content.

HUNGARIAN CHEESE MOLD

8 ounces cream cheese

¼ pound unsalted butter

3 tablespoons sour cream or plain yogurt

¼ pound ricotta or cottage cheese

4 scallions, finely chopped

1 tablespoon Hungarian sweet paprika

1 1/2 teaspoons caraway seeds

1/2 teaspoon salt (optional)

1 tablespoon capers

Chives

Small can chopped anchovies

Thin slices rye bread

Black radish curls*

Allow the cream cheese, butter, sour cream and cottage cheese to reach room temperature. Combine in a food processor with steel blade, pulsing to blend ingredients. Into the bowl add the chopped scallions, paprika, caraway seeds and salt; taste before adding the salt for both the capers and anchovies are salty. Whirl the mixture until well mixed and smooth. Remove from the bowl into a mixing bowl and fold in the capers. Transfer to a serving plate and shape into a smooth round mold. Sprinkle the top with chopped chives. The mold may be refrigerated until ready to serve. Separately beside the mold serve the chopped anchovies and bread slices. Surround the mold with black radish curls. The mixture makes 2 cups.

*Black Radish Curls: Black radishes lend drama to this hors d'oeuvre. Wash the radishes thoroughly. Do not peel. Cut into thin slices with a mandoline or a very sharp knife. Soak in ice water to make the slices curl. These may be prepared ahead, placed in plastic bags and refrigerated.

From São Paulo, Brazil, comes the following intriguing appetizer, given to me by a charming friend, Ana Maria Jones. Ana Maria is married to an eminent Tulsa journalist. With her Brazilian background, exotic touches give excitement to her cuisine. We both agree these appetizers are best when served warm, for the banana seems to melt into the other ingredients. Most satisfying and stimulating — and they can be made in any quantity desired, so no ingredient amounts are given.

A BRAZILIAN HORS D'OEUVRE

Toasted bread rounds, 1 1/2 inches in diameter

Pimento cheese, soft and spreadable

Slices of banana

Cinnamon sugar

Cut 1½-inch bread rounds with a biscuit cutter and toast until just lightly golden in a 350° oven. White, whole wheat or sourdough bread may be used. Remove from the oven and allow to cool on the baking sheet. Spread each round with soft pimento cheese and top with a slice of banana. Combine 2 tablespoons of cinnamon with 1 cup of sugar and mix well. Sprinkle cinnamon-sugar atop the banana slices. These may be made about two hours before guests arrive. Pop into an oven, set on broil, about 6 to 8 inches from the element. Broil until the cinnamon mixture begins to bubble, which will take only a few moments. Remove from oven and arrange the appetizers on a serving plate. Serve as soon as possible, while still warm.

Shrimp de Jonghe is an enchanting appetizer served in ramekins or for a light luncheon entree. The complete dish may be prepared ahead and frozen or prepared the morning of a party, covered and refrigerated. Remove an hour before guests arrive and bake immediately as wine and cocktails are served.

SHRIMP DE JONGHE

1½ cups dry white bread crumbs

¼ cup finely chopped green onions

¼ cup finely chopped parsley

¾ teaspoon dried tarragon

4 cloves garlic, minced

¼ teaspoon nutmeg

Dash of mace

Dash of thyme

Grindings of black pepper

1 cup melted butter

½ cup dry sherry

2 pounds cooked medium shrimp

Combine all ingredients except the shrimp, mixing thoroughly. In a separate bowl blend one-half the mixture with the shrimp. Divide the shrimp among 8 buttered ramekins or scallop shells. Top each with the remaining crumb mixture. Bake in a preheated 400° oven 10 to 15 minutes or until hot and lightly browned.

La Posta, a fine Mexican restaurant, was established many years ago in Messilla, New Mexico, north of El Paso. I met Katy, the owner, who explained as we walked through the five dining rooms that La Posta had been on the Butterfield Express and was the spot where Billy the Kid was tried. Katy unlocked a back kitchen door and we stepped into her private apartment — a Hollywood setting, including an indoor swimming pool, lavish rugs and furniture, and a huge round bed. One would never suspect all this was behind the restaurant. I loved Katy's guacamole salad, fried pies, tacos — in fact all the food was excellent. But for this recipe I have chosen to follow the directions of a friend whose home is in Taos, Rosalie Talbott. Serve as an appetizer accompanied with corn chips or blue corn chips or as a salad placed on a large leaf of red tipped lettuce. Dark-skinned avocados such as Haas will have the richest flavor.

GUACAMOLE

2 ripe avocados, medium sized

2 tablespoons lemon juice

1 clove garlic pressed or $\frac{1}{4}$ teaspoon garlic powder

2 tablespoons grated onion

4 tablespoons finely chopped tomato

Tabasco to taste

Salt, optional

Cut the avocados in half, discarding the seeds and scoop the flesh into a shallow mixing bowl. Mash with a fork. (Guacamole must have texture; do not use a food processor.) Add the lemon juice, pressed garlic and onion. Mix very well and stir in the tomato and several dashes of Tabasco. Taste for salt content and Tabasco, for it is up to your taste how hot you wish the guacamole to be. This amount will serve 4 as a salad and 10 as an appetizer.

Note: A delightful Mexican cook taught me that if a really fiery guacamole is preferred, add one small finely chopped jalepeño pepper. That will do it!

There are far more salmon in Alaska than people, for the population of our forty-ninth state is no larger than my city of Tulsa. Alaska is a land of mountains, gorgeous inland lakes, wildlife, valleys, ice cold river glaciers, fifty below zero temperatures (at which point the fog crackles when an automobile drives through) and hundreds of miles of beautiful wilderness. We spent four weeks covering as much as humanly possible from Pt. Barrow above the Arctic Circle to Valdez, the southernmost point, landing on a Mt. McKinley glacier in a tiny plane, cruising a glacial lake watching two enormous glaciers "calve" under the midnight sun with seals diving around us and hundreds of Arctic birds perched on small icebergs. We enjoyed Matanuska Valley where cabbages grew twice as large as my head, flew over huge converging glaciers larger than Delaware and Vermont put together and watched salmon swim up river to spawn and die. For a fisherman who lands beautiful salmon, there are smoke houses to have them finished and mailed home. Serve salmon with elegant simplicity for perfect enjoyment.

If a fragment of the beautiful smoke salmon is left over, make a salmon mold — the best way to stretch a small amount of smoked salmon. Any remaining portion of the mold will make a beautiful sandwich on a sourdough rye bread — so nothing is wasted!

SMOKED SALMON

Serving a Whole Smoked Salmon: Line a long platter with crisp leaf lettuce and place the salmon on top. At one end, arrange a mound of drained aromatic capers and at the opposite end about ½ pound of chilled cream cheese. A tiny spoon should be placed beside the capers. Provide triangles of rye or whole wheat bread on the side and guests will have a delightful time stacking all these lovely goodies to create their own hors d'oeuvres. I have noticed at my cocktail parties that smoked salmon disappears first, down to tiny flakes, for guests literally hover over this colorful fish.

SMOKED SALMON MOLD

8 ounces smoked salmon

20 ounces cream cheese, softened

2 tablespoons capers with a little juice

Lemon juice to taste

Chop the salmon in coarse pieces. In a mixing bowl, combine the salmon with the softened cheese (allow cheese to become room temperature or place in a microwave oven for a few seconds). Add the capers and several drops of lemon juice. Stir until well mixed. Taste and adjust for the lemon flavor. Transfer to a crystal plate and mold smoothly into a mound. Serve with small slices of rye bread or whole wheat crackers. Serves 25-30.

Lunch was served at our Kiev hotel at two in the afternoon and from there we flew to Moscow for our final night in Russia. On the flight our tour guide announced that dinner would be at six that evening. There was no way in such a short time that I could possibly ingest another four-course meal served en masse to 2000 people. My husband and I slipped away to do some last-minute shopping in the hotel store and to our delight found a jar of caviar, a pint of vodka and a large can of Greek orange juice. Happily we returned to our room with our treasures and arranged seats by the windows of our room overlooking Red Square. We enjoyed caviar on English wheatmeal crackers I had tucked in my suitcase and drank toasts with orange juice and vodka, laughing over the hard pallet beds, the rigidity of the tour guides, and the lack of communication between countries within the Soviet Union. (This was in the mid-seventies.)

Suddenly we wondered if our conversation was being recorded by the KGB. This cold-war-era superpower seemed like a third world country all dressed up with a huge military machine. There were no refrigerated trains or planes, few paved highways, and the airplanes seemed to be held together with rubber bands. However, we certainly did enjoy the caviar!

Russian caviar makes a splendid and handsome first course or an appetizer that can be made completely the day before a party. Red caviar is a must here for its brilliant color.

RED CAVIAR SOUFFLÉ ROLL

Melted butter

1/4 cup butter

1/2 cup all purpose flour

1/2 teaspoon salt

2 cups milk

4 egg yolks

1 teaspoon salt

1 teaspoon sugar

4 egg whites, stiffly beaten

FILLING

6 ounces cream cheese

4 ounces red caviar

Sour cream

Red caviar for decoration

Preheat oven to 325°. Brush a 10x15" baking sheet heavily with melted butter. Cut a piece of wax or parchment paper to fit into the baking sheet. Brush again with melted butter. Dust lightly with flour and set aside.

Melt the ¼ cup of butter in a saucepan. Whisk in the flour and salt; stir over medium heat for 2 minutes. Gradually add the milk continuing to whisk constantly 4-5 minutes or until the mixture is thick and smooth. Remove from the burner and blend in the egg yolks and sugar. Transfer to a mixing bowl and fold in the beaten egg whites. Spread batter evenly on prepared baking sheet. Bake in preheated oven 40 minutes.

While the soufflé is baking, prepare the filling. Allow cream cheese to soften — it may be placed in a microwave oven for about one minute. Beat the cheese in a small bowl of an electric mixer until fluffy. Fold in the caviar. If the mixture seems too soft, refrigerate until the soufflé has finished baking.

Spread a large, thin tea cloth on a counter. When the soufflé is golden, turn out immediately on the cloth. Remove paper and discard. Spread the caviar filling over the soufflé. Roll from the long side with the aid of the tea cloth, jelly-roll style. Hold tea cloth firmly and turn the roll on the seam. Tighten the roll and place in the refrigerator to chill.

If serving the following day, wrap the roll in plastic wrap and refrigerate. Slice and serve on small plates as an appetizer or a first course. With a first course, add a dollop of sour cream on top of each slice and decorate with half a teaspoon of red caviar. The soufflé roll will serve 10 to 12.

The most beautiful sausage in brioche I've tasted was a first course in the famous restaurant of Chef Paul Bocuse in Lyons, France. The sausage was studded with pistachios; the brioche melted in my mouth. I could have eaten every bite but dared not, as there were six courses yet to come! Unfortunately, it is rare to find such magnificent sausage in our country.

For the sausage in brioche that follows, find a good summer sausage about 12 inches long and 2 inches in diameter. This will easily feed ten to twenty people depending on the thickness of the slices.

The sausage in pastry makes a most delightful attraction for a buffet table, and it can be prepared the morning of a party with no loss of quality.

SAUSAGE IN BRIOCHE

FOR THE SAUSAGE

1 summer beef sausage, 12 inches long

2 cups dry red wine

1 recipe brioche (recipe following)

1 egg yolk

Flour

1 whole egg, beaten

Place the sausage in cold water, bring to a boil, lower heat and simmer 30 minutes. Remove pan from heat and cool sausage in the water 30 minutes. With a sharp knife remove skin from the sausage. Measure the wine into a skillet and immerse the sausage in the wine. Bring to a simmer, turning the sausage occasionally, until the wine has evaporated. Cool the sausage.

Sprinkle a counter or pastry cloth with flour and roll out the brioche dough, making a rectangle 3 inches larger than the sausage. The dough must be wide and long enough to cover the sausage. Brush the cooled sausage with beaten egg yolk and sprinkle lightly with flour. Place on the brioche dough and roll around the sausage, sealing tightly by using a little water and pressing down the dough. Fold or pleat the ends, dab with a bit of water and press tightly to seal. Place on a baking sheet seam side down. Let rise 45 minutes. Brush with the beaten whole egg. While the dough is rising, preheat the oven to 400°. Bake the sausage about 30 minutes or until the brioche is golden. Cool slightly before slicing.

FOR THE BRIOCHE

¼ cup warm water

1 package quick-rising yeast

3 cups all purpose flour

4 large eggs

½ teaspoon salt

½ pound butter, at room temperature

Combine the water and yeast in a small bowl, stirring with a fork until dissolved. Place the remaining ingredients in a large bowl of an electric mixer. Start mixing on low speed, adding the yeast mixture slowly. When the ingredients hold together, scrape down the sides of the bowl and then beat at medium speed 8 minutes. Place the dough in a bowl, cover with plastic wrap and a towel. Allow to double in bulk about 1 to 1½ hours. If desired, knead down and refrigerate, covered, overnight and finish rolling with the sausage the next morning. Otherwise knead down, cover and let rest 10 minutes and roll out as directed above.

Along with cheese, seafood, and pastry of all sorts, soups make splendid appetizers and first courses. In our travels, we found Tangiers to be the place for soups. To my delight and that of my companions, we were wafted into a lush Arabian dining room carpeted with deep Persian rugs and huge, comfortable pillows on banquet seats. I slid into one corner and reclined comfortably on two pillows — Ah, a loaf of bread and jug of wine! The first course was a sensational soup. The energetic Moroccan brought the soup pot to offer more and I could not resist asking how the soup was prepared. In other words, could I obtain the recipe? He was most pleased, disappeared and returned bearing a plate with an onion, celery, tomato, parsley and some chick peas. He explained the preparation. The entire group of Americans laughed with delight as they followed his elaborately descriptive gestures. From there on it was up to me to hurriedly scribble down the information. He and I exchanged cards and parted great friends.

A MOROCCAN SOUP

2 large tomatoes, peeled, seeded, chopped

2 cups chopped celery

1 large onion, coarsely chopped

1 cup coarsely chopped parsley

8 cups beef or chicken broth

4 sprinklings of paprika

2 dashes cayenne pepper

2 tablespoons flour

2 tablespoons soft butter

1 cup canned garbanzos (chick peas)

1 cup broken spaghetti (bite-size)

In a large soup pot combine the tomatoes, celery, onion, parsley and broth. Bring to a boil, lower heat to simmer and add the paprika and cayenne pepper. Continue to simmer, stirring occasionally until vegetables are tender, about 30 minutes. Remove from heat and whirl in a food processor fitted with a steel blade or use a blender. Return to a clean soup pot and place over medium heat. With a fork mash the flour and butter together into a paste. Add ½ cup of hot soup stirring until smooth. Add this mixture to the simmering soup whisking constantly until lightly thickened. Add the garbanzos and spaghetti and let boil 15 minutes. When I first prepared this soup, I made cornbread and a fruit salad and relished my Arabian-American dinner! Serves 8.

After another fine meal in Tangiers, I awakened suddenly one night staring into a darkened room and realized the heartwarming soup we had for dinner was French, for I had enjoyed it many times in southern France. But, of course, the waiters were French, the manager, French — for Morocco was imbued with French influence. A light, cool breeze came through the door opened to our secure balcony, the city quiet at two in the morning. We were in a five-star hotel, Moroccan style—no air conditioning. I smiled in the darkness knowing a talk with the manager could easily produce the recipe or at least a list of the ingredients. The next morning the manager enumerated the contents of the soup, all vegetables. An inexpensive, delicious, healthful dish — do try it.

COUNTRY FRENCH SOUP

2 large potatoes (baking), peeled and cut in cubes

2 large carrots, scraped and thinly sliced

1 large onion, peeled and coarsely chopped

2 tomatoes, peeled, seeded and chopped

5 cups water

4 tablespoons butter

Salt and grindings of pepper to taste

$^1/_2$ cup freshly chopped parsley

Combine the potatoes, carrots, onion and tomatoes in a large saucepan and add the five cups of water. The vegetables should be well covered with water so add more if necessary. Bring to a rapid boil over medium high heat and cook about 30 minutes or until all vegetables are very very tender. Remove from burner and whirl in a food processor fitted with a steel blade. If necessary, stop and scrape down the sides. Remove to a clean saucepan and add the butter. Over medium heat bring to a simmer adding salt and pepper tasting to your satisfaction. The parsley may be added to the soup or sprinkled on top when served. In Tangiers the cook had added the parsley when being whirled in the food processor. Serves 8.

Note: Only the ingredients were given to me, not how much of each. One could add another carrot or tomato but personally I was pleased with the result. If the soup becomes too thick, add a little water to gain the consistency desired but not too thin for this is a robust vegetable soup.

Another light and delightfully refreshing soup course that can be put together in minutes is Consommé Madrilène. For an appetizer, serve in flared liqueur glasses or demitasse cups using small demitasse spoons. For larger portions, cream soup bowls are excellent. Ingredients given will be for one appetizer — from there triple and quadruple to the number being served.

CONSOMMÉ MADRILÈNE WITH CAVIAR

2 tablespoons consommé madrilène

1 tablespoon light sour cream

1 heaping teaspoon red caviar

Several excellent brands of canned consommé madrilène are on the market. Select one can and refrigerate until thoroughly chilled. Spoon the consommé in chosen receptacle and top with sour cream. Spread the caviar across the sour cream, place spoon with the appetizer and serve. A different and intriguing beginning for an elegant dinner that is most refreshing to the palate.

JELLIED CONSOMMÉ MADRILÈNE

Spoon chilled jellied consommé madrilène into small porcelain bowls or demitasse cups. Add a slice of fresh lemon or lime, a touch of chopped parsley and serve with a demitasse spoon. Refreshing and delicious.

Like the French, the Italians make wonderful soups. As souvenirs of Italy, we brought back memories of a kind Italian couple who helped us secure a hotel room when we were lost in Turin — and also this soup, served that evening. After a few experiments I discovered how easily pasta soup can be prepared with the variety of excellent tortellini available in most supermarkets. The vegetables listed are optional; without them the soup can be prepared in 30 minutes.

TORTELLINI SOUP

2 quarts chicken broth, preferably homemade

1 or 2 packages (9 ounces each) tortellini

$\frac{1}{2}$ cup slivered carrots, optional

$\frac{1}{2}$ cup slivered celery, optional

$\frac{1}{2}$ cup diced tomato, peeled and seeded, optional

Bring the chicken broth to a rapid boil in a large saucepan or kettle. If just the tortellini are preferred, add 2 packages to the broth, bring back to a boil and cook until very tender and more than tripled in size, 20 to 25 minutes. Here is a list of the tortellini that are especially good: chicken and vegetable, cheese and basil, chicken and rosemary, sweet Italian sausage, beef and herbs. There will be others to choose but avoid just plain cheese as there is little flavor.

If the vegetables are desired, add those first to the boiling broth and cook 10 minutes. Add one package of tortellini and continue boiling until tender, 20 to 25 minutes. Either recipe will serve 6 generously.

In so many parts of the world, delicious little bites are likely to accompany whatever refreshing beverage is served. To round out an hors d'oeuvre table, or just to present with drinks, the following simple dishes are perfect.

PRUNES WITH BACON

Marinate 2 to 3 pounds of pitted prunes in a bowl, crock or a glass jar with sufficient dry red wine to cover, for one week or longer. The fruit will keep indefinitely if left in the wine, covered and refrigerated-great for emergencies or just to nibble on for yourself.

Thinly slice bacon, drained prunes and toothpicks will be needed. Slice each piece of bacon in half. Wrap the prunes with the bacon and secure with a toothpick.

Place on a baking sheet and set aside until ready to serve. Preheat broiler and broil the fruit on one side until bacon is lightly browned. Turn fruit over and broil the other side. Serve while hot.

LEBANESE OLIVES

$\frac{1}{2}$ pound green cracked olives

$\frac{1}{2}$ pound black Greek olives

1 tablespoon vinegar

2 stalks celery, cleaned and cut diagonally

1 medium onion, quartered and sliced diagonally

2 teaspoons oregano

2 tablespoons olive oil

Both types of olives may be found in import stores and fine supermarkets. Place the olives in a bowl. Add the remaining ingredients and mix thoroughly. Transfer to a glass jar, cover and refrigerate one week before serving.

The Bewitching Egg

Traveling abroad can present charming food, beautiful vistas, and excitement with awesome, dreadful and dreamy events. One incident, for me, simply became tricky. In the fascinating city of Manila, my husband and I went shopping. While he was being fitted for a shirt, I watched several employees preparing lunch, which seems to be a custom in all Asian countries. (If pots and pans aren't provided they bring their own, cooking a meal in the back but usually eating in the front part of the store, to avoid missing any customers, I presume.) Because of my great interest in breads, I asked one Filipino woman if her national cuisine included special breads. Her response was an immediate negative but she wanted to know if I had eaten Filipino eggs. It so happens that when I travel I read prodigiously about each country on that specific journey. I knew immediately what she meant by "our eggs." Their egg is called a *balut*. It is a boiled duck's egg with embryo (all intact inside) and is considered a delicacy. My knowledge emanated from Fodor's book on Southeast Asia. I do relish his books for they provide many such little gems of information. *Balut* are supposed to be great with beer — lots of beer. To my surprise, the woman scurried into the back and returned with a large bowl filled with hot eggs. I knew exactly what was inside each egg and I had absolutely no desire to eat a hot, dead, unborn baby duckling. Generously she brought a paper plate with a sprinkling of salt and gave me two eggs. There I was face to face with two hot *balut*. No doubt this could lead to a tricky international situation.

My mind was racing; there was no way I could bite into one of those eggs. I thanked her profusely and asked if I could take the eggs to my hotel where I had happily left my camera explaining I wished to take a picture when I opened the *balut*. She was most agreeable, nodding her head, and so proudly I picked up those two intact warm eggs and walked out. When I entered the sanctity of our room, I whipped out the camera, placed it in my husband's hands, and broke open the *balut*.

There was the complete little embryo with feet, beak, eyes and body all wrapped around what I suppose was a portion of the yolk — there was no white left, just a little juice. I flushed it away but took the second *balut* downstairs where a bus was waiting to take our group to the airport. Quite a few fellow travelers gathered around when they heard I had this funny egg. I broke the egg over some paper and I thought the women were going to faint. The men sort of edged away — chicken, you know.

The chicken before the egg or the egg before the chicken? The egg came first, of course, for in very ancient Greece, ducks and geese and other such birds were found nesting with eggs. This preceded the chicken, and it was long before eggs were accepted as food. After all, the egg is in the chicken and the chicken is in the egg.

By the thirteenth century eggs were important in the diet of western Europeans and in many odd ways used to cure coughs, irritation of the windpipe, hoarse voice and to warm the blood. One ancient recipe describes "Eggs on a Spit — Pierce eggs lengthwise with a well-heated spit and turn them over the fire as if they were meat. They should be eaten hot. This is a stupid invention and foolish behavior and sport for cooks" — 1475.

With eggs in the refrigerator, no modern cook need be at a loss for an emergency meal. Eggs may be scrambled, baked, sautéed, steamed, coddled and transformed into elegant Eggs Benedict. During the seven days of a week, one can have a differently prepared egg each morning with ideas to spare. They lend themselves to beautiful desserts, sauces for meats and fish, and they give lightness to cakes. Without eggs there would be no angel food cake, mayonnaise, or Hollandaise. So, a tribute to the indispensable egg!

If there is a cholesterol problem in your family, you can, in many instances, throw the yolk away and just use the whites. Egg substitute products are principally egg whites with a myriad of flavors added to (hopefully) make the product taste and act like an egg. In many dishes the substitute can be used successfully in place of the real egg.

Eggs have an amazing affinity for cheese, and, as the knowledgeable Clifton Fadiman stated, "cheese is milk's leap toward immortality."

In the following pages, I have had great pleasure in giving a few directions to deal happily with eggs. In many instances they should be treated gently and cooked slowly to produce a tender, perfect egg. During the first year of my marriage, I met a woman who taught me that egg dishes were some of the most elegant foods in the world. I had to learn what she meant for at that point in my life most eggs had been fried, scrambled and boiled — hard. (That prepared me for my first journey to Russia where we were often served huge bowls of hot, hard-boiled eggs for breakfast.)

Break an egg into a saucer and if the white spreads out over the dish, the egg is several weeks old. If the albumen concentrates around the yolk, the egg is fresh. A fresh egg dropped into a glass of water will stay flat on the bottom. As the egg becomes older an air pocket enlarges and as a result the egg will stand straight in the water. For hard boiling it is best to have eggs about two weeks old simply because they peel easier. In selecting eggs for breakfast, fresh is the ultimate for not only are they more tasteful, but much more attractive when finished. Following are several easy methods of preparing breakfast eggs.

CODDLED EGGS

For one egg, use a small saucepan; for four, a larger pan will be necessary. Fill the pan with water two-thirds full. Bring to a boil.. Remove from burner and with a large spoon slip the egg into the saucepan and cover immediately. For one egg in a small saucepan, set a timer for 8 minutes. Remove cover and break the egg into a small compote or custard cup. Or serve in an egg cup accompanied with a demitasse spoon and scissors to snip off top of the egg. I prefer coddled eggs to soft boiled as the albumen is delicately cooked to perfection. Add a bit of butter as my mother used to do. If preparing a number of eggs in a large saucepan, place the eggs in a wire basket. If there are more than four eggs, increase the time 3 to 4 minutes. (Note: The lid must fit tightly, even with the wire basket inside the saucepan.)

POACHED EGGS

Bring water to a boil in a skillet. Remove from burner, break an egg into a saucer and slide from the saucer into the hot water. A ten inch skillet will hold four to six eggs. I prefer poaching 4 at one time. Cover immediately and allow to sit until congealed. To finish poached eggs, especially when there are several in the skillet, turn off the electric burner, then set the pan back on the cooling element.. With gas burner, turn the fire to the lowest point) Return the skillet to the burner to finish eggs.

(An egg cooked in an electric poacher in little buttered cups can be quite delicious but is not a true poached egg. It is more like a steamed egg and lacks the delicacy of a water-poached egg.)

The French method for poaching is fun and intriguing. Have water boiling in a deep skillet or shallow saucepan. Add one tablespoon of vinegar (helps stabilize the egg). With a spoon stir the hot water around in a circle until it makes a small whirlpool. Break an egg in a saucer and slip from the saucer into the whirling water. The force of the whirling water will encase the albumen around the yolk making a perfect little egg. This is the method used in such places as Brennans in New Orleans.

Eggs poached in milk are exceptionally delicate. Add sufficient milk to fill a skillet two-thirds full. Bring to a simmer, add 2 tablespoons of butter (a perfect amount of butter for 4 eggs), and slip the eggs into the milk. Cover and remove from burner, returning if necessary to finish the eggs. Lift an egg with a spatula to check for doneness.

Serve milk-poached eggs on toast in a shallow soup bowl.

STEAMED EGGS

Melt 2 to 3 tablespoons of butter in a skillet and break four eggs into a saucer one at a time and slip (one at a time) from the saucer into the pan. Add 2 tablespoons of water, cover and let eggs steam for only a minute or two over medium heat until the yolks are glazed over and the whites delicately done.

FRIED EGGS

Measure 2 to 3 tablespoons of butter into a skillet over medium heat. Break eggs into the bubbling butter. A fried egg should never be cooked rapidly for then the albumen becomes tough. Sunny side up, allow them to cook until the whites are softly finished. For those who wish the egg turned, do so with a spatula quickly and cook only a minute. Serve immediately.

EGGS IN TOAST

One of my sons calls this method "Toad in the Hole," which does seem quite appropriate. Cut a small square from the center of a slice of good homemade bread. Have butter lightly bubbling in a small skillet over medium heat. Place the bread in the butter and grill on both sides, then break the egg into the hole. Let cook for a few minutes, then flip the toast and egg over to cook 2 to 3 minutes. A dish my sons loved for it was different, yummy and they liked watching it cook.

OVEN-BAKED EGGS

Brush a small ceramic gratin dish with butter. Break an egg into the dish and pour a small amount of milk or light cream over the yolk. Grate about 2 tablespoons of cheddar or Colby cheese over the top. Place in a preheated 350° oven for 10 minutes. The egg will be perfect. There are gratin dishes just the right size for one egg or two. Small cooked sausages or some slivered ham may be added on the side. All of my house guests ask for baked eggs and that is a delight for they are easy to prepare and quite elegant with a handsome coffee cake.

HARD-BOILED EGGS

Place the number of eggs desired in a saucepan. Fill the pan with cool water so the eggs are covered and place on medium high heat. Bring just to a boil, lower heat to simmer for 10 minutes, no longer. Remove from burner, pour off the hot water and run cool water over the eggs to stop the cooking.

SCRAMBLED EGGS

Use two eggs per person. Break them into a mixing bowl and stir with a fork or whisk just until they are mixed, no more. Melt butter (about 1 teaspoon per egg) in a skillet and when the butter begins to foam, slowly pour the eggs into the skillet. With a large silver or wooden spoon stir carefully. Until the eggs begin to congeal, lower heat as they should not cook too fast. Continue to stir until softly done. Transfer to a warm platter with your choice of bacon, sausage or ham.

Classically, one small slice of truffle always topped Eggs Benedict, but after truffles rose to $100 per can, most cooks turned to olive slices. A visit with my sister, Kay Loring (who was a restaurant columnist for the *Chicago Tribune*) into the kitchens of the famous Brennans in New Orleans presented some interesting facts. Brennans poaches a million eggs each year and that is accomplished in pans that can hold 24 eggs at one time. Usually one or two eggs are ruined and tossed away. Eggs Benedict is the most popular of their egg dishes and each that I have had at Brennans has been perfect. I prefer to use Holland rusks and found that this, too, is Brennans' preference. If you are an English muffin fan, they certainly work very well; they're just more difficult to cut. No specific number of ingredients will be given, just general directions.

EGGS BENEDICT

Holland rusks, English muffins or toast

Canadian bacon

Soft Poached Eggs, page 41

Blender Hollandaise Sauce, 231

Paprika

Truffle or black olive slices

Parsley

Holland rusks may be toasted lightly or untoasted. English muffins must be split and toasted. Sauté or grill the Canadian bacon and poach the eggs. Top a rusk with one slice of grilled bacon, then a soft poached egg. Ladle Hollandaise sauce over all, sprinkle with a bit of paprika for color and top with an olive slice. Garnish with parsley sprigs.

These puffed savory eggs are excellent for an emergency breakfast as all ingredients are simple. Toast and bacon can be prepared while the eggs bake. The omelet will serve four to six. More people? Make two at one time!

A BAKED OMELET

1 cup grated American or cheddar cheese

2 tablespoons butter

$\frac{1}{2}$ cup light cream or milk

1 teaspoon dry mustard

$\frac{1}{2}$ teaspoon salt

Grindings of black pepper

6 eggs, lightly beaten

Preheat oven to 325°.

Thoroughly brush soft butter over an 8-inch round, deep glass pie plate or similar dish. (Pottery is attractive.) Spread the cheese on the bottom. Dot with the 2 tablespoons of butter, cut in pieces. Combine the cream or milk, mustard, salt and pepper. Pour half the cream mixture over the cheese. Add the beaten eggs atop this mixture. Swirl the remainder of the cream mixture over the eggs. Bake in preheated oven for 25 to 30 minutes or until puffed and golden. Serve immediately.

BAKED OMELET WITH EGG SUBSTITUTE

Allow a large box of egg substitute (4 eggs) to thaw completely. Follow
directions for A Baked Omelet, but use the egg substitute. I have tested this
with Fleishchman's Egg Beaters and the result was most successful. The
omelet will not rise as high as the original, but is most tasty and satisfying.
Makes 4 large servings or 6 smaller portions.

For a satisfying and easy method of serving poached eggs (with fewer calories
than Eggs Benedict), turn to the trusty tomato. Bacon or ham could be added but
I enjoy this for its simplicity, especially when tomatoes are at their best.

POACHED EGGS WITH TOMATOES

4 Poached Eggs, page 41

4 thick tomato slices

4 Holland rusks

Grated low-fat cheese

Poach the eggs and set aside. Place the tomatoes in a small baking sheet and
bake in a preheated 350° oven 5 to 8 minutes just until warm. Arrange the
rusks on a baking sheet and top each with a slice of tomato and then a
poached egg. Sprinkle grated cheese over each and broil about 10 inches
from the element until the cheese has melted and is bubbling. Serve on
warm plates immediately. Serve 4.

Often I stood in my tiny kitchen aboard our boat, the Queen Mary, and served
25 people the special breakfast dish that follows. Even though there was just room
for me, I had eggs poaching in one skillet, ham sautéing in another and the sauce,
made at home, reheating on a third burner while coffee perked on the fourth.

BAKED EGGS WITH HERBED CHEESE SAUCE

6 large eggs

$1/2$ cup bread crumbs

$1/2$ teaspoon dried basil

1 tablespoon chopped parsley

2 tablespoons butter

Preheat oven to 350°. Brush a glass baking dish or a round attractive pottery plate. Pour one-half the hot herbed cheese sauce in choice of dish. Break the six eggs, one at a time, into a saucer and slip each into the cheese sauce. Spoon a little sauce over each egg. Combine the bread crumbs, basil, parsley and butter.

Sprinkle the crumb mixture over the eggs. Place the baking dish in shallow pan of hot water and cover loosely with aluminum foil. Bake the eggs about 25 to 30 minutes. If you are concerned about how done the eggs are, take a spatula and lift one of the eggs. If not done, bake a few more minutes. Serve each egg atop toast or a Holland rusk. Serves 6.

HERBED CHEESE SAUCE

6 tablespoons butter

6 tablespoons flour

$3/4$ teaspoon oregano

$1/2$ teaspoon savory

$1/8$ teaspoon cayenne pepper

Dash Worcestershire sauce

3 cups hot milk

3 cups grated cheddar cheese

Melt butter in a saucepan and whisk in the flour, stirring rapidly. Add the oregano, savory, cayenne and Worcestershire. Whisk thoroughly and let bubble 1 minute to give the herbs a chance to meld into the roux. Remove from the burner and add the hot milk all at once. Stir quickly with the whisk until smooth. Return to burner and continue cooking until thick and smooth. Add the cheese and blend until melted.

For the baked eggs; this will be more sauce than needed but the remainder can be used over broccoli or cauliflower or may be frozen for future use.

Another good egg recipe for a crowd is poached eggs. The poached eggs that follow are enriched with ham and herbed cheese sauce. Double the cheese sauce recipe if serving 24 guests.

I shall not give a specified number of eggs or other ingredients for this can be prepared for four or twenty-four.

MARY'S SPECIAL POACHED EGGS

Holland rusks

Thin slices ham

Sliced tomatoes

Poached Eggs, page 41

Herbed Cheese Sauce

Have plates ready for serving. Place a Holland rusk in center of each plate. Sauté the ham quickly and place a slice on each rusk. Top that with a slice of tomato. Poach no more than six eggs in one skillet. Lift each egg carefully with a pancake spatula so the water will run off and place an egg on top the tomato. Now pour hot Herbed Cheese Sauce over each and serve immediately. Instead of ham, bacon can be used —2 to 3 slices per rusk. I have tried this with split and toasted English muffins and although quite delicious, they are difficult to cut. I assure you this was always a favorite with both grown-ups and teenagers.

Baked Eggs make a magnificent casserole that can be prepared the day before, refrigerated and baked an hour before serving, relieving the tension of last minute chores. Offer two or three coffee cakes or toasted English muffins, a large bowl of fruit and the menu is complete. The casserole will serve 25.

BAKED EGG CASSEROLE

THE MUSHROOM MIXTURE

1 ½ pounds bacon

¼ cup butter or margarine

1 ½ pounds mushrooms, cleaned and sliced

Sauté bacon in a skillet until crisp and drain on paper toweling. Discard the fat from the skillet, wipe the skillet clean with paper toweling and add the butter. Over medium high heat sauté the mushrooms until tender. Set aside.

THE CREAM SAUCE

½ cup butter or margarine

1 cup flour

6 cups hot milk

Salt to taste

Melt the butter in a large saucepan. Whisk in the flour until smooth and bubbling. Remove pan from burner and add half the hot milk, whisking vigorously. Return to burner and add remaining milk. Cook and stir until mixture is creamy and smooth. Crumble the bacon into pieces and add to the cream sauce with the mushrooms. With the bacon, little salt may be needed but check for seasoning and adjust.

THE EGGS

24 eggs

1 teaspoon salt

1 1/2 cups condensed milk

3/4 cup butter or margarine

Parmesan cheese

Combine the eggs with salt and milk, whisking until smooth. Melt the butter in a large skillet. Add the egg mixture and over moderate heat, stir until a soft mass. Do not cook too long for the casserole will bake for an hour the following day.

Brush a large casserole with melted butter. Beginning with the egg mixture, make alternate layers of egg mixture and sauce. Sprinkle the top with Parmesan cheese. Cover and refrigerate overnight. An hour before guests arrive, remove casserole from refrigerator and bake for one hour in a preheated 275 ° oven. Check to see that the contents are piping hot and serve immediately.

Another delectable make-ahead egg dish is Eggs Chamay. Try them for a breakfast, brunch or luncheon — they fit perfectly in a handsome 8x12″ oval copper pan. The eggs may be prepared and served from such a baking pan or covered and refrigerated overnight, then baked at the last minute until hot and bubbling.

EGGS CHAMAY

4 tablespoons butter

4 tablespoons all purpose flour

2 cups warm milk

Salt to taste

Pinch cayenne pepper

1 $\frac{1}{2}$ cups finely chopped mushrooms

2 tablespoons finely chopped shallots

2 tablespoons butter

10 Hard-Boiled Eggs, page 43

1 tablespoon each chopped parsley and chives

$\frac{1}{2}$ teaspoon each tarragon and chervil

Grindings of black pepper

Salt to taste

1 teaspoon Dijon-type mustard

2 tablespoons soft butter

$\frac{3}{4}$ cup heavy cream

$\frac{1}{2}$ cup grated Gruyère cheese

Freshly grated Parmesan cheese

Fresh bread crumbs

2-3 tablespoons butter, cut in pieces

Prepare a béchamel sauce: Melt the 4 tablespoons of butter in a saucepan and whisk in the flour until smooth. Add the warm milk all at once stirring vigorously until smooth and thickened. Add salt to taste and a pinch of cayenne pepper. Set aside.

Chop the mushrooms finely in a food processor fitted with the steel blade. Slice the shallots and add to the processor pulsing until chopped and mixed into the mushrooms. Melt the 2 tablespoons of butter in a skillet and sauté the mushroom mixture (duxelle) until dry, stirring to avoid burning. Divide the hard-boiled eggs lengthwise. Mash the egg yolks in a bowl and add the mushrooms duxelle. Stir in the parsley, chives, tarragon and chervil. Add the black pepper, salt to taste and mustard. If the mixture seems to be a bit dry, add more soft butter. Stuff each of the egg white halves with the egg yolk mixture. Brush the baking pan lightly with soft butter.

To the béchamel sauce add the cream and Gruyère cheese. Return to a burner and bring just to a simmer, stirring constantly. Pour a thin film of the sauce in the baking pan spreading evenly and arrange the stuffed eggs to fit atop the sauce. Cover the eggs with the remaining sauce. Sprinkle with freshly grated Parmesan cheese and bread crumbs. Dot with pieces of butter. Bake in a preheated 350° oven 20 to 30 minutes or until hot and bubbling. Serve one or two half eggs per person.

Note: If the Eggs Chamay have been prepared and allowed to refrigerate overnight, remove at least one hour before heating. Bake until the complete dish is piping hot and sauce is bubbling.

The Salad Bar

Fresh, crisp, green salads all year around have become one of America's favorite foods. When I was a young girl, cabbage, iceberg lettuce with summer tomatoes, cucumbers and leaf lettuce completed the offerings available. Salad bars mushroomed soon after World War II in motel restaurants, delicatessens, supermarkets and even in fast food chains.

Most importantly, salads are an integral part of our cuisine at home, even at times becoming the main entree. Greens are the basis of any salad, and have been since the days of ancient Rome. How fortunate we are these days to have a tremendous abundance of lettuce and amazing choice of greens. Preparation of a fine, well dressed salad can be delightfully easy with a bit of preplanning, selection and cleaning.

When salad greens are brought home, either wash the leaves under running water or fill a sink with cool tap water and immerse the leaves, swishing around to remove sand and dirt. Shake off the water and spin in a salad dryer. Then place leaves on sheets of paper toweling, roll up loosely to absorb the last of the water on those leaves. (We remove the water so that the salad dressing will cling easily to the leaves.) For the crispest leaves, tuck them in a small plastic bag and refrigerate overnight before using. With other greens such as iceberg lettuce, cut out the core and run water through the head and shake thoroughly. Place on paper toweling cut side down and let drain. Pat as dry as possible, place in a plastic bag and refrigerate. With parsley and similar greens, wash under running water, shake thoroughly or spin as dry as possible. Tuck away in the refrigerator.

The Greens

....

BELGIAN ENDIVE (SOMETIMES CALLED FRENCH ENDIVE):
This is a slender head, 6-8 inches long, with tightly packed leaves shading from white to delicate yellow green tips. New endive plants are tinged with a lovely light

reddish color, some even with lavender! With crisp texture and a delicately bitter flavor, endive blends well with other greens, particularly Bibb lettuce and watercress. Do not wash endive until ready to use. A clean lettuce that keeps well a number of days refrigerated requires a minimum of washing. Core, split and clean under running water. Let drain on paper toweling and pat dry.

BIBB OR LIMESTONE

The sweet flavor and exceptionally delicate texture gives this lettuce a number one place with fine chefs. Often dirt and sand catch in the loosely packed head, but the leaves separate easily for washing. The name Bibb comes from John Bibb, a nineteenth century pioneer in developing this butter lettuce. Perfect for a salad alone or mixed with favorite greens and tossed with choice of vinaigrette dressing. One of my favorite chefs in Ft. Worth, Texas, composes a Bibb lettuce flower for each salad; it looks like a large, loose rose.

BOSTON OR BUTTER

Often confused with Bibb but the leaves are quite fragile and must be washed with care. A soft, mild flavor, Boston may often be found in a perforated plastic box for protection. Both Bibb and Boston are expensive.

CURLY ENDIVE OR CHICORY

A large spreading head with prickly leaves that add a delightful essence to a salad. The leaves are a lovely pale green shading into a darker green. With a light bitter flavor, it is an effective addition to a very large buffet salad mixed with other greens.

ESCAROLE

Similar to curly endive in appearance but the leaves are smoother with wavy edges. The head shades from light to dark green. The enticing flavor gives zip to salads.

ICEBERG OR HEAD LETTUCE

A round, firm head with tightly packed leaves is the best selling of all salad greens, for it is inexpensive, almost always available. Though often maligned because of its bland flavor, the hearts when well crisped can be quite delicious. Select heads that are firm but avoid any that are rusty. With its bald flavor but delightful crispness, iceberg is particularly satisfying combined with oranges and onions and the stronger-flavored dressings.

LEAF LETTUCE

Varies in shades from all green to red tipped. The large, leafy bunches are quite delicate in flavor — another favorite of chefs and caterers, for the leaves are easily handled for use as an under layer with salads, patés, poached or smoked salmon. The leaves should be washed, dried and used quickly as they wilt easily. Medium crisp with a light, lovely flavor, and shading from green to reddish bronze, the leaves mix beautifully with any salad.

OAK LEAF

Shaped similar to leaves of a huge oak tree although indentations are much deeper. Velvety in texture, expensive and found only in well stocked markets.

ROCKET OR ARUGULA

Small, flat tender leaves with a light bitter, peppery flavor adding excitement to a bland salad. Should be used in small quantities, is expensive and not too easily found in American markets but very popular in Italy.

ROMAINE OR COS

Originated on the lovely Greek island of Kos and is one of the highly nutritious members of the lettuce family. Elongated head with crisp, slightly cupped leaves shading from a dark to pale green. It takes particularly well to a vinaigrette dressing. Always a favorite of chefs, romaine became famous as the principle ingredient in Caesar Salad. Break off the outer leaves if they are at all discolored, and wash as directed for leaf lettuce.

SPINACH

Superb for a salad alone when using only the tender young leaves, but must be well washed. Spinach is excellent when combined with other greens, so stop thinking of it as just a cooked vegetable. Spinach salad with bacon, mushrooms and grated hard-boiled eggs has become a favorite of Americans, but spinach blends beautifully with a variety of greens and fruit such as oranges and even strawberries.

RADICCHIO

Small compact head with red leaves embellished with white center and veins. The leaves are so tightly packed that it seems unnecessary to wash them. Usually all the leaves will be edible but discard any on the outside that look discolored or wilted. A mildly, assertive flavor, it is beautiful as an addition to salads. Usually quite expensive.

WATERCRESS

Long stems with dark green leaves which are usually tied in bunches. Be certain to examine the inside of a bunch for any discoloration. The leaves are delicate and should be stored in a tight container or placed in water, for watercress grows in fresh water ponds and streams. I have seen leaves as large as the palm of my hand in a crystal clear Arkansas Ozark Mountain stream. Its light pungent flavor is a marvelous addition to salads and for decoration. Fairly inexpensive and available most of the year.

Leaves can be broad and long but the tender young leaves add a delicious tartness to salads. The French love adding sorrel to soups. Appears only occasionally in American markets but is quite easy to grow. Remember eating sheep's sorrel as children? The flavor is very much the same.

CABBAGE

Green, Red or Savoy. The green solid head is always available, inexpensive and is the basis for many salads and an addition to soups. Riding the train from Moscow to St. Petersburg, we passed mile after mile of cabbages, ready for that cabbage soup thrust at us twice a day. Red cabbage is often used for color in salads, particularly in restaurants - rather like a filler. Savoy is the elegant cabbage both for salads and cooking, having a milder flavor than its cousins.

The Adornments

Herbs, flowers, fruit and an almost limitless variety of vegetables create lovely, satisfying salads for those willing to experiment or desiring only a light green touch for dinner. Listed will be suggestions on the availability of a great variety of these exciting ingredients. From that point it is up to the personality of a family or the occasion, special tastes and willingness to try something a bit new and perhaps exotic. A magnificent salad served me at the Biltmore Estate in North Carolina of fresh fruits and sliced chicken breast was topped with a gorgeous, light lavender flower that I tucked in my hair to enjoy as I drove on through the state of Kentucky. Do expose children to salads. To my enjoyment, I've watched my grandchildren enjoy fresh green salads with a vinaigrette dressing that they love sopping up with a piece of bread.

HERBS

Herbs to think about are basil (good in everything), chervil (for a light salad), dill (most agreeable but particularly adaptive with cucumber and tomatoes), all the parsleys (giving both a bland and a pungent flavor), tarragon (tantalizing on anything but ice cream) and coriander (imparts an exotic flavor). Explore in special sections of the market and you may find fresh mint, marjoram, rosemary, thyme, savory, fennel, wonderful pods of garlic and enticing long leaves of chive.

EDIBLE FLOWERS

Petals of a few edible flowers are enchanting to add in small quantities to a salad for unusual flavor and beauty. Use only those that you know are edible. Petals of nasturtiums (as well as the leaves) are popular. With fruit, try a few petals of roses. I can remember as a child nibbling on rose petals and enjoying the velvety enticing flavor. Violets are particularly lovely with Bibb lettuce; use a vinaigrette dressing made with lemon juice for best effect. Recently in a St. Louis special supermarket, I found plastic boxes with mixed edible flowers among the salad greens.

Making the Salad

Avoid crowding a salad with so many different ingredients that it results in a slippery texture. Greens should be the main interest, so consider color and texture along with flavor. For color, use a few red radishes, red, yellow, orange and green peppers and lovely summer tomatoes. In the winter cherry tomatoes do have a decent flavor. Possibilities are exciting — just walk down the aisle of a beautifully stocked supermarket and choose from a superb variety of mushrooms (such as the delightful Enoki), broccoli, cauliflower, zucchini, red and green onions, shredded carrots, celery and sprouts of all kinds. I always stop when I see an outdoor farmer's market. Recently in Boulder, Colorado, I discovered organic vegetables, hanging baskets filled with lovely herbs, unusual vinegars, plus an amazing variety of hard-to-find lettuces.

Go to a Chinese or Vietnamese grocer for exotic vegetables and excellent sprouts. Grapefruit, orange, avocado, walnuts, capers, hearts of palm, artichoke hearts and gorgeous asparagus make beautiful adornments for salads. Don't forget the star fruit — two slices on the side of a salad is most intriguing and quite delicious. But handsome, crisp, carefully broken lettuce leaves (never slice for the leaves bruise easily) is the prima donna of a salad. Now in many cities, mixed lettuces of superb variety are available in bulk form. They are sometimes called *mesclun*, from the French word *mesclumo*, meaning "mix" or "melange." Select with handy tongs as much as desired placing in a plastic bag — a wonderful and unusual salad is ready for your favorite dressing.

Serving the Salad

Wooden, clear Lucite, ceramic and glass receptacles are my favorites. The bowl must be large enough to toss all the greens and "insides" with no trouble. (By all means, wash salad bowls! An unwashed wooden bowl will soon become rancid, and bugs are attracted to the residue of oil.) Large wooden spoons or Lucite tongs are excellent for tossing, although I often use my hands. (Yes, I wash my hands first.) At a buffet table guests prefer to serve themselves from the salad bowl with tongs; it's difficult to serve oneself salad with two spoons while balancing a plate — and perhaps a glass of wine — in one hand.

Preparing the correct amount of salad is not always easy. Try measuring for a while with a four-cup measure until you get the feel of just how much to prepare. If a leftover salad is not too wilted, cover with plastic wrap and enjoy the following day for lunch. Or try whirling the remains of a salad in a food processor with tomato juice for a tangy soup to sip!

Dressing the Salad

The dressing on a salad will determine its ultimate success and excellence. Heavy dressing will wilt any of the delightful greens and accompaniments, actually making the preparation soggy. A simple vinaigrette dressing is amazingly easy and far superior to any of the multitude of commercial dressings filled with additives. Here's an elementary oil and vinegar dressing from which a number of different versions can be easily prepared. Always use the finest and freshest olive oil or canola oil; both are now recommended for low cholesterol. Red and white wine vinegars are lovely either plain or with herbs added.

BASIC VINAIGRETTE AND VARIATIONS

I cup olive oil

$1/3$ cup red or white wine vinegar

Salt to taste

Grindings of black pepper

Combine all the ingredients in a small bowl and beat with a fork or small whisk until smooth and creamy. Or, place the contents in a jar with a tight lid and shake thoroughly. Or, try a food processor with steel blade in place and pulse ingredients until well mixed and creamy. The dressing will keep very well at room temperature but, remember, the dressing will be at its best when freshly made. (The above recipe may always be cut in half.)

VARIATIONS FOR BASIC VINAIGRETTE

Add any of the following:

2 to 3 teaspoons Dijon-type mustard

I to 2 teaspoons Pommery mustard

1 clove garlic, peeled and halved

1 tablespoon chopped dried tomatoes

A choice of herbs or combination of herbs: tarragon, oregano, thyme, basil, dill, parsley and mixed Italian herbs.

LEMON VINAIGRETTE

Combine ⅓ cup olive oil, 3 tablespoons fresh lemon juice, grindings of black pepper, salt to taste. Whisk or shake the ingredients vigorously. To this dressing may be added 2 tablespoons chopped fresh parsley, 2 tablespoons fresh chopped mint or 1 teaspoon dried mint, 1 clove garlic, peeled and halved. Or add 1 teaspoon Dijon-type mustard. If a stronger and more piquant flavor is desired, try using fresh lime juice instead of lemon.

BALSAMIC VINAIGRETTE

1 garlic clove

1 tablespoon Dijon-type mustard

3 tablespoons Balsamic vinegar

Salt to taste

Freshly ground black pepper

1 cup olive oil

Cut the garlic in half and rub the inside of a small bowl. Reserve the garlic. Whisk the mustard and vinegar together seasoning with salt and pepper. Slowly add the oil in a steady stream whisking constantly until the dressing is creamy and thickened. Taste and correct seasoning. Add the reserved garlic, cover bowl and leave at room temperature several hours. Remove garlic and whisk the dressing just before using.

In the north woods of Wisconsin, where I visited my friend Jo Spencer, chipmunks outnumber the squirrels and a fawn may meander into the yard. (—or even a bear. In my room there was a magnificent bear skin on the wall; rangers had told my host to shoot this bear which kept coming into the yard to forage from the garbage.) Ducks and loons swam gracefully on Lake Shishebogama in a perfect reflection of the beautiful trees and low shrubs as I watched one quiet morning. The whole scene was simply breathtaking. Jo and I talked about the birds and the glacial action over this country several million years ago. Then our thoughts, as always, turned to cooking. Jo had become enamored, as many fine cooks do, with Balsamic vinegar. We created a vinaigrette dressing for our dinner salad that evening, to enhance the fresh whitefish we had purchased on Lake Superior close to the famous Rittenhouse Inn.

BALSAMIC VINAIGRETTE II

1 cup olive oil

1/3 cup Balsamic vinegar

1 teaspoon mixed Italian herbs

1 clove garlic, peeled and pressed

Freshly ground black pepper

Combine all ingredients in a bowl and whisk until light and creamy. Transfer to a jar with a tight lid and set aside. Shake thoroughly just before dressing the salad.

Note: We also tried the addition of 2 teaspoons of Dijon mustard which gives an even more piquant flavor. The mustard is optional.

AVOCADO DRESSING

1/2 cup buttermilk

2 green onions, sliced

1 clove garlic, peeled

2 tablespoons olive oil

2 teaspoons red wine vinegar

1/2 teaspoon dried tarragon

Grindings of black pepper

Salt to tast

1 large avocado, peeled, seeded and diced

Lemon juice

Combine all the ingredients except the avocado and lemon juice in a food processor fitted with a steel blade. Rub a few drops of lemon juice over the peeled avocado to maintain its color, cut it into cubes and drop it into the processor. Pulse several times, remove lid and scrape down the sides. Continue to whirl until smooth. Transfer to a jar with a cover and refrigerate until ready to use. Makes about 1½ cups.

Once I met a chef who told me he could enjoy tarragon on anything except ice cream. I agreed, for I love the herb, especially on veal, chicken, and in salads and sauces. Dried tarragon has a most distinctive flavor and should be used discreetly. Interestingly, the arctic region of Siberia is the original home of tarragon and was not used in Europe until the sixteenth century.

TARRAGON DRESSING

1 medium egg

1 teaspoon dried tarragon

2 tablespoons chopped parsley

1 teaspoon dry mustard

$^3/_4$ teaspoon salt

1 $^1/_2$ tablespoons lemon juice

1 tablespoon chopped shallot

$^1/_2$ cup cider vinegar

1 $^1/_2$ cups olive or canola oil

Place all ingredients except the oil in a food processor fitted with a steel blade. Pulse several times to mix ingredients then blend slowly adding the oil. When all the oil has been added allow to whirl several seconds. The dressing will be creamy, a lovely light color. Makes a bit over 2 cups.

Some Favorite Salads

TOMATOES AND CUCUMBERS

In the summer when tomatoes and cucumbers are at their peak for freshness and flavor, select a long narrow cut glass or white china dish. Peel both the tomatoes and cucumbers and slice evenly. Arrange the two vegetables alternately on the dish. Make one of the Basic Vinaigrette dressings on pages 56-58 and dress the two vegetables. Finely chop fresh parsley, and perhaps a few leaves of chives, and sprinkle atop the tomatoes and cucumbers. All so very simple to accomplish but quite pretty and inviting. For a buffet serving a number of guests, I have used a long narrow fish-shaped dish and placed two rows of tomatoes and cucumbers — certainly a delightful salad that can be prepared a few hours ahead and refrigerated.

All tomato salads were popular on the Queen Mary. Someone would always bring a large sack of fresh tomatoes purchased from a farmer on the way to the lake. Then everyone griped because I insisted they be peeled; but, to me, the peeled tomatoes seemed to absorb the piquant dressing better and were more delicate on the tongue. After all the ingredients were together and drenched with dressing, I would always tuck the large bowl in the Queen Mary's refrigerator — that is if it was running. (Each weekend I opened the door fearfully, for the machine operated on butane which had sometimes evaporated during the week. While someone drove to the nearest spot to obtain a tank of butane, I would throw away all the molded junk and hurriedly wash the little refrigerator clean. There were many ice chests that lined the decks filled with ice, pop, beer and melons, but that refrigerator was my "baby" and very important for all the cooking afloat.) I always had plenty of fresh basil, for once started, this herb will grow like a weed. Indeed, this is a favorite salad for my family and friends.

SUMMER TOMATO-BASIL SALAD

1 large clove garlic, peeled and minced

$\frac{1}{2}$ teaspoon salt

Freshly ground black pepper

2 teaspoons Dijon-type mustard

$\frac{1}{4}$ cup olive oil

2 tablespoons red wine vinegar

6 to 8 medium-size tomatoes

5-ounce can water chestnuts

$\frac{1}{2}$ cup fresh basil, snipped in pieces

Bibb or red leaf lettuce, cleaned and crisped

Combine the garlic, salt, pepper and mustard in a small bowl. With a fork beat in the oil and vinegar until creamy and smooth. Peel the tomatoes and cut in wedges. Slice the water chestnuts. In a large bowl, combine the dressing, tomatoes, water chestnuts and basil. Let stand at room temperature about 20 minutes or in the refrigerator, covered, for one hour. Serve atop leaves of Bibb or red leaf lettuce. Serves 6.

The salad may be increased to any amount desired. If using on a picnic or a boat, the lettuce can be omitted.

During the years that we floated on the Queen Mary, another favorite salad of fresh summer tomatoes was drenched in a vinaigrette dressing and redolent with basil leaves, actually a very simple salad easy to prepare. Peel and quarter 8 large tomatoes and place in a large ceramic bowl. Prepare the basic Vinaigrette Dressing, page 56 with 3 teaspoons of Dijon-type mustard and pour over the tomatoes. Now add a fistful of fresh, big basil leaves — about 1 cup. Mix altogether with your hands, gently. Cover with plastic wrap and place in an ice chest. An alternative would be placing the finished salad in wide-mouth quart jars or large plastic containers with tight lids. This amount will feed about 10 hungry teenagers.

Like tomatoes, citrus fruit is wonderfully refreshing in summer. Oranges and grapefruit combine in a lovely combination of citrus fruit with avocado that is popular across our country. It is often served with a sweet dressing, but I much prefer a Lemon Vinaigrette that enhances the flavor of all the ingredients.

ORANGE AND GRAPEFRUIT SALAD

6 cups Bibb lettuce, washed and dried

3 large oranges, peeled, seeded, and sectioned

I cup grapefruit sections, more if desired

I large avocado, peeled and sliced

$^{3}/_{4}$ cup thinly sliced green onions

Lemon Vinaigrette, page 57

Divide the lettuce among six salad plates. Arrange orange and grapefruit sections interspersed with slices of avocado over the lettuce. Sprinkle green onions atop the fruit. Swirl each salad with a portion of the Lemon Vinaigrette. Serves 6.

Note: Always prepare the avocado at the last minute to maintain color.

RADICCHIO AND RED PEPPER SALAD

I head Bibb lettuce

I head radicchio

$^{1}/_{2}$ pound mushrooms

I-2 sweet red peppers, julienne-cut

Leaves of Belgian endive, optional

Balsamic Vinaigrette, page 57

Discard any blemished outer leaves of the Bibb lettuce. Separate the leaves, rinse in cool water and spin dry. Remove any of the outer leaves of the radicchio if necessary. (Many times these small heads will be almost perfect.) Separate the leaves, wash and dry. Place all the leaves in plastic bags and refrigerate to crisp. Remove stems from mushrooms and save to add to soups. Wipe the mushrooms with a damp cloth, slice and refrigerate, covered. Slice the peppers open and discard the ribs, stems and seeds. Slice, julienne, lengthwise in thin strips. Cover and refrigerate.

For formal presentation: On chilled salad plates divide both types of lettuces — this amount will serve eight. Divide the sliced mushrooms among the salads and arrange the julienned red pepper atop the mushrooms. If desired, tuck in the pale green leaves of the Belgian endive. Drizzle each plate with Balsamic Vinaigrette. For an informal presentation: into a large salad bowl, break the lettuce leaves in bite-size pieces and add the remaining ingredients. Toss thoroughly with the Balsamic Vinaigrette.

A fresh green salad can sometimes be a problem to finish and serve for a dinner party. The following method describes how to keep the greens and "insides" of the salad crisp and chilled so that at the last minute all can be tossed together and served on chilled plates. All the ingredients can be substituted according to your whim or what is available and very fresh on the market.

DINNER SALAD FOR TWELVE

I head Boston or Bibb lettuce

I head romaine lettuce

$^{1}/_{2}$ clove garlic

2 medium ripe tomatoes

I cucumber

6-8 scallions

5-6 radishes, cleaned and sliced

I cup orange sections, fresh or canned mandarin

Roquefort cheese or walnuts

Wash and thoroughly dry the lettuce leaves discarding any that are discolored. Rub a wooden bowl with the garlic, discarding the garlic. Break the lettuce in the bowl and cover with plastic wrap. Peel tomatoes and cut in bite-size pieces. Peel and slice the cucumber. Pull the outer skin from the scallions and slice in pieces. Section the oranges. Add the tomatoes, cucumber, scallions, radishes and oranges on top of the plastic wrap and cover with another layer of plastic. Refrigerate until ready to serve. Remove the sheets of plastic and toss the salad with choice of dressing. Sprinkle over each serving cheese or walnuts - perhaps a little of both. Serves 12.

Brilliat-Savarian commended salad, for it refreshes without weakening and soothes without irritating. This is the way I feel about Belgian endive, the queen of salad greens. Around the middle of the nineteenth century gardeners grew chicory in cellars with dim light. The leaves became elongated as they sought light. One farmer made mounds of dirt around his plants. When he unearthed them, he had plants with broad, tightly wrapped leaves and a delicious bitter flavor. After World War II, with selection and improvement, the plants became beautiful endive, mostly grown in Belgium and northern France. The spears keep well when properly refrigerated and certainly there is no more elegant salad than Belgian endive lightly dressed.

BELGIAN ENDIVE WITH WATERCRESS

4 spears of Belgian endive

I head of Bibb lettuce, washed, dried and refrigerated

I bunch of watercress

Fresh crisp sprouts

Lemon Vinaigrette, page 57

Slice each endive in half and clean under running water. Discard any discolored outside leaves. Turn flat on a terry cloth towel to drain. Divide the Bibb lettuce leaves among four salad plates. Wash and dry the watercress. Then choose the prettiest leaves and stems. Place two halves of endive in center of each arranged lettuce leaves and add the watercress around and in between the endive. Cover lightly with crisp sprouts.

Alfalfa sprouts, when fresh, washed and drained, are light and lovely. Or, if you have access to a Chinese or Vietnamese store, buy fresh mung bean sprouts. Swirl with the Lemon Vinaigrette and serve as a separate course. Serves 4.

The selection of American apples has become so magnificent that Waldorf salad has developed into an even more pleasurable winter salad than when it originated at the famous New York hotel many years ago. Waldorf salad always is perfect for a Thanksgiving dinner. The original classic salad had a bit of cream and Worcestershire sauce added to the dressing. I have made a lighter dressing using part yogurt to decrease fat content. When preparing the apples, do leave a bright red or green skin on for this adds beautiful color as well as nutritive value.

WALDORF SALAD

3 cups celery, cut diagonally

2 cups cut dates or dark raisins

2 cups pecans

4 cups apples, cored and cut in pieces

Leaves of leaf lettuce

DRESSING

$^1\!/_2$ cup plain yogurt

$^1\!/_2$ cup mayonnaise

1 $^1\!/_2$ teaspoons fresh lime juice

Combine the celery, dates or raisins and pecans. My mother often used dates which I loved, for we seldom had dates back in the 1920's. Use a tart, firm apple, preferably Granny Smith or Gala. In a small bowl combine the yogurt, mayonnaise and lime juice, mixing thoroughly. Add to the apple mixture, stirring well to cover all the fruit. If this recipe makes insufficient dressing, add more yogurt or mayonnaise according to taste. Arrange lettuce leaves on chilled salad plates and distribute the salad among the plates. This amount will serve 10 to 20.

High on a mountainside east of Beirut, Helen Yeni-Komshian stopped at a cave converted into a bakery. Inside, a fire of intense heat flared against the back wall of the cave. The baker rolled bread dough paper thin, placed it over a huge black pillow and with his hand under that pillow slapped the dough on the hot wall above the fire. The bread turned golden brown in just minutes, was loosened, folded gently into a small triangle of Lebanese mountain bread, which was offered to me. I tucked the bread in my purse, for the following day we were flying back to the States and I would be able to show this amazingly thin mountain bread to my cooking class students. The following day as Helen drove us to the airport, she presented a second going-home present of an enormous bag of pine nuts, fresh and fat, the very best I have had the pleasure of receiving. The succulent aroma and flavor of pine nuts adapts superbly to a great variety of foods.

SPINACH SALAD WITH PINE NUTS

⅔ cup pine nuts, toasted

10 tablespoons olive oil

4 tablespoons red wine vinegar

1 teaspoon grated lemon rind

1 teaspoon dried tarragon

1 pound fresh spinach leaves

2 cups orange sections

¼ cup slices green onion

1 cup sliced fresh mushrooms

To toast pine nuts, place nuts in a cake or pie tin and toast in a 300° oven five minutes. (Watch carefully as they burn easily.) Cool and chop the nuts coarsley. Combine the oil, vinegar, lemon rind and tarragon. Beat well with a fork or small whisk and add the pine nuts. Set aside.

Wash and dry the spinach leaves removing stems. Tear the spinach into bite-size pieces and place in a wooden salad bowl. To the spinach add the orange sections, onions and mushrooms. Toss with the pine nut dressing until all the spinach leaves glisten. Serve from the salad bowl or in individual plates. Serves 8.

On my first trip to Greece I fell in love with the fresh and uncomplicated salads served in all the little *tavernas*. Often the cooks would escort me into the kitchen to choose my main entree, and what fun it was to peek into all the big pots and skillets and a drawer filled with ice where fresh fish resided. But first would come the salad and always there was excellent feta sprinkled on top. Once, in mid afternoon, we stopped at a *teverna* to rest, have a little feta cheese and coffee. The room was filled with men and the only available table was with a very elderly man, quite drunk. We ordered and had wine brought for the old man. Now this was the time when the Kennedy half dollar had begun to spread in Europe and at the suggestion of friends we had brought several with us. When we finished my husband decided to see what would happen if he offered the waitress a Kennedy half dollar.

She held it up crying, "Kennedy! Kennedy!" and all the men in the *taverna* jumped to their feet to look. They were so delighted with this coin we couldn't leave the *taverna* without handing out several more Kennedy half dollars.

A GRECIAN SALAD

3 quarts romaine lettuce, torn in bite-size pieces

1 medium cucumber, sliced

2 medium tomatoes, peeled and cut in eighths

$\frac{2}{3}$ cup olive oil

6 tablespoons fresh lemon juice

Grindings of black pepper

Salt to taste

1 cup feta cheese, crumbled

Black Greek olives

Wash and dry lettuce thoroughly. Place in a large plastic bag and refrigerate to crisp. Tear lettuce in bite-size pieces and combine with the cucumber and tomatoes in a large salad bowl. Whisk the oil, lemon juice, pepper and salt until light and creamy. Pour enough dressing over the salad to thoroughly coat all ingredients. Reserve any leftover dressing for future use. Toss the salad lightly and sprinkle the feta cheese over the top and garnish with black olives, or divide ingredients equally among bowls for individual servings. Serves 8 to 10.

Not until my son Peter married a young woman from Beirut, Lebanon did I understand the proper way to serve taboulie. This has always been one of my favorite salads, despite some of the weird notions I've encountered of just how this mideastern salad should be prepared. When Annie made the salad, showing me the finishing touches, I was delighted and charmed, for the complete bowl became a huge flower. Taboulie keeps wonderfully for several days so even with a small family there is no need to fear making the complete recipe.

TABOULIE

1 cup fine bulgur wheat

Water to cover

$\frac{1}{2}$ teaspoon salt

4 cups chopped parsley

$\frac{1}{2}$ cup finely chopped green onions, including green part

2 cups peeled, chopped cucumbers

1 teaspoon salt

$\frac{1}{3}$ cup lemon juice

$\frac{1}{3}$ cup chopped fresh mint

$\frac{1}{2}$ cup olive oil

Romaine lettuce

2 cups chopped tomatoes

Combine the wheat and sufficient water to barely cover adding $\frac{1}{2}$ teaspoon salt. Let soak 5 to 10 minutes. Squeeze excess water from the wheat and place in a large bowl.

Add parsley to a food processor fitted with the steel blade. Pulse until finely chopped but not mushy — there must be some texture. The parsley should be measured after chopping. When finished with the parsley, transfer to the bowl with the wheat and add the green onions to the processor, pulsing until just chopped. Peel the cucumbers and slice in small pieces with a sharp knife. Combine the wheat, parsley, onions and cucumber stirring thoroughly. Blend in the salt, lemon juice, mint and oil. Taste carefully for the amount of lemon juice and salt. Annie taught me that tasting is most important especially for the amounts of lemon juice and salt.

Line a large salad bowl with romaine lettuce leaves allowing them to flare above the top of the bowl. Transfer the taboulie into the lined bowl, packing gently, smoothing into a round mold. Arrange chopped tomatoes in a circle around the edge of the salad and another circle on top of the taboulie. The resulting appearance is like a lovely green and red flower — the way taboulie should be served. The recipe will serve 10 to 12.

During our first journey into the Middle East we hired a taxi for the day each morning in Beirut. Our son Peter served as our guide and linguist. Peter sat with the driver to give instructions for a trip to Damascus, Byblos and other ancient areas. The driver was always enchanted with this young American who could speak Arabic so fluently and the fact that I was the mother of three sons gave me a position of great honor. Early one morning on our way to Byblos we stopped at a huge seaside warehouse on the Mediterranean. Suddenly we were wafted inside and perched atop piles of Persian carpets to sip tiny cups of hot, Turkish coffee. I was so charmed that I felt all I needed was a magic lamp to rub! It was fascinating to watch the Persian salesman in his jaunty gray fur hat dashing from one customer to another. Of course, we purchased a rug which I still treasure. Enjoy my Persian salad, for it brings nostalgic dreams of a country that once was the center of learning and banking in the mideast.

A PERSIAN SALAD

3 cups orange sections

1 cup sliced black olives

1 cup thinly sliced mild onions

¾ cup olive oil

⅓ cup red wine vinegar

1 teaspoon Dijon-type mustard

3 dashes cayenne pepper

1 tablespoon chopped fresh basil

Leaf, Boston, or Bibb lettuce

2 tablespoons chopped fresh mint

2 tablespoons chopped fresh parsley

In a mixing bowl combine the orange sections, olives and onions. Measure the oil into a jar and add the vinegar, mustard, cayenne pepper and basil. Shake well until creamy. Pour sufficient dressing over the salad ingredients until well coated. Cover the bowl and refrigerate for at least one hour or longer. Place leaves of lettuce on each salad and divide the prepared chilled salad among them. Sprinkle each salad with a portion of mint and parsley. Serves 4.

The origin of the wonderfully innovative salad called Caesar Salad is supposed to be that exciting, wild border city of Tijuana, Mexico. The most amusing Caesar salad we had as a family was in Yboe City in Florida at the Columbian Restaurant. The waiter dramatically swished snow-white napkins into our laps, stood back, looked at our three sons and said, "Only three, I have five!" Then he took a napkin from the youngest boy and made a rabbit with very tall ears. By then the boys were captivated and watched carefully as he proceeded to make the salad, pouring "gasoline" and "oil" into the dressing and greatly entertaining our sons.

Many versions of this salad have appeared on both sides of our border with Mexico and properly there should be anchovies in the dressing. If this is too much salt, simply eliminate the little fish. Caesar salad should be tossed and served immediately as a separate course.

CAESAR SALAD

2 small heads romaine lettuce

1 clove garlic, peeled and crushed

¾ cup olive oil

2 cups croutons, preferably French bread

6 anchovy fillets, diced

4 tablespoons garlic oil

Juice of 2 lemons

2 tablespoons red wine vinegar

Grindings of black pepper

2-3 tablespoons grated Parmesan cheese

1 egg, coddled,* optional

Strip any blemished leaves from the two heads of lettuce and cut off the ends. Wash thoroughly, dry and wrap in paper toweling. Refrigerate to crisp. Combine the garlic and oil in a jar to stand overnight or all day. Sauté the croutons in a heavy skillet with ¼ of the garlic oil stirring carefully until golden brown on all sides. Drain and cool on paper toweling.

Place the anchovies in a wooden salad bowl and crush with a fork into a paste. Add the 4 tablespoons of garlic oil, lemon juice, vinegar and pepper. Beat the mixture with the fork until well blended.

Break the romaine into bite-size pieces and place in the salad bowl. Mix with two spoons until each piece of romaine is lightly coated. Add more garlic oil if necessary. Add the croutons and sprinkle on the cheese. Add the egg and toss until the romaine has a thick creamy coating.

Taste the salad and add more cheese if necessary. Offer grindings of black pepper and serve immediately. Serves 8.

*Coddled Egg: place egg in a saucepan and cover with boiling water. Let stand 1 minute. Remove immediately and break into the salad. If you are not certain about the freshness of the egg, eliminate it.

I do believe I've tried over fifty varieties of pasta salad, finding most rather bland and unappetizing. With such a wonderfully healthful food offering so many possibilities, I decided to construct a salad to suit my taste and, I hope, yours. I've chosen my favorite ingredients with suggestions of many others.

PASTA-VEGETABLE SALAD

6 cups cooked tricolor rotelle pasta (spiral pasta)

2 cups broccoli flowerettes, blanched

1 cup snow peas, blanched

$1/3$ cup sweet red pepper, cut in bite-size pieces

1 jar ($6\frac{1}{2}$ ounces) artichokes in oil, cut in quarters

$2/3$ cup thinly sliced red onion

12 to 14 Greek olives

Vinaigrette dressing:

$2/3$ cup olive oil

$1/4$ cup red wine vinegar

$1/2$ teaspoon dried basil

$1/2$ teaspoon dried oregano

2 teaspoons Dijon mustard, preferably Poupon

To cook the pasta: Boil 4 to 5 quarts of salted water in a large saucepan. Drop 10 ounces of the spiral pasta into the boiling water and cook 15 minutes or until tender. Pour into a colander, running water over briefly. Let stand until cool, stirring occasionally.

To blanch vegetables: cut off the flowerettes of broccoli and drop into boiling water for 1 minute. Drain in a sieve running cool water over the vegetable to stop the cooking. Allow to cook. Repeat with the snow peas, cutting them in half for ease of eating. Transfer the cooked pasta to a large glass bowl, for this is a beautiful salad when finished. Add the broccoli, snow peas, artichokes, red pepper, onion and olives. Stir very well and taste for salt content. Combine all the ingredients for the vinaigrette dressing in a separate bowl and whisk until creamy. Pour over the salad ingredients and stir until all is shining and inundated with the pungent dressing. Serves 8.

Optional ingredients: celery, carrots, green pepper, blanched cauliflowerettes, tomatoes.

The combination of goat cheese and vinaigrette is in no danger of being bland and I have tried it from the famous Chez Panisse restaurant in San Francisco to the Arcadia in New York. Although each serving of warm goat cheese on delectable greens was a little different, I loved the concept. It is a salad that should be served separately on chilled plates. The combination of hot cheese and very cold greens is an intensely pleasurable experience. Here is my version of this now famous salad, serving six.

GRILLED GOAT CHEESE WITH MIXED GREENS

6 slices of goat cheese, about 1 inch in diameter and 1 inch thick

Olive oil

$^{1}/_{2}$ teaspoon dried basil

1 large head Bibb lettuce, washed, dried and chilled

Spears of Belgian endive

Radicchio leaves

Arugula or watercress

1 cup soft bread crumbs

1 teaspoon dried basil

Basic Vinaigrette (page 56) with 1 teaspoon dried basil

Imported and domestic goat cheese are both available in slender packages. Occasionally a goat cheese impregnated with basil can be found and, if so, use for this salad. Cut the cheese in 1-inch slices pressing each to retain any small pieces that might fall off. Place in a bowl large enough for the cheese to be in one layer. Cover with olive oil and sprinkle with the ½ teaspoon of dried basil. Let marinate at room temperature for at least five hours turning occasionally. Prepare all the greens and refrigerate to chill thoroughly. When ready to serve, arrange Bibb lettuce first on individual plates and garnish with spears of the endive, and for color use the radicchio and arugula or watercress. Preheat oven to broil. Dip each slice of cheese in the bread crumbs mixed with 1 teaspoon basil to cover completely. Place in a small pan and broil 8 inches from the element about 5 to 6 minutes or until hot and lightly browned. With a spatula, scoop up each piece of cheese and place in the center of the salads. Swirl the vinaigrette quickly on the greens and serve immediately. Serves 6.

Even more exotic, perhaps, than goat cheese with greens is the luxurious and beautiful enoki salad to be prepared and served on individual plates. Enoki mushrooms are usually available in well stocked supermarkets encased in air-tight plastic bags for preservation. Remove the plastic and cut off one-third of the bottom of the mushrooms. Rinse the mushrooms in tap water and place in a small bowl to drain. Enoki mushrooms are delicate and should be used within two days of opening the package.

WALNUT ENOKI MUSHROOM SALAD

Lemon Vinaigrette (page 57) with 1 teaspoon Dijon-type mustard
1 small head Bibb lettuce, rinsed and dried
1 cup walnuts
1 package enoki mushrooms

Combine all the ingredients for the lemon vinaigrette and beat with a fork until smooth and creamy. Divide the Bibb lettuce among four plates. Sprinkle each with walnuts. If walnuts are in halves, I suggest slicing each half in two pieces for ease in eating. Spread the enoki mushrooms, fan shape, atop each salad. Swirl each salad with the lemon vinaigrette. Serves 4.

Rarely had I seen cabbage growing, for it is a northern vegetable and not an agricultural product of Oklahoma or Texas. But I made up for that on my second journey to Russia. We boarded a train in Moscow for St. Petersburg at midnight, slept a few hours and as the sun was rising, I peeked out the window and discovered we were passing mile after mile of cabbages — row after row dropped over the horizon. Yet, we were never served fresh cabbage in Russia; only cooked cabbage in soups. How delightful it is to enjoy a fresh, crisp slaw, mixed with sweet fruits and a yogurt dressing.

SLAW WITH FRUIT AND YOGURT

1 cup fresh orange sections
5 cups finely shredded cabbage
1 cup celery, sliced diagonally
¾ cup chopped dates
2 tablespoons lemon juice

1 cup fresh pineapple, diced

1 tart apple, unpeeled, cored, cut in bite size pieces

$^1/_2$ cup coarsley chopped pecans or walnuts

8 ounces plain yogurt

Grated rind of 1 orange

1-2 tablespoons orange juice

$^3/_4$ teaspoons poppy seeds

In a large salad bowl combine the oranges, cabbage, celery and dates. Brush the lemon juice over the pineapple and apple and add them to the salad with the nuts. Combine the yogurt, grated rind and 1 tablespoon orange juice. Taste the yogurt and add more orange juice, or, if you wish a sweeter dressing, sugar to taste. Pour the dressing over the prepared ingredients with the poppy seeds and stir very well. Cover and refrigerate until ready to serve. Serves 6 to 8.

The beauty of salads is in the combination. The title of the following recipe foretells an exciting blend of flavors that makes this salad a perfect luncheon offering or a delightful light supper accompanied by crusty French bread.

SHRIMP SALAD WITH CAPERS AND FETA CHEESE

THE DRESSING

$^1/_4$ cup fresh lemon juice

$^3/_4$ cup olive oil

1 teaspoon dried oregano

THE SALAD

3 medium tomatoes, peeled and cut in bite-size pieces

1 cup diagonally sliced celery

1 head of Bibb or Boston lettuce, washed, dried, and crisped

1 pound tiny salad shrimp

$^1/_2$ cup capers, drained

$^1/_4$ pound feta cheese, crumbled

Black olives

Freshly ground black pepper

Salt to taste, optional

Combine all the ingredients for the dressing in a jar, cover tightly and shake thoroughly until well blended and creamy.

Preparation of salad for four: Use four plates or large salad bowls. Tear lettuce and divide among the four plates. Arrange the tomatoes and celery atop the lettuce. Then top each with an equal amount of shrimp. Sprinkle capers and feta cheese over the shrimp and spoon dressing over each salad. Add several black olives (preferably a pungent Greek olive) to each plate. Offer grindings of black pepper to guests. With both the feta cheese and capers, no salt is actually needed. Serve immediately.

Luncheon in England can be a Ploughman's Lunch at any pub in the kingdom. But the French apply a bit more imagination to lunch, particularly in Provence, where it seems there is always a good soup available — along with Salade Niçoise which is healthful, delightful to eat and easily prepared.

NIÇOISE SALAD

THE DRESSING

¼ cup fresh lemon juice

½ cup olive oil

1 garlic clove, minced

2 teaspoons Dijon-type mustard

Freshly ground black pepper

Salt to taste

THE SALAD

Red leaf or Boston lettuce leaves, washed, dried, and crisped in refrigerator

7-ounce can solid white tuna in water, drained

3 to 4 medium red new potatoes, cooked (peel left on), cut in ½ inch slices

1 shallot, minced

2 cups fresh green beans, cooked 5 minutes (frozen beans may be used)

1 sweet red or green pepper, cut in strips

4 medium tomatoes, peeled and cut in quarters

3 hard-boiled eggs, sliced lengthwise in quarters

1 cup black or Spanish green olives

2-ounce can rolled anchovy fillets with capers (optional)

Place the ingredients for the dressing in a jar with a tight fitting lid and shake until well mixed and creamy. Place the warm sliced potatoes in a small bowl and spoon a little dressing over them. Sprinkle the chopped shallot over the potatoes, cover and refrigerate 1 hour.

Line a large platter with the crisped lettuce and mound the tuna in the center. Divide the green beans in several portions and arrange around the fish. Add the olive and anchovies in between the vegetables. Pour remaining dressing over the salad and serve. Serves 6 for luncheon.

Presumably Cobb Salad originated in the famous Brown Derby of Hollywood during the glamorous years of the 1930s — at least that was what I was told while dining at the Brown Derby in Disney World with my youngest grandchildren. The exciting combination of ingredients presents a light alfresco supper on the patio, especially in the fall when good vegetables are still available. A sturdy lettuce is necessary so use either iceberg or romaine or a combination of both.

COBB SALAD

THE SALAD

1 head iceberg or romaine lettuce

1 poached chicken breast, cut in pieces

2 medium tomatoes, peeled and sliced

3 hard-boiled eggs, chopped

6 slices bacon, cooked crisp and crumbled

3 ounces crumbled Roquefort cheese

2 medium or 1 large avocado, halved, peeled and cut in wedges

1 head French endive, optional

Chopped chives or parsley for topping

THE DRESSING

1 cup red wine vinegar

Grindings of black pepper

1 tablespoon Dijon-type mustard

1 teaspoon Worcestershire sauce

1 clove garlic, minced

1 $\frac{1}{2}$ cups olive oil

Remove damaged leaves of lettuce. Section out the core and shred the lettuce to line a large salad bowl. Arrange the chicken over the lettuce and follow with layers of tomatoes, eggs, bacon and cheese. The salad may be covered and refrigerated one hour.

Combine all the ingredients for the dressing in a jar and shake vigorously or whirl in a food processor until well mixed and smooth. Toss the salad gently with the prepared dressing. Garnish with wedges of avocado and endive leaves. Sprinkle with chives or parsley. Serves 6 to 8.

I became intrigued with barley many years ago. I had read ancient history describing the first grains man cultivated and knew from my childhood as a Methodist preacher's daughter that barley was important in the Old Testament. First I discovered how marvelous barley was in soups instead of potatoes and rice, then I tried it in pilafs with herbs that I loved. Knowing that this grain has been used for thousands of years gives one the feeling of its health and strength. And here is a different idea for a salad using this wonderful ancient grain as a base. This salad can be used as a complete meal or served for a buffet supper and is quite lovely garnished with fresh tomatoes and cubes of cheese. Do purchase the pearl barley rather than instant; it has much better flavor and texture.

A FULL MEAL SALAD

THE SALAD

2 cups cooked salad shrimp

2 cups cubed cooked chicken

2 cups cubed spicy salami

2 cups fresh zucchini, cubed

$^1\!/_2$ cup capers, drained

I cup chopped pimento

2 cups cooked barley

THE DRESSING:

I bunch parsley

$^1\!/_2$ cup fresh basil or I $^1\!/_2$ teaspoons dried

$^1\!/_3$ cup red wine vinegar

$^1\!/_3$ cup fresh lemon juice

2 cups olive oil

2 cups fresh tomatoes, peeled and chopped

2 cups Monterey Jack or Muenster cheese, cubed

Combine the first seven ingredients for the salad in a large bowl. Use either the tiny salad shrimp, sometimes called popcorn shrimp, or large cooked shrimp, sliced.

It will take ¾ to 1 cup barley to make 2 cups of cooked barley. Cover with water and boil rapidly about 30 minutes or until tender. Drain and let cool. After all these ingredients are combined, set aside while preparing the dressing.

To make the dressing, discard the parsley stems and place in a food processor with steel blade in place. Add the basil, vinegar and lemon juice. Pulse off and on until the parsley is chopped. Slowly begin adding the oil. Stop and scrape down the sides and continue to pulse until a fairly smooth dressing has formed. Blend thoroughly into the salad ingredients, cover and refrigerate overnight. Toss the salad, smooth the top and decorate with a row of chopped tomatoes around the edge and inside the tomatoes, a row of cubed cheese. Since the salad is marinated overnight, this makes an easy presentation for luncheon with a French bread and fruit dessert. Serves 8, but more for a buffet.

Entrees

Beef

....

My nephew quietly stopped his ranch wagon and said, "Mary, look in the shadow of that huge rock! There's a golden eagle." I gasped at the sight of this gorgeous, huge bird tearing at a rabbit. It was beautiful and horrible at the same time. Suddenly the eagle noticed us, picked up the rabbit and flew away, lifting off on enormous wings. I caught my breath in frustration and wished I could have been faster with my camera. I love walking or riding over the huge ranch owned by Bill Loring, my nephew, for he knows every bird, animal, and species of tree. He knows stories about the land, too — stories of bandits hiding in a deep canyon open at both ends giving them an easy escape. Bill loves the land and takes great care in moving a thousand head of cattle from the winter pasture to the high summer area. We walked a sturdy swinging bridge over a raging river to check on needed repairs before the cattle drive and watched a work train dumping rocks on the siding, shoring up the sides in anticipation of the flooding caused by melting snows. I learned much from Bill about leasing land from the government versus limited private sources. We walked the 40 acres where he lives, which is bordered by the Colorado River. It was expected to crest in a week, and he was anxious about the flooding of planted fields and a neighbor's house. Geese have made a permanent home on the inland lakes, which were created long ago when the Colorado changed course. Such beautiful, rugged country is well cared for by both ranchers and the Bureau of Land Management.

The robustness of beef will always appeal to Americans, for no other food seems as satisfying and nourishing. The Pilgrims imported heifers and a bull while the Spanish introduced the sturdy longhorn cattle into the west. Few countries in the world can match the United States for producing beef of excellent flavor and tenderness. Here we have a vast expanse of land for grazing and years of expertise in feeding cattle.

Countries in South America feed only on grass for there is little corn production. My eldest son, who has climbed mountains in the Andes, related that the beef had a good flavor but was a bit tough to chew. Once the grain produced in the midwest proliferated, cattle were then driven to points in Kansas, Nebraska, Iowa and other areas to be fed in enormous feed lots for a year before slaughtering.

Beef in the United States has become leaner on demand. Also, cooks have learned to trim extra fat when purchasing any cut, from roast to steaks. Since our beef is so well fed and cared for, this does not destroy the flavor. When buying ground beef, look at the contents of the package carefully, for one can easily tell when there is a great deal of fat left in the meat. Buy ground sirloin or purchase a desired cut of beef and grind it in a food processor. Most butchers will be happy to grind a cut of your choice.

My experience cooking with beef began with Grandmother's roaster, for she purchased a new one and gave me the old one, big, slightly bent in places but strongly made. The boys were quite small when I received this gem. I love it because it holds a huge turkey, ham or pot roast with vegetables. There are two vents on top that can be opened or closed and that is most important, for with no vent a roast becomes a steamed or boiled piece of meat. With those vents I learned how to cook a pot roast all crispy and brown. For a roaster with no vents, forget the top and cover with aluminum foil, crimping the edges. Make a hole the size of a half-dollar in the center. Works beautifully. Now I've promised this roaster to my youngest son, but not yet, for I still use that wonderful old utensil that must be over 80 years old. Grandmother died at age 104!

POT ROAST WITH VEGETABLES

4 to 5 pound pot roast

2-3 cloves garlic, peeled

Salt and grindings of pepper, optional

Canola oil

6 medium potatoes, peeled

6 carrots, scraped and trimmed

6 medium onions, peeled

6 parsnips, scraped and trimmed, optional

The best pot roast is a blade cut with a bone down the center but now since so many meats are precut, the bone is gone. Too bad, for the bone did add flavor. Occasionally at a fine butcher shop where they cut their own meats a blade roast will be available. Otherwise use the boneless roast or a similar cut. Cut the garlic in thick slices, make slits in both sides of the roast and insert the pieces of garlic. Sprinkle with salt and pepper if you wish but I find the meat has sufficient natural salt. Pour a small amount (about ½ cup) of canola oil in bottom section of the roaster and place over a medium high burner. When hot, sear the roast on both sides quickly until browned. Preheat oven to 325°. Place cover on the roaster (never add any water) and open one vent. If the roast is room temperature, bake 1 hour, otherwise add 20 minutes. During this time prepare the vegetables. When the roast has cooked the allotted time, remove the cover and arrange the vegetables around the roast. Replace the top and return to the oven. Bake another 1 to 1½ hours or until the vegetables are tender and the roast is brown and crispy. There is an alternative if you have an electric skillet: set it at 350° and place a small amount of water in the bottom. Arrange all the vegetables in the skillet, cover and let cook one hour. Quite good, but then I love the flavor of roast juices on the vegetables. Place the roast on a big platter with the vegetables surrounding it. With a good salad, either vegetable or fruit, this is a happy and very satisfying dinner. Serves 6.

The filet is the most tender and most delicate of all beef cuts simply because the animal does not use those muscles as much as the rest of the body. Have the butcher remove the fat (which in an untrimmed filet will be about 25 percent) and also fold the tail end over and tie. For best results, have the filet at room temperature before cooking.

FILET OF BEEF

5 to 6 pounds filet of beef, trimmed

Soft butter

Salt and grindings of pepper, optional

Watercress or parsley to garnish

I have specified a 5 or 6 pound filet, but either a larger or smaller one is fine. Let beef come to room temperature. Rub the filet with soft butter and place in a shallow baking pan. Preheat oven to broiling, 500°. Salt and pepper may be sprinkled over the filet if desired. Broil on lowest rack (about 10 inches from the heating element) for 15 minutes, turning three times. Reduce heat to 250° and bake the filet about 30 minutes for rare. This depends on whether the beef was room temperature at the beginning. For medium, bake 10 to 15 minutes longer, but don't ruin a beautiful piece of beef! Never cook well done—just use another cut of beef. Five minutes before serving, broil again, turning once for even browning. Remove beef to a large wooden platter. It is best at this point to add a little salt and pepper rather than before cooking, but I do neither as I am interested in the flavor of the beef. Let stand 10 to 15 minutes before carving. Garnish with watercress or parsley. A large filet will serve 8 to 10, depending on how thick you slice it.

Marinating a filet of beef is an excellent preparation for grilling it outside. Even when a filet is already very tender, the marinade imparts a marvelous flavor, most agreeable when using charcoal briquettes. (If preferred the filet can always be broiled in the oven as described in Filet of Beef, page 80)

MARINATED FILET OF BEEF

4 to 6 cups dry red wine

½ cup red wine vinegar

1 teaspoon salt

2 cloves garlic, cut in half

1 cup thinly sliced onion

1 teaspoon each oregano and thyme

1 bay leaf

Grindings of black pepper

5 to 6 pounds filet of beef, trimmed

In a mixing bowl, combine the wine, vinegar, salt, garlic, onion, oregano, thyme, bay leaf, and pepper. Mix well. Place the beef in a large bowl or shallow dish and pour the marinade over the beef. There should be sufficient wine mixture to cover half the beef. Turn the beef over several times in the marinade, cover and refrigerate for at least 24 hours or longer, turning several times during the period. Remove from refrigerator two hours before grilling. Let the charcoal briquettes (and any choice mesquite wood) burn until bright coals. Grill the beef for approximately 30 to 45 minutes, turning several times. Press finger on meat to determine doneness. When the meat is soft, the filet will be rare; if firm, too well done! Serves 10.

Sautéed filet mignon touched with herb and napped with a piquant mustard-yogurt sauce served with Arborio rice is a handsome main entree. An equally pleasurable enticement is created by slicing any leftover rare filet of beef into thick portions and using it in the following recipe:

FILET MIGNON WITH MUSTARD SAUCE

2 tablespoons butter or oil

4 filet mignon steaks, 1 to 1 1/2 inches thick

Salt, optional

Grindings of black pepper

1 teaspoon rosemary

1 teaspoon thyme

1/4 cup brandy

4 teaspoons Dijon-type mustard

2 teaspoons Pommery mustard

1/2 cup plain yogurt

Heat the butter or oil in a heavy skillet over medium high heat and sauté the steaks 4 minutes on one side. Turn and sprinkle with a little salt (if desired), pepper, rosemary and thyme. Cook 4 more minutes and lower heat to medium. If the steaks are room temperature the time will be about 10 minutes total for rare. Press with a finger atop the meat. When beginning to be firm, the steaks are rare to medium rare. (Never cook a filet well done — choose some other type of steak.)

Pour off excess fat. Warm the brandy lightly and flame the steaks. Transfer steaks to a warm oven, 150°. Lower heat under the skillet and add both mustards and the yogurt. Stir for 2 minutes or until hot and just beginning to simmer. (Do not have the burner too hot or the yogurt will curdle.) Pour sauce over the filets and serve immediately. Serves 4.

Back in the good old days before cholesterol and calories, I had a wonderful butcher who would hang prime ribs of beef at a special temperature for six weeks. He trimmed the mold and fat off the meat and the aroma while roasting was unbelievable, the flavor superb. These days, prime rib is leaner but still flavorful. I love preparing a special English Christmas dinner for my family with Yorkshire pudding, roasted potatoes, and rich gravy with all the extra trimmings.

PRIME RIBS OF BEEF

Prime ribs of beef, 4 ribs, approximately 10 to 12 pounds
Salt and grindings of black pepper, optional

Preheat oven to 325° fifteen minutes before roasting the beef. It is important that the roast is removed from the refrigerator, placed in a roaster and let come to room temperature. A prime rib needs neither salt nor pepper unless necessary to your taste buds. When the beef is room temperature, place in preheated oven. Timing can be determined with a meat thermometer, plunging it into the center of the roast. When the temperature reaches 130°, the roast will be rare; 140° and it will be medium rare. Timing by minutes: for a rare roast, 20 minutes per pound, for medium rare, 25 minutes per pound and longer for well done. Always bake the roast uncovered. Never cover a fine piece of beef, for it will be steamed rather than roasted. During the last hour, scrubbed small new potatoes may be placed around the meat. Or if Idaho baking potatoes are preferred, scrub and peel off ½ inch of the skin around the middle. All this timing is predicated on the roast being room temperature. When the roast is removed and placed on a carving platter or board, let the beef rest for at least 20 minutes and it will be easier to carve. This size roast will feed 10 to 12 people.

Gravy: pour off all but ¾ cup of hot beef fat and sprinkle in ½ cup of flour. Stir rapidly with a whisk until it begins to turn brown. Add sufficient water to create the consistency you prefer. Whisk until smooth and turn heat to lowest point to keep warm until the roast has been carved. Transfer to a gravy boat.

Brisket is an excellent choice for picnics, buffets and informal dinners. It may be sliced ahead, wrapped in foil and reheated if necessary. Actually, it is good hot, at room temperature, or chilled.

BRISKET OF BEEF

4 cloves garlic
1 tablespoon salt
6 to 7 pound brisket of beef
⅓ cup pickling spices
3 tablespoons celery seeds

Grate the garlic into the salt, rubbing together with fingers until well mixed. Rub this over and into the brisket. Combine the pickling spices and celery seeds. Place the brisket in a shallow baking pan. Rub the pickling spice mixture over the beef. Some will fall off but most can be picked up and pressed into the beef. Let the beef stand 4 hours at room temperature or overnight, refrigerated and covered.

Preheat oven to 425°. Roast the brisket 20 minutes, turning over once. Reduce heat to 325° and continue to bake until fork tender, about 3 to 4 hours. Serve either hot or cold. This size brisket will feed 20 people and possibly more. If preferred, two small briskets may be cooked in the same manner but roasting time will be less. Use the same amount of ingredients as with the large brisket.

My youngest son wanted to know if I would include something in this book as mundane as steak and onions, a dish he loved as a child. There is nothing mundane when excellent beef is combined with Vidalia or those wonderful Texas onions. Then it becomes a superb entree.

ROUND STEAK WITH ONIONS

1 1/2 to 2 pound steak
Salt and grindings of black pepper
Flour
4 tablespoons canola oil
4 cups sliced onions
1 cup beef broth

Lightly salt and pepper the steak and sprinkle with flour. Smooth the flour over the steak and shake off any excess. Measure the oil into a large skillet over high heat and brown the steak. Transfer the steak to a plate, lower heat to medium high and add the onions. Cook and stir the onions about ten minutes or until limp and just beginning to be tender. Place the steak atop the onions and add the beef broth. Lower heat to simmer, cover and allow to cook very slowly 1½ to 2 hours. Check for tenderness. Serve in a large platter with the onions piled on top. Pour all the liquid from the skillet over the steak and onions. Do have some crusty French bread to sop up the juices — delicious! Serves 6.

My husband found two men who built twin pontoons, 44 feet long and 3½ feet wide. A 34-foot mobile home was placed between the pontoons, a large deck constructed in front while the top of the pontoons became side decks. We added two motors, a butane tank, a crow's nest in the back for the pilot and a diving board off the stern, and the Queen Mary was born. We could cruise comfortably over Grand Lake O' the Cherokees during the day, and spend the nights tied to a huge log on some bank in a protected cove. There was a master bedroom with bath, a second walk-through bedroom with bunk beds, tiny kitchen and living area which became a grand dining room for buffets. The bar was the kitchen counter. Each weekend the Queen Mary became a floating dock with six or eight ski boats coming and going. Twenty deck chairs were arranged on the front deck. Our tricolor collie could always be found reclining in the center of the deck, enduring the whole scene of adults yelling at teenagers to BE CAREFUL and teenagers leaving contact lenses in anyone's care, grabbing ropes, jumping into the water and taking off on waterskiis behind one of the six or eight boats. The skiers became so proficient that the final summer my youngest son and two girls made a pyramid just as exciting as a show at Cypress Gardens in Florida.

Everyone brought food for a weekend on the Queen Mary. We always had a great variety and one main entree the kids loved was drip beef which I prepared at home, refrigerated, and then reheated in the oven of my small stove.

DRIP BEEF

6 to 8 pounds beef roast: English cut, rump, Pike Peak's pot roast or brisket

2 to 3 cloves garlic

Salt and grindings of black pepper, optional

Preheat oven to 250°. Choose any size roast that is solid meat with little fat. The size will be determined by the number of people to be served. An 8-pound roast will feed 25 to 30 people. A much smaller roast, 4 pounds, will take less time to cook. Make incisions over the meat, cut the garlic in slivers and insert into the slits. To me, good beef needs no salt or pepper, but that is a personal choice. Place the beef in a baking pan deep enough to hold the wonderful juices, about 2 inches deep. Cover slightly with aluminum foil and place in preheated oven. Let the roast cook all day. (A large one will take at least eight hours.) Remove the foil and test for tenderness; the meat should fall apart with the touch of a fork and if not, recover and cook longer. While the beef is warm, chop it into shreds. The beef may be

refrigerated at this point and the next day remove all accumulated fat. If
more au jus is necessary, add 2 to 4 cups of beef broth, especially for a very
large roast. The drip beef can then be transported to boat, pot luck supper
or the back patio. Serve on thickly sliced French bread (preferably toasted)
or hamburger buns.

With a combination of lean ground beef, part-skim milk mozzarella, ricotta
cheese and light regular noodles, this very old recipe of mine is both savory and
delicate in texture. Add a crusty Italian bread and a big green salad for a most satisfying dinner.

AMERICAN LASAGNA

2 tablespoons olive oil

1 pound ground sirloin

2 cloves garlic, minced

8 ounces tomato sauce

2 cups canned tomatoes

1 teaspoon salt

Grindings of black pepper

$^1\!/_2$ teaspoon oregano

8 ounces noodles*

$^1\!/_2$ pound mozzarella cheese

15 ounce ricotta cheese

$^1\!/_2$ cup grated Parmesan cheese

Measure the oil into a skillet over medium high heat. Add the ground sirloin and garlic. Stir constantly until the meat begins to brown. Stir in the
tomato sauce, tomatoes, salt, black pepper and oregano. Cover and simmer
20 minutes or until slightly thickened. Taste and add more oregano if
desired. Cook the noodles in boiling water until just tender. Drain in a
colander and rinse. Set aside to drain. Slice the mozzarella cheese into slivers. Fill a rectangular or oval casserole with layers: first a layer of noodles,
sliced mozzarella, ricotta and meat mixture. Repeat a second layer ending
with the tomato sauce on top and sprinkle over all the Parmesan cheese.
Bake in a preheated 350° oven 45 minutes or until bubbling and very hot.
Serves 6 to 8.

*Being slightly averse to the heavy lasagna noodles, I have tried several different kinds of regular noodles, but particularly enjoy an organic pasta made of sifted durum wheat because of lightness in texture. These noodles can be found in fine supermarkets.

The cuisine of Middle Eastern countries involves combinations of fascinating spices and herbs. One of my favorites is the blending of mint and cinnamon, which to an American sounds a bit odd, but can be most stimulating, as in these meatballs. Each meatball should be small and as a result this recipe takes a bit of time to prepare. Turn on the radio, enjoy your favorite music and roll away!

MIDDLE EASTERN MEATBALLS WITH RICE PILAF

MEATBALLS

3 medium onions, minced (approximately 3 cups)

4 tablespoons olive oil

3 pounds lean ground beef

1 1/2 teaspoons cinnamon

Grindings of black pepper

2 tablespoons chopped fresh mint or 2 teaspoons dried mint

2 teaspoons salt

1/2 cup dry bread crumbs

1/2 cup milk

2 eggs

Whirl the onions in a food processor fitted with a steel blade until finely minced but not mushy. Sauté the onions in a skillet in the oil over moderate heat approximately 10 to 12 minutes or until wilted, stirring constantly; do not allow to burn. In a large mixing bowl combine the onions with the meat, cinnamon, pepper, mint, salt, crumbs, milk and eggs. (The amount of salt is just a suggestion.) If using a heavy mixer, mix thoroughly with the flat beater until well blended. Line a baking sheet with foil and coat with a vegetable spray. Shape the meat mixture in 1-inch balls and place on the prepared baking sheet. Preheat oven to 400° while making the balls. Bake the meatballs 20 minutes or until browned. Combine with the rice pilaf and serve from a very large platter or bowl.

⅓ cup olive oil

⅓ cup pine nuts or slivered almonds

I medium onion, minced

I cup rice

2 cups chicken broth

I-inch cinnamon stick

¼ teaspoon ground coriander

2 whole cloves

Measure the oil into a skillet and add choice of nuts. Over moderate heat sauté until golden, stirring constantly. (Do not allow to burn or they will become bitter.) Use a slotted spoon to remove the nuts to paper toweling. Add the onion to the skillet and sauté until just soft, about 8 minutes. Blend in the rice and cook until clear, stirring continually. Add the broth and spices. Bring to a boil, lower heat and simmer until tender, about 15 minutes.

Actually I think the following recipe should be entitled Continental Ground Steak, for I do believe Europeans would relish such a choice, flavorful hamburger! Purchase the best ground sirloin available or buy a sirloin steak, cut in pieces and chop in a food processor using the steel blade.

HAMBURGERS IN WINE

I ½ pounds ground sirloin

2 tablespoons olive oil

2 tablespoons chopped shallots or green onions

I clove garlic, peeled and minced

I teaspoon Dijon-type mustard

I cup dry red wine

3 tablespoons butter

4 English muffins

Shape the meat into 4 patties a bit wider than the English muffins. Heat oil in a large skillet over moderately high heat, and add the meat patties. Brown on both sides, lower heat to medium and cook to desired degree of doneness. With such fine beef, these ground steaks are particularly good on the rare side—much more succulent. While the meat is cooking, split and toast the muffins. Place the muffins in a 150° oven to keep warm. Remove meat when done and place a patty on top of one-half muffin. Leave in the oven.

Add the shallots and garlic to the skillet and cook 3 to 4 minutes stirring constantly. Blend in the mustard and wine. Bring to a rapid boil, reducing by half. Add the butter and stir to melt. Place each hamburger with muffin on a warm serving plate. Spoon the wine sauce over each. Serve the remaining toasted muffins on the side. Accompanied with a big salad, this will be a most pleasurable meal! Serves 4.

Wine sauce is one way of customizing the classic hamburger. But the Lebanese enjoy ground beef in a way few Americans do. The forerunner of this special recipe was actually steak tartare. Ground raw meat mixed with spices, onion and egg is an appetizer the Lebanese love. The following recipe is similar to steak tartare, but, of course, cooked and preferably served in pita bread topped with shredded lettuce, fresh tomato, Middle Eastern olives and a dollop of yogurt. Truly a delicious repast.

LEBANESE HAMBURGERS

2 pounds ground beef

1 1/2 cups minced onion

1 cup finely chopped parsley

1 teaspoon salt

1 teaspoon cinnamon

1 teaspoon paprika

Dash cayenne pepper

2-3 tablespoons olive oil

Place the meat in a large bowl of a heavy mixer fitted with the flat beater. In a food processor with steel blade in place whirl the onion until finely minced but not mushy. While pulsing, stop and scrape down the sides. Add the onion to the meat and add the parsley to the food processor. Again, pulse until finely chopped, stopping to scrape down the sides. Add the parsley to the meat. Mix in 1 teaspoon salt and fry a tiny portion of the meat mixture to taste and adjust. Add the cinnamon, paprika and cayenne pepper. Beat at medium speed until well mixed. Form into the number of patties desired. This amount of mixture will make 8 regular-size patties.

Add the olive oil to a skillet and sauté the hamburgers over moderately high heat. Turn once and cook to desired doneness. To broil the hamburgers in the oven, brush a pan with olive oil and place patties on the baking sheet. Broil on one side and finish on the other.

Another favorite with my sons was Flaming Ground Steak, which they loved standing around the stove to watch flame — better than playing with matches! Since this is a simple ground steak, purchase the best ground meat — ground round or sirloin — a meat with flavor.

FLAMING GROUND STEAK

1 1/2 pounds ground round or sirloin steak

Freshly ground black pepper

5 pats butter or margarine

Worcestershire sauce

Lemon juice

4 tablespoons brandy

Finely chopped parsley

Shape the meat into 6 patties. Place them on a counter close to the stove, pat firmly and sprinkle each with the pepper. Let stand for 30 minutes. Heat a heavy skillet (such as cast iron) and sprinkle heavily with salt. When this begins to smoke sauté the patties quickly, browning on one side and then the other on high heat. Lower heat and cook to the desired doneness. Place a pat of butter on each, top each with several drops of Worcestershire sauce and lemon juice. When they have cooked the correct length of time, drain off any extra fat. Heat the brandy until just barely warm. Turn off the heat, pour on the brandy and set ablaze. Shake the pan until the flame subsides. Sprinkle each with parsley. Serves 6.

Lamb

....

Lamb has been with us a very long time. It is a meat adaptable to many different ways of cooking and seasoning — from being covered with herbs to stewed with fruits. The progenitors of lamb were domesticated thousands of years ago primarily in the area of northern Iran and Kurdistan. In the beginning they were used primarily for their luxurious wool, but their ability to survive anywhere in the world and to flourish rapidly was recognized and valued; then their milk and meat became priceless. When the sirocco winds blew, they survived the drought, for sheep store and live off fat similar to camels. Gradually Jewish and Christian religions used lamb for such special occasions as Easter and Passover and the Muslims used it for their New Year. Up until the time of the Englishman Robert Blakewell, the ancients had to tenderize their meat or simmer it for a very long time. Mr. Blakewell developed a chunky, compact animal and these are the sheep that were brought to America. The states of Colorado, Wyoming, Idaho and Texas produce some of our finest lamb. The sheepherders in the northern states are often Basques — immigrants from northern Spain. Once, driving through Idaho, my husband and I observed at least 3000 sheep guarded by a Basque sheepherder with his quaint small covered wagon hung with pots and pans, most distinctive and practical, for a Basque could live out of this wagon for months.

My first experience in cooking lamb was only a few weeks after my wedding. I discovered my young husband adored roast leg of lamb. In small towns of Oklahoma where I grew up lamb was never available; only occasionally could my mother buy a leg of mutton, which is just an elderly lamb. The flavor was musky and strong, but my father loved it and I did too. Desperate for information, I talked to my butcher, Fred, and from him I received explicit directions for tackling a leg of lamb. I have changed methods since my first lesson, but particularly enjoy simple preparations with herbs and vegetables.

I've tried different methods of roasting a leg of lamb but this preparation has become my favorite. Following this recipe is a suggestion for grilling a butterflied leg of lamb using the same coating ingredients. Always inquire from the butcher where his lamb was raised and if the answer is either Colorado or Wyoming, the lamb should be excellent.

HERBED LEG OF LAMB

5 to 6 pound leg of lamb

$1/3$ cup Dijon type mustard

1 teaspoon rosemary

1 teaspoon thyme

$1/4$ teaspoon oregano or basil

2 cloves garlic, peeled and minced

1 tablespoon dry red wine

Wipe the leg of lamb and trim off any excess fat. With a sharp knife, make several slits in the lamb. Combine the mustard, rosemary, thyme, oregano and garlic. Stir and add just enough wine to make this combination easily spreadable. Rub the mixture (with your hands) over the lamb and into the slits. Place in a shallow baking pan and set aside to marinate and come to room temperature.

Preheat oven to 375°. For medium rare, which is best, roast for 1½hours. If the lamb is cold or weighs more than 6 pounds, roasting time will be longer. Roast 2 hours for the meat to be medium. Baste occasionally. If desired, small new potatoes, scrubbed and unpeeled, may be placed around the roast the last 45 minutes of roasting. Serves 8 to 10.

GRILLED BUTTERFLIED LEG OF LAMB

5 to 6 pounds leg of lamb
Coating ingredients from Herbed Leg of Lamb, page 91

Have a butcher bone the leg of lamb or with a little patience and a very sharp boning knife, perform this operation at home. Cut off as much fat as possible. Without the bone the meat will be almost flat. Don't worry about any scraggly ends for they will be delicious tidbits to nibble on when cooked and crispy (just for the cook!). Make slits over the lamb, combine all the coating ingredients and thoroughly rub into the boned leg and into the slits. Place in a shallow baking pan and set aside to marinate and come to room temperature.

Preheat the oven broiler and for medium rare, broil 15 to 20 minutes on each side. Broil longer for medium. Remove from the oven to rest 20 minutes before carving. Carve at the table, rather thinly and on the bias.

To grill outside, let coals reduce to glowing red and grill the lamb 6 to 8 inches from the heat. Follow the timing as for broiling in the oven but test with a fork to check color of juices. Serves 8 to 10 easily.

When properly trimmed, tied, baked and decorated, a crown roast of lamb is the most elegant of meats. Find a butcher who knows how to prepare a crown roast and he can make it most any size from a single rack of lamb to a double rack. Allow 2 chops per person — a good butcher can add lamb chops to enlarge these racks. Be certain the roast has been prepared for easy carving.

CROWN ROAST OF LAMB

Crown roast of lamb, serving 6 to 8

Salt and freshly ground black pepper

Rosemary or tarragon

Aluminum foil

Paper frills, available in culinary shops and fine butcher shops

Preheat oven to 325°. Have the roast at room temperature. Season lightly with salt, pepper and herb. Wrap a small piece of foil around the end of each bone to prevent charring. Make a ball out of foil and stuff the center to keep the round shape. Place in a shallow baking pan and roast 13 to 15 minutes per pound for pink meat. A crown roast is difficult to test with a thermometer but if the meat is room temperature the timing by minutes will work splendidly.

Remove roast to an easy carving platter. Discard the foil from bones and center of roast. Place a paper frill on each bone and allow the roast to stand 10 to 15 minutes before carving. The center may be filled with any of the following:

New fresh peas cooked with tiny onions

Rice and Wheat Pilaf, page 168

Whole mushrooms sautéed in butter with a splash of lemon juice

Cracked Wheat and Mushrooms, page 170

Wild rice and almonds, pine nuts or mushrooms

A single rack of lamb will be about 6 chops. The whole rack of lamb, called a bracelet, consists of 12 to 16 chops, and usually will have to be ordered, but makes for an elegant and memorable dinner. I was amazed recently to have a friend recall to me a dinner party I had forty years ago featuring a bracelet of lamb. Have the butcher cut the rack so that it may be carved right through the chops without having to struggle with the bones. The ingredients for this recipe are for a single rack of lamb; double the coating ingredients for a bracelet.

RACK OF LAMB PERSILLÉ

1 rack of lamb, (6 chops)

Salt, if desired

Grindings of black pepper

Foil

1 cup bread crumbs

2 cloves garlic, peeled and minced

$\frac{1}{2}$ cup finely chopped parsley

$\frac{1}{2}$ teaspoon dried basil

$\frac{1}{2}$ teaspoon thyme

$\frac{1}{4}$ cup melted butter, approximately

Sprinkle the rack of lamb lightly with salt, if desired, and grindings of black pepper. Wrap the ends of the bones with small pieces of foil to avoid burning. Preheat oven to 375°.

Blend the bread crumbs, parsley, basil and thyme together. Add sufficient melted butter to combine the mixture for spreading. Set aside. Place the rack in a shallow baking pan and roast in preheated oven 25 minutes for medium rare if the roast started out at room temperature. If roast is still chilled, bake another five minutes. For testing with a thermometer, it should register 130°.

Remove the rack to a workable space and spread the crumb mixture over the fat side of the lamb. Return to the oven and continue to roast until the topping has browned nicely and the roast is done, about 15 minutes. Serve immediately on a wooden carving board. One rack of lamb will feed only four guests. For a larger group, I would suggest preparing two racks of lamb or ordering a bracelet.

Lamb patties make easy main entree, light in calories. Cooking in wine gives the lamb a succulent flavor. Try serving with something a bit different such as the earthy but light Quinoa, page 176, and a green vegetable.

LAMB PATTIES IN WINE

$1\frac{1}{2}$ pounds lean ground lamb

Grated rind from 1 lemon

2 tablespoons finely chopped parsley

$1\frac{1}{2}$ tablespoons lemon juice

1 teaspoon salt

Grindings of black pepper

I large bay leaf, crushed

½ teaspoon crushed rosemary

I cup dry white wine

In a large mixing bowl, combine the lamb, grated rind, parsley, lemon juice, salt, pepper, bay leaf and rosemary. (The salt content can be cut in half.) Mix very well and form into 6 patties. Pour the wine in a skillet large enough to place all the patties in one layer. Or cook three at a time. Cook over moderate heat turning once. Test for doneness — just a bit pink makes the patties juicy and flavorful. Serves 6.

Several lamb shanks are not easily found at one time. Buy, when available, and freeze until the quantity desired has been acquired. Small shanks are best and one will serve one person. The larger ones will hopefully take care of two people unless they are big healthy boys that love this most tender of meats so full of flavor with crispy edges to nibble.

LAMB SHANKS

6 lamb shanks

Flour for dredging

⅓ cup canola or olive oil

Salt and freshly ground black pepper

I teaspoon oregano

I teaspoon thyme

2 cloves garlic, peeled and minced

½ cup dry red wine

½ cup beef bouillon

Preheat oven to 350°. Wipe the lamb shanks with a damp cloth. Measure the oil in a large, heavy skillet. Dredge the lamb shanks in flour and brown over medium high heat. As the shanks are browning, sprinkle lightly with salt, if desired, the pepper, oregano, and thyme. Transfer the shanks to a large casserole or Dutch oven. Sprinkle with the minced garlic and add the wine and bouillon. Cover and bake in preheated oven for 1½ hours. Remove the cover and continue baking another 30 minutes to crisp the shanks. Serves 6.

Shish means skewer; *kebab*, broiled or roasted meat. These are the middle eastern terms which Americans use predominantly, rather than the French, *en brochette*, or the Russian *shashlik*. In the Middle East shish kebab is served with an aromatic Persian chello or rice combined with toasted pine nuts. Kebabs are versatile for they may be cooked outside over charcoal or broiled in the oven. A glowing bed of hot charcoal will brown meat quickly without making it dry; the temperature at the grill level should be about 350°. For oven broiling, preheat the broiler and cook kebabs 5 to 6 inches from the heat.

I was behind the former Iron Curtain hunting for a special Georgian bread when I discovered a handsome restaurant in Tibilisi, Georgia. No one could speak English and certainly I had no knowledge of Georgian or Russian. The kitchen staff, after seeing one of my cookbooks, guided me into their large kitchen. Here the men proudly pointed to show me how they made bread from a sourdough starter., bubbling on the floor in a commodious pot.. Beautifully prepared vegetables and lush caviar were in a refrigerator, but the most fascinating appliance was a broiler especially for shish kebab. Made of black iron, about two feet tall, and open in the front it had slots on each side of the interior to place the skewers filled with meat. At the bottom glowed red coals. I thought it most ingenious, for I had seen nothing like this in America. I clapped my hands to show my enjoyment and suddenly three men appeared playing music on strange instruments, singing folks songs. Soon everyone in the restaurant began dancing excitingly fast. What a charming, whirling adventure!

Suggested equipment for broiling shish kebab: a bowl for marinating, a knife for chopping, basting brushes, skewers and heatproof mittens for turning skewers. Shish kebab does not have to be just meat; poultry, fish and vegetables are equally good.

My very first day in Beirut in the year 1966 was a Sunday. My husband and I walked with our son, Peter, who was working on his master's degree at the American University of Beirut. We stood beside the Mediterranean Sea watching the waves beat against the huge rocks and cliffs below and swirl around and through one enormous rock arch that is as familiar to this part of the world as Diamond Head is in the Hawaiian Islands. Groups of people were sitting at tables smoking hubbly bubblies (truly my imagination wafted me off on a Persian carpet). We stopped to have lunch in a second story cafe with a huge window open toward the street and the sea. To my amazement a herd of cattle was led right down this main thoroughfare in this sophisticated city. Our luncheon was chicken shish kebab — no vegetables — with a lovely bowl of hummus tahini, freshly sliced raw carrots and the flat Arabic bread.

Tenderloin, sirloin and loin strips are the most tender cuts of beef for shish kebabs and do not need overnight marinating. Four hours will be quite sufficient. Leg of lamb is excellent. Cut pieces off the leg for the kebabs and roast the remainder. At the end of the recipe will be suggestions for a variety of seasonings and additional vegetables.

Try adding hunks of green or red sweet peppers to your kebabs. Or you may enjoy one small eggplant, unpeeled and cut in cubes. Slice large tomatoes one inch thick and grill them on one side only and serve on the side — an excellent addition. For a different flavor, especially for lamb, add ¼ teaspoon ground cloves and ¼ teaspoon cinnamon to the marinade. Chop fresh mint finely and brush over the meats when serving. The following herbs may be added or substituted — any combination of rosemary, marjoram, thyme, or basil. Add dashes of Tabasco or cayenne pepper for a highly spiced flavor.

SHISH KEBAB WITH LAMB OR BEEF

1½ cups dry red wine

¾ cup olive oil

½ large onion, chopped

1 clove garlic, minced

Freshly ground black pepper

1 teaspoon salt

½ teaspoon each thyme and savory

3 pounds cubed beef or lamb

½ pound mushrooms

½ pound small onions, parboiled

Combine the wine, oil, chopped onion, garlic, pepper, salt, thyme and savory in a large bowl. Add the cubed meat and marinate 4 hours to overnight. (Refrigerate if marinating overnight.) Wipe off the mushrooms with a damp cloth; trim the stem but do not remove. String the meat on skewers and the vegetables on separate skewers. Brush well with the marinade and either broil in the oven about 6 inches from the element or grill over hot coals in an outside grill. Grill the meat 10 to 15 minutes but the vegetables half that time. Serves 6 to 8.

Ready for a picnic supper? Have plenty of towels for this succulent pita bread filled with broiled chicken kebabs, topped with a green salad and a touch of the Middle East in a luscious tahini sauce. *Tahini* is equally delicious on baked or broiled fish and cauliflower. It is available in specialty shops, health food stores and fine supermarkets. *Tahini* is delicious and exceptionally healthful for it is pure sesame seed. A jar, once opened and refrigerated, will keep just like peanut butter.

Pork

....

When a loin of pork is trimmed and then marinated overnight, there is a minimum of fat and the meat becomes luscious and tender. The roast slices easily when hot and any left over is marvelous chilled for sandwiches or luncheon slices with a salad.

TENDERLOIN OF PORK STUFFED WITH PRUNES

$1/2$ cup lemon juice

$1/2$ cup light soy sauce

$1/2$ cup Marsala wine

3 cloves garlic, peeled and sliced

2 tablespoons chopped fresh ginger

10 pitted prunes

5 to 6 pounds loin of pork

Combine the lemon juice, soy sauce, Marsala, garlic and fresh ginger in a small mixing bowl; stir well. Slice the prunes in half. With a sharp knife, make incisions in the meat and insert a half prune into each slit. Place the meat in a shallow dish and pour the marinade over the roast. Cover and let stand at room temperature several hours or preferably overnight, refrigerated, turning several times.

Preheat oven to 350°. Place the pork tenderloin in a shallow baking pan and roast approximately 2 hours if room temperature. Baste every 20 to 30 minutes with the marinade. Serves 8.

The Brazilians have a hearty peasant dish called *feijoada* similar to the French cassoulet but using different beans and meats. Although the preparation does take time, it is not difficult. The result is an enticing wintertime casserole for a buffet needing only a green or fruit salad and French or pumpernickel bread.

BRAZILIAN FEIJOADA

4 cups dried black beans

3 pounds uncooked corned beef

$1/4$ pound sliced bacon, cut in fourths

$1/2$ pound ham, cubed

1 pound smoked sausage links

1 1/2 pounds lean pork, cubed

1 1/2 cups dry red wine

1 1/2 cups orange juice

4 tablespoons olive oil

2 large onions, chopped

3 large cloves garlic, minced

1/2-1 teaspoon dried chili pepper flakes

Grindings of black pepper

Salt to taste

2 cups uncooked rice

1 tablespoon olive oil

1 teaspoon salt

4 cups sliced oranges or canned mandarin oranges

Place beans in a large kettle, cover with water and soak overnight. The next morning, transfer beans to a colander and wash well. Return to a clean kettle, cover with water, place on a moderate burner and simmer for 2 hours uncovered. Check occasionally to add more water if necessary.

In a separate pan, cover the corned beef with water to cover. Bring to a boil and drain immediately. Add fresh water to cover, bring to a simmer and cook for one hour. Sauté the bacon until half done. Drain on paper toweling. When the corned beef has cooked for 1 hour, add the bacon, ham and sausage. Barely cover meats with water and simmer for one hour. Add the cubed pork the last 30 minutes of cooking.

Drain the beans, reserving the liquid. Combine the meats and their cooking liquid with the drained beans in a large casserole. Barely simmer for 2 hours. If the mixture becomes dry, add some of the reserved bean liquid. Test the beans for tenderness. If not done, simmer another 30 minutes. Pour off any excess liquid. Remove the corned beef and cut in bite size pieces; return to the bean mixture. Add the wine and orange juice. Return casserole to low heat and simmer 30 minutes.

Measure the 4 tablespoons of oil into a skillet. Sauté the onions and garlic until limp, about 8 minutes, stirring occasionally. Add the onions, garlic, chili pepper flakes and grindings of black pepper to the bean mixture. Stir thoroughly and check for flavoring, adding more chili peppers to increase spiciness, if desired. Very little salt will be needed as some of the meats contain salt. Cook over low heat or place in a preheated 325° oven 30 to 40 minutes.

Combine the rice with 4 cups of water, the tablespoon of oil and 1 teaspoon of salt in a saucepan. Cover, bring to a boil, lower heat and simmer until liquid is evaporated, about 20 minutes.

Presentation: leave the feijoada in the casserole and sprinkle the top with orange sections. When serving, offer the rice first, then top with the Feijoada. Any remaining orange sections should be placed in a serving dish to be offered with the casserole. Serves 12 to 16.

In the Parisian family our sons came to know so well during their years of hitchhiking the world, is a daughter-in-law, Denise, a superb cook. For two years Denise and her husband loved living in the United States but finally returned permanently to Paris. On one evening while in Paris we joined the family for dinner and to my complete delight, Denise had painted a mural of the Mississippi River complete with paddle wheel boat on a wall in their apartment.

Denise has served us several charming dinners, but one I shall never forget began with Pompadour au Jambon, a luscious soufflé encased in thin slices of superb French ham, the whole surrounded with a beautiful tomato sauce. Denise taught me her secret which I give to you.

POMPADOUR AU JAMBON

Melted butter

Thin slices baked or boiled ham (approximately 7)

2 tablespoons butter

2 tablespoons all purpose flour

I cup milk

Salt and grindings of black pepper

1/4 cup grated Gruyère cheese, packed

1/2 cup finely chopped cooked ham

6 egg yolks

6 egg whites

Tomato sauce*

Brush a 4-cup charlotte mold with butter thoroughly. Line the bottom and sides with the slices of ham. Set aside. Melt the 2 tablespoons of butter in a saucepan and whisk in the flour, cooking until bubbling, stirring constantly. Add the milk and whisk constantly until thick and smooth. Season lightly with salt and pepper. Remove pan from burner and add the cheese and chopped ham, stirring until the cheese is melted. Allow to cool slightly, 5 to 10 minutes. To this mixture add the 6 egg yolks, blending very well. In an electric mixer, beat the egg whites until soft, stiff peaks. Fold a little of the yolk mixture into the egg whites. Then fold the remaining two mixtures together until smooth. Pour into the ham-lined mold.

Preheat oven to 350.° Place the mold in a pan of hot water and set on a moderate burner to cook for 20 minutes. Transfer the mold in the pan of water to the oven, baking 35 minutes. Remove and take the mold out of the water wiping off excess moisture off the bottom and unmold on a serving platter. Denise used a lovely white oblong dish that held all the sauce. The soufflé may be served as is but I prefer a lovely, bright red tomato sauce swirled around the shimmering Pompadour au Jambon. Serves 6 to 8.

TOMATO SAUCE

2 pounds fresh tomatoes or 2 cups canned tomatoes with juice

1/2 cup olive oil

1/3 cup finely chopped onion

1/3 cup chopped carrots

1/3 cup finely chopped celery

1 teaspoon salt

1/4 teaspoon granulated sugar

Note: The sauce should be made ahead so that it will be ready for serving with the soufflé.

Peel fresh tomatoes and remove seeds. Chop coarsely. Chop canned tomatoes and save the juice. Measure the oil into a saucepan and lightly sauté the onion until just translucent; do not allow to brown. Add the carrot and celery, continuing to sauté for another minute. Add the tomatoes and juice (if canned) blending the mixture well. Stir in the salt and sugar and simmer 45 minutes. Purée in a blender, and if using canned tomatoes, run through a coarse sieve. The sauce can be made a day ahead and then heated just before serving.

Pigs have never been one of my favorite animals. I do not trust a pig, nor do I care for their manners — except for three pink pigs in Italy on the Amalfi Drive.

With a little difficulty we found where our hotel on the Amalfi Drive was or was supposed to be. There was a tiny shrine and beside it a door and from there one looked down a tremendously high ridge into the Mediterranean. Four narrow parking places were in front of the shrine and Gene was attempting to maneuver our Fiat into the last spot but the car was at a most awkward position. I stepped out of the car hoping to be of some assistance when two handsome strong Italian men saw our predicament, picked up the back of the car and set it over in the correct position. I thought the whole scene was hilarious. We entered the elevator and after pushing the lobby button, we descended rather fast. The door opened to a stunning room, the floor paved in intricate, magnificent Italian tile. We were escorted to our rooms with a balcony overlooking the ocean—but the bathtub was my love. It was set in a huge curved window encircled with sumptuous bougainvillea. One could soak in this beautiful tub and look down at the blue Mediterranean. What bliss! For luncheon the following day I chose a special restaurant that I had discovered in *Gourmet* Magazine. An old hotel just half a mile off the Amalfi Drive was owned by a cousin of Enrico Caruso. Despite the hotel's age, all was in perfect order. Since no one was present, we decided to explore, and wandered around to the back. Beautifully kept vineyards draped down the hillside as we followed a path to a fence. And there were three really beautiful pigs, pink and scrubbed completely clean. Even the yard had been swept; never had I seen a pig pen such as this. Mr. Caruso joined us, knew immediately what we wanted for lunch, gave us lovely wine from his vineyards and one of the most elegant meals we had in Italy.

There is nothing difficult about baking a ham, the problem is finding a really fine ham that is not precooked and pumped full of water. Look, for they are available and what a difference in the aroma and flavor!

BAKED HAM

15-pound ham

1 cup brown sugar, packed

5 tablespoons apple cider vinegar

Whole cloves

Canned pineapple, optional

Remove wrapping from ham and the mesh that will probably cover it. Check the directions for cooking on the wrapper for this may be of some help in determining amount of cooking time. Most will suggest covering the ham but I prefer the meat to be left uncovered. For a 15-pound ham, 15 to 16 minutes per pound will be sufficient. By that time the ham should be crusted and brown. If there is any heavy skin, remove it. In a mixing bowl stir together the brown sugar and vinegar. Remove ham to a counter, still in the roaster, and with a sharp knife score the ham across diagonally both directions so that small squares are made. Stick a clove in center of each square. If there is to be a buffet party, arrange drained canned pineapple slices across the top and sides securing with toothpicks. One can go even further and pin a red candied cherry in the center of each pineapple. The cooks of my childhood loved decorating a ham with everything. Spoon the brown sugar mixture over all the ham. Return to the oven for 30 minutes. Remove and place ham on a large wooden carving board. One large ham will serve many people, 30 to 40, with scraps left for a great split pea soup.

During a truly memorable month in Italy, we walked the ancient streets of Rome, spent a week in Florence, then a night in northern Italy close to the Austrian border wandering through desolate, gray, abandoned, huge square German military buildings. We enjoyed superb food in Venice and an Italian opera in Naples. We had a horrible experience being mugged in Naples, were fascinated by a prostitute wearing an orange wig walking the streets after the opera, were enthralled by Paestium, Pompeii and Herculaneum. We drove the magnificent Amalfi Drive curving high above the Mediterranean, traveling the complete length of the Italian boot simply because it was there. We took the last plane from Palmero, returning to Rome to find everything on strike. We ate a tiny early breakfast and then found no international planes could land for six hours and no food was available in the airport. We boarded an American plane where we were offered a cocktail and almost fell on the floor. Despite a few difficulties we loved it all, from the elegant hotels to the highway motels, the antiquities, museums, and exhilarating buildings. But most of all we loved the superb Italian cuisine.

ITALIAN CREPES STUFFED WITH RICOTTA AND HAM

MEAT SAUCE

1/2 cup butter or margarine

1/2 cup olive oil

2 cups finely chopped onions

3 cloves garlic, peeled and minced

3 large stalks celery, finely chopped

3 pounds ground sirloin

4 cans (16 ounces each) plum tomatoes

8 ounce can tomato sauce

Freshly ground black pepper

2 cloves

3 teaspoons Italian mixed herbs, page ??

1 teaspoon oregano

$\frac{1}{2}$ cup chopped fresh parsley

Salt to taste

In a large skillet melt the butter and oil. Sauté the onions, garlic and celery until tender, about 10 minutes. Add the ground meat and stir well browning very lightly. Blend in the tomatoes and tomato sauce. Bring mixture to a simmer and add the pepper, cloves, Italian herbs, oregano and parsley. Stir very well, add salt, taste and adjust. Cover and let just barely simmer for 1 hour. Remove cover and continue to simmer until the meat sauce has become thicker. Taste again for seasoning. The sauce may be cooled and refrigerated and then congealed fat may be removed. The complete dish can be finished the following day.

BÉCHAMEL SAUCE WITH HERBS

4 tablespoons butter or margarine

3 tablespoons onion, finely minced

10 tablespoons all purpose flour

6 cups hot milk

$\frac{1}{2}$ teaspoon salt

$\frac{1}{2}$ teaspoon white pepper

2 sprigs parsley, snipped in pieces

$\frac{1}{8}$ teaspoon nutmeg

Melt butter in a large saucepan. Sauté onion until soft over moderate heat. Whisk in the flour and cook the roux slowly, stirring constantly until the mixture just begins to turn golden. Gradually add the hot milk stirring vigorously with a whisk until thick and smooth. Add the salt, white pepper, parsley and nutmeg. Allow sauce to just barely simmer for 30 minutes, stirring occasionally. It should be reduced by one-third. Strain sauce through a fine sieve.

1 cup all purpose flour

¼ teaspoon salt

3 eggs

1½ cups milk

¼ cup oil

Combine the flour, salt, eggs and milk in a blender. Blend until smooth, removing the top once to scrape down the sides with a rubber spatula. Blend again and refrigerate for 1 to 2 hours. Brush a crepe pan with oil and place on moderate burner. The crepes should be about 5 inches in diameter. Use 1 tablespoon of batter for each crepe. Cook in the center of the crepe pan for about one minute on each side. Crepes can be stacked when cooled with oiled paper between each crepe, wrapped and frozen. This amount of batter will make approximately 20 to 22 crepes.

THE FILLING

1 pound ricotta cheese

1 cup grated Parmesan cheese

1 cup cooked ground ham

¼ cup finely chopped parsley

1 clove garlic, minced

1 teaspoon dried basil

2 eggs

Salt to taste

Grindings of black pepper

Parmesan cheese, for topping

Combine all ingredients except the final Parmesan cheese for topping. Stir until very well mixed. Place one large tablespoon of the filling in each crepe and roll, laying them seam side down in a buttered baking dish. Brush each crepe with melted butter and sprinkle with Parmesan cheese. Preheat oven to 375° and cook the crepes for 25 minutes or until completely hot.

To serve: Place two crepes on each plate and have both sauces hot. Pour the meat sauce on one side and the Béchamel on the other. Or several crepes may be placed in a baking dish with sauces arranged on each side. Heat until bubbling hot. Serves 10 with two crepes each.

Note: There will be extra meat sauce. Sauté one pound of Italian sausage, sliced, and add to the sauce. Serve on spaghetti for 4.

Veal

....

For the following veal roast, choose either a rolled veal roast which frequently will be the shoulder of veal, or a sirloin tip roast which is good solid meat with little fat. Serve hot the first evening and later chilled as Vitello Tonnato, page 107.

BRAISED VEAL ROAST

4 to 6 pound veal roast

2 tablespoons soft butter

Salt and grindings of black pepper

2 cups chopped onions

3 carrots, scraped and chopped

2 large stalks celery, chopped

3 cloves of garlic, minced

2 bay leaves

2 cups dry white wine

1 1/2 cups water

1/4 cup all purpose flour

Preheat oven to 500°.

Rub the butter over the roast and sprinkle lightly with salt and pepper. Place the roast in a heavy casserole with a cover, large enough to hold all the vegetables. Place the roast, uncovered, in hot oven and brown, turning after 10 minutes and turning again if necessary.

Make a mirepoix by combining the onions, carrots, celery, garlic and bay leaves. (For ease in handling remove the casserole from the oven and arrange the mirepoix around the roast.) Return to the oven. Let the vegetables cook in the high heat until just beginning to turn color, about 10 to 15 minutes. Browning particularly brings out the flavor of the onion. Again, remove casserole and sprinkle the flour on top of the roast. Turn the roast several times until there is no flour visible. Add the wine and sufficient water to come just to top of the roast. Cover, return to oven and lower heat to 325°. Veal roast will become flavorful and tender when braised in the combination of wine and the mirepoix. Bake about 1½ hours and test for tenderness. Remove the roast to a serving platter and drain the juices from the casserole into a saucepan. Boil rapidly until reduced to half the original amount. Slice a portion of the roast and ladle the reduced liquid over the slices. Serves 8-10.

As we reclined happily in a charming room with windows open wide to a magnificent view of the Mediterranean in the city of Taormina, Sicily, we looked back over our drive down the complete boot of Italy. We'd stopped once in an Italian roadside motel, we'd accepted two enormous lemons from a filling station attendant and we'd gotten lost in the city of Reggio at the toe of the boot, trying to locate the boat dock to ferry across to Sicily. We had four superb weeks in Italy and soon it would be time to return home. But now a beautiful plate of chilled Vitello Tonnato was placed in front of us. It was a sumptuous dish worthy of our last few nights on a splendid journey. If you are fortunate enough to have cold sliced veal, try the following recipe.

VITELLO TONNATO

6½-ounce can tuna fish

2 tablespoons lemon juice

6 anchovy fillets

¾ cup mayonnaise

Cold sliced veal

Capers

Lemon slices

Place the tuna in a small bowl. Spoon the lemon juice over the fish and let marinate for one hour. Transfer to a food processor fitted with a steel blade and add the anchovy fillets and mayonnaise. Pulse until well mixed. Remove cover and scrape down the sides with a rubber spatula. Continue to pulse until the mixture is smooth and creamy. Arrange slices of chilled veal on a serving tray. Mask with the tonnato sauce and sprinkle capers down the center. Decorate with lemon slices. A beautiful tray for a buffet or a Sunday evening supper made from leftover Braised Roast of Veal. No salt is necessary for both the anchovies and the capers are salty.

Several years ago I watched an incredible performance of two men milking fifty cows in one hour on a Wisconsin dairy farm. Fifty huge Holstein cows patiently walked into an enormous barn, each selecting her own stall. The milking machine had been thoroughly cleansed and in rapid succession the two men cleaned udders, clamped on the machine and milk poured through sterilized tubes running overhead across this vast barn and into a pasteurized vat. With such an enormous dairy industry, the finest of milk-fed veal is produced in this beautiful state. Too bad so many Americans shun this delicate meat, but the Italians love it and Osso Bucco is a triumph of their culinary art.

OSSO BUCCO

4 veal shanks (about 7 pounds), cut 1-2 inches thick

Flour for dredging

Salt (optional)

Grindings of black pepper

1/4 cup butter

1/2 cup olive oil

4 cloves garlic, peeled and thinly sliced

1 medium onion, peeled and thinly sliced

3 medium carrots, scraped and sliced

2 stalks celery, sliced

Rosemary

Thyme

Basil

2 bay leaves

14-ounce can sliced tomatoes

2 sprigs parsley

1 1/2 cups dry white wine

2 cups chicken broth

2 slices lemon

2 slices orange

Preheat oven to 325°. Choose a heavy casserole that can be served at the table for baking the shanks.

Dredge the shanks in flour, shake off the excess and sprinkle with optional salt and pepper. Combine the butter and oil in a large skillet and brown the shanks, a few at a time. Place the meat in the casserole, standing each piece against the other. On top of the shanks add the garlic, onion, carrots and celery. Sprinkle liberally with rosemary, thyme and basil. Tuck in the bay leaves. Add the tomatoes, parsley, wine and chicken broth and top with the lemon and orange slices. Bring the contents to a boil over medium heat and transfer to the preheated oven. Cover and bake 1½ to 2 hours or until the meat is fork tender. More wine or broth may be added if liquid becomes low. Osso Bucco will be better if cooked one day, cooled and refrigerated to serve a day or two later. Depending on the number of veal slices, the recipe will serve about eight. Do try this with Italian Arborio rice.

Late in the afternoon on a drive from Switzerland to southern France, I suggested stopping in a French village for the night. My husband insisted it was much too early and that we should drive on, which landed us in northern Italy and in the huge, industrial city of Turin. Neither of us knew anything of this city and we actually had not intended to be in Italy, but by this time dusk was enveloping us and we could see nothing that resembled a hotel. In the dim light, we spotted a tiny taverna, actually a pizza parlor with a bar in front. After pulling into a convenient parking place in front we entered this establishment and were greeted by an Italian stocky, pleasant woman who spoke no English. Our Italian was limited to two words — yes and no. After much sign language, my husband suddenly found his way behind the bar and mixed two drinks with the lady smiling and nodding. Well, he did have a way with women! Then her husband appeared to rescue us. Although he could speak no English, either he seemed to understand from our sign language that we had sleeping and eating in mind. To our delighted amazement, he brought his own car around and indicated that we should follow. With elaborate good-byes we drove across this unknown city ending at the airport. Our guide pointed to a handsome hotel, we waved our thanks and relief, and he disappeared. After freshening up in a most pleasant room, we entered a busy dining room at ten p.m. Our waiter was most attentive. Since we were actually in Italy, I wanted Lemon Veal, which they do so beautifully, a good soup and gelato, their superb ice cream. The waiter nodded and returned soon with large soup bowls filled with a beautiful clear broth swimming with luscious tortellini. And finally, just as I had hoped, he brought lovely veal scallops redolent with lemon. Never shall I forget the hospitality of our unknown Italian friends whom we will never see again. Here is my own recipe for veal cooked in lemon and wine with the addition of green grapes.

SCALLOPS OF VEAL WITH GREEN GRAPES

2 pounds veal scallops

Light sprinkling of salt

Grindings of black pepper

Juice of 1 large lemon

Flour for dredging

⅓ cup butter

½ cup dry white wine

½ cup chicken broth

2 cups green grapes

Lemon wedges

Slice the veal scallops in half if they are long and ungainly to handle.
Season the scallops lightly with salt and pepper and rub with the lemon
juice. Dredge lightly with flour shaking off any excess. Melt butter in a
skillet and brown scallops quickly for one minute on each side. Remove to a
plate. Add the wine and broth to the skillet, stir well and return the veal to
the skillet with the grapes. Let simmer 2 to 3 minutes, moving the scallops
around to allow the grapes to heat completely. Arrange the scallops and
grapes on a serving platter pouring over any of the pan juices left. Decorate
with lemon wedges. These delicate morsels disappear quickly; they are
excellent with rice or tiny new potatoes. Serves 6.

Poultry and Game

The redoubtable chicken is prepared in hundreds of ways but a few of them have
attained the status of classics. The French *coq au vin* is one of those. There is no other
chicken dish that is quite as succulent and pleasurable as this classic French composi-
tion of flavors. What great satisfaction it is to end such a meal by breaking off pieces
of French bread and sopping the whole plate! The French enjoy using salt pork for the
flavor it adds to a dish. In part of this process much of the salt is removed but, if you
prefer, in sautéing the chicken, drain off the pork fat and substitute olive oil and the
butter.

COQ AU VIN (CHICKEN IN WINE)

1/2 pound salt pork

5 pounds chicken pieces

Salt, optional

Grindings of black pepper

2 tablespoons butter

1/4 cup minced shallots or scallions

1/2 pound mushrooms, sliced

1 clove garlic, minced

2 cups dry red wine

1/4 teaspoon thyme

1 bay leaf

2 cups chicken broth

1/2 cup tomato sauce

2 tablespoons butter

1 pound small boiling onions

1 cup beef broth

2 tablespoons flour

2 tablespoons melted butter

Slice the rind off the salt pork and dice. Place in a saucepan, cover with water, bring to boiling and cook 6 minutes. Drain in a sieve. Dry with paper toweling. Sauté the pork in a heavy skillet or a Dutch oven until golden, stirring occasionally. Remove with a slotted spoon to paper toweling.

Remove skin from chicken, if preferred, and any excess fat. Dry pieces thoroughly. Sprinkle lightly with salt and pepper. Add 2 tablespoons of butter to the fat in the skillet and brown chicken on all sides, removing pieces to a plate. Do not crowd the chicken while sautéing. When finished, add the shallots and mushrooms to the skillet and sauté 3 minutes, stirring constantly. Add the garlic and cook 1 minute. Drain off any excess fat. Return the chicken and salt pork to the skillet atop the mushrooms. Add the wine, thyme and bay leaf and bring to a boil. Cook uncovered 10 minutes. Add the broth and tomato sauce. If there is not sufficient liquid to barely cover the chicken, add a little more wine or broth. Cover and simmer 30 minutes or until the chicken is tender.

Melt the two tablespoons of butter in a small skillet and add the onions, shaking the pan until they are lightly golden. Add the beef broth, cover and simmer until tender. This may be accomplished while the chicken is simmering.

Arrange the chicken, drained onions and mushrooms on a large serving platter. Keep warm in a very low oven. Bring sauce to a rapid boil. Blend the flour and melted butter together in a small bowl. Add some of the boiling liquid, stirring until smooth. Slowly add the flour mixture to the boiling sauce stirring constantly. Cook about 5 minutes. Strain over the chicken. The chicken may be decorated with a little parsley, then served with rice or noodles and, of course, French bread. Serves 8.

When I last tested this savory entree, I gave half to a friend. Her husband called the next morning extolling the virtues of my cooking — he was most emphatic that I could cook for him anytime!

CHICKEN BREASTS WITH SPINACH

3 whole boned chicken breasts, cut in half

1 cup cooked, well squeezed spinach

¾ cup ricotta cheese

½ cup minced prosciutto or mild cooked ham

1 egg, lightly beaten

3 tablespoons milk

¼ teaspoon ground nutmeg

Salt to taste

¼ cup butter or margarine

⅓ cup dry white wine

⅓ cup chicken broth

Grindings of white pepper

Place chicken breasts, one at a time, between sheets of plastic wrap or wax paper. Flatten the chicken with the side of a mallet or a cleaver. In a mixing bowl combine the spinach, ricotta, proscuitto, egg, milk, nutmeg and salt. Place an equal amount of spinach mixture on each chicken breast. Fold the chicken over the filling pressing edges together and transfer to a platter. Cover and chill 1 hour.

Preheat oven to 350°. Melt the butter and pour into a baking dish just large enough to hold the chicken in one layer. Carefully pick up each breast and turn in the butter, placing seam side down. Add the wine and broth. Bake in preheated oven 30 minutes, basting twice during that time. Turn oven to broil and brown the chicken lightly for 5 minutes. Arrange the chicken on a serving platter and add the white pepper to the juices and then pour all over the chicken breasts. Serves 6 and will be wonderful with Middle Eastern rice, or quinoa, page 176

Chicken is fondly regarded in part because of its ability to blend with so many other delicious ingredients, and the recipe that follows demonstrates this trait. No, zucchini is not stuffed into the cavity of a young chicken, but under the skin. This dish is fascinating and fun to prepare, resulting in a finished entree that is one of the most succulent birds to adorn any table. Serve with an elegant rice ring and a big, fresh green salad. No vegetable is needed for it is all inside the chicken!

CHICKEN STUFFED WITH ZUCCHINI

THE CHICKEN

> 3 ½ to 4 pound chicken
> Olive oil
> Thyme, oregano, savory

Using poultry shears or a sharp, heavy knife, split the chicken down the back just to the neck. STOP! Turn the chicken, skin side up, and flatten the bird with the palm of your hand by giving it a good whack. Don't worry, it will not come apart.

With one hand holding the bird, gently loosen the skin with the other hand. Start with the breast and work down into the thigh and leg until finally, your hand and wrist will nearly be lost from view! Be careful with fingernails to avoid piercing the skin. Stick one finger down into the leg and twist around; the skin will loosen easily.

Fold under the wings and rub olive oil atop the skin and sprinkle with the dried thyme, oregano and savory. Set aside in a large baking pan and let rest one to two hours.

1 pound small zucchini

Salt

1/3 cup butter

1 medium onion, finely chopped

6 ounces ricotta cheese

3/4 cup Parmesan cheese

1 to 2 teaspoons dried herbs: thyme, oregano, savory

Salt and pepper, optional

Grate the zucchini by hand or in a food processor. Place in a mixing bowl and salt lightly. Allow to stand 35 minutes. Squeeze out as much water from the zucchini as possible. Melt the butter in a skillet and sauté the onion 5 minutes. Add the zucchini and continue to sauté another 8 minutes, stirring to mix well. Remove from burner and combine with the ricotta and Parmesan cheese, adding the amount of herbs desired. Preheat oven to 450°. Stuff the dressing underneath the loosened skin. Indeed, this is messy but just keep pushing the dressing down into the legs, thigh and breast to make the chicken round and plump. Sprinkle lightly with salt and grindings of pepper. Return to the baking pan. Bake the chicken 10 minutes; lower heat to 375° and bake 50 minutes, basting occasionally. The bird will be a luscious, dark golden brown. Transfer to a big wooden carving platter and serve with pride! Two birds can easily be prepared to serve 8 to 10 guests.

There is nothing quite so enchanting for Americans than wandering through the Casbah in Casablanca or a *souk* in Beirut or Cairo listening to the strange sounds, breathing the unusual aromas, wildly imagining the secrets behind the curtained or beaded doorways and seeing strange people dressed in an enticing array of colors. The flavors and exotic atmosphere of Casablanca are represented in this chicken dish, cooked with garbanzos and served with couscous that seems to literally inhale the aromatic juices. One could dream of having dinner with Pepe le Moko or perhaps Humphrey Bogart.

MOROCCAN CHICKEN

4-5 pounds chicken pieces

$\frac{1}{4}$ - $\frac{1}{2}$ teaspoon ground cumin

Salt

Freshly ground black pepper

6 tablespoons butter

6 tablespoons canola oil

2 onions, sliced

2-inch strip of lemon peel

1 can (15 ounces) chick peas, drained (garbanzos)

2-3 cups chicken broth

4 tablespoons chopped parsley

3 cups cooked rice or couscous*

Lemon juice

Season the chicken pieces lightly with cumin, salt and pepper. (If preferred, remove skin from chicken.) Combine the butter and oil in a large, heavy skillet and sauté the chicken pieces. When golden, remove to a plate or paper toweling. Add the onions to the skillet and sauté until golden. Place the chicken atop the onions and add the lemon peel and chick peas. Add sufficient broth to barely cover the chicken. Lower heat to simmer and cook slowly, uncovered, about 1 hour until chicken is very tender.

Serving: Spoon half the rice on a serving platter and place the chicken on top. Pour the sauce from the skillet over the chicken and top with remaining rice and parsley. Sprinkle with lemon juice. If using couscous, serve separately from the chicken, as this grain rapidly absorbs liquid. Serves 8.

COUSCOUS

2 cups boiling water

1 cup couscous

2 tablespoons butter

Bring 2 cups of water to a boil in a saucepan. Add the couscous and bring back to a boil. Let cook rapidly 2 minutes. Add the butter, stir, cover and remove from burner. Let stand 15 minutes. Fluff the couscous with a fork before serving.

CHICKEN KEBABS WITH TAHINI SAUCE

2 1/2 pounds boned chicken breasts

1/2 cup dry white wine

4 tablespoons lemon juice

1/2 cup olive oil

4 large garlic cloves, peeled and mashed

1 teaspoon oregano

1 teaspoon thyme

Salt, optional

Cut the chicken in bite-size cubes, trimming off fat and the tendon. In a mixing bowl combine the wine, lemon juice, oil, garlic, oregano and thyme with a light sprinkling of salt, if desired. Mix well and add the chicken. Stir until all is well mixed and cover with plastic wrap. Refrigerate overnight.

TAHINI SAUCE

1 cup tahini (sesame seed paste)

5 tablespoons lemon juice

1 cup water, approximately

3 cloves garlic peeled

1/2 teaspoon salt

In a mixing bowl combine the tahini with the lemon juice; this mixture will become a very thick paste. Add sufficient water continuing to stir vigorously, until the mixture becomes the consistency of mayonnaise. In a mortar and pestle work the garlic and ½ teaspoon of salt until the garlic is well mashed and dissolved. Add to the tahini sauce. This amount will be sufficient for about 8 sandwiches; it doubles easily and can be done in a food processor with a larger amount.

THE SALAD AND VINAIGRETTE DRESSING

1 head Romaine lettuce

Green onions

Tomatoes

2/3 cup olive oil

1/4 cup red wine vinegar

3 teaspoons Dijon-type mustard

Break in small pieces all of the inside, tender leaves of 1 head of romaine lettuce. Chop one bunch (about 6) green onions, white part only and add to the lettuce. Cut 2-3 tomatoes in small pieces and add to the salad. Salad ingredients must be in small pieces for ease in stuffing into the sandwich and eating. Combine the oil, vinegar and mustard, beating until creamy. Toss the salad thoroughly with the dressing. A dressing redolent with mustard is essential in the amalgamation of all the ingredients.

Pita Bread: buy whole wheat or white. The small pita is my favorite with just the top sliced off. If a really fine and sturdy pita is available, buy the large size and cut in half. One, per person will probably be ample but there are always those ready to split another one — they are so good!

Final Procedures: Place the chicken pieces on wooden Japanese skewers, about 5 pieces per skewer. Broil in the oven six inches from the element until they begin to brown, turning the skewers twice. With small pieces of chicken this process should take no longer than 10 minutes. If broiled outside, let the coals burn down to just glowing and cook the chicken until golden brown, about 10 minutes. The wooden skewers may scorch a bit but metal tears the chicken. Have the bread ready and scoop off the chicken from a skewer into the bread. Top with the tahini sauce and then the salad. One layer of each is sufficient for my appetite but two layers of each can be added in the larger bread — chicken sauce, salad and the same layers again. Provide lots of paper napkins or small Turkish towels. All this can become a bit messy but much fun and absolutely delectable.

BROILED CHICKEN WITH MAÎTRE D'HÔTEL BUTTER

Melt ½ cup butter or margarine and add the juice of 2 lemons. For 2 split chickens or 4 Cornish hens, cut in halves, brush the lemon butter on both sides of the birds and let marinate until room temperature.

For the chickens, broil skin side down on bottom rack of an electric stove, about 25 minutes or until quite golden brown. Remove from oven, sprinkle lightly with salt and pepper and turn over to brown on the skin side. Brush with remaining marinade. Broil 15 to 20 minutes or until golden and the juices run clear. The Cornish hens will take less time, about 20 minutes per side.

MAÎTRE D'HÔTEL BUTTER

1/2 cup butter or margarine

2 tablespoons minced parsley

2 tablespoons minced chives or shallots

2 tablespoons lemon juice

Combine the butter, parsley and chives in small bowl of an electric mixer. Stir until thoroughly mixed and gradually add the lemon juice, continuing to beat until the juice is absorbed. Refrigerate until the mixture becomes slightly solid. Spread plastic wrap on a counter and place the butter mixture in a straight line about 1 inch thick. Roll tightly and refrigerate. When solid, cut in 1 inch slices and freeze, ready to use at anytime. The butter mixture is delightful on fish and steaks.

For chickens: Rub split broilers with oil, salt and pepper. Place in broiler pan skin side down so that most of the heat can pass through without tearing the skin. Let cook until the bones become quite brown. Turn the skin side up, broiling until golden and the skin is puffing and bubbling. This will take about 20 minutes per side. Immediately spread a piece of maitre d'hôtel butter over the chickens. Serve immediately.

Note: for a more pungent flavor add 1 tablespoon of Pommery mustard to the maître d'hôtel butter. Both the suggestions for broiling chickens and Cornish hens in the oven may be switched to grilling outside. Let the coals become red hot with no flame and grill as suggested on both sides. The timing will depend on the type of grill you posses. Twenty to 30 minutes per side should be ample as long as the coals maintain their heat.

Pat Biggs, my niece and artist, enjoys a big family — six children and four grandchildren. Pat's husband Bill loves cooking outside so half their meals are grilled. Pat made up a wonderful slightly sweet but piquant marinade that is most savory and enticing while on the grill — and on the table.

GRILLED CHICKEN WITH HONEY MARINADE

FOR TWO CHICKENS

1/2 cup honey

1/4 cup low-sodium soy sauce

¾ teaspoon powdered ginger

¼ teaspoon garlic powder

½ cup ketchup

Combine all the ingredients for the marinade, mixing very well. Brush the chickens that have been either split or quartered. Let them marinate for at least 2 hours allowing them to come to room temperature. Spray the rack on the grill with a vegetable spray to avoid sticking. Grill the chicken skin side up over glowing red coals turning to brown at the last. For Cornish hens, serve each person half a bird. Do distribute plenty of paper napkins or small terry cloth towels for one must really use the hands for this delicious chicken.

The little chickens called Cornish hens make a very appealing presentation, and when combined with a touch of lime and green grapes, are also delicious. Serve with baked brown rice for a hearty and lovely dinner. This dish is light in calories which you may squander on a wicked dessert!

CORNISH HEN WITH LIME MARINADE

¾ cup canola oil

¾ cup fresh lime juice

I tablespoon dried tarragon

Salt

Grindings of black pepper

½ teaspoon Tabasco sauce

4 Cornish hens

Green seedless grapes

Combine the oil, lime juice, tarragon, salt if desired, and pepper. Beat with a small whisk until creamy, similar to a vinaigrette. Clean the hens, dry thoroughly and tuck the wings under. Brush the hens completely with the marinade and allow to sit at least one hour. When ready to bake, preheat the oven to 350°. Stuff the hens with grapes, tie the legs with twine to keep the birds straight and attractive. Bake one hour if the birds are room temperature, longer if cold. Brush with remaining marinade twice during the baking process. Delicious with Baked Brown Rice, page 172.

The phrase "chicken and noodles" conjures up comforting home cooking in our part of the world, but chicken with pasta is beloved elsewhere too. The following aromatic chicken is reminiscent of Italy and Greece. It makes a complete dinner that may be partially cooked ahead and finished just before serving. Just add a crisp, green salad and a crusty Italian bread.

CHICKEN WITH PARMESAN NOODLES

4 cups tomatoes, peeled, seeded, chopped

1/4 cup finely chopped parsley

3 tablespoons finely chopped fresh basil or 2 teaspoons dried

2 tablespoons fresh oregano or 2 teaspoons dried

Grindings of black pepper

4 whole cloves

6 pounds frying chicken, cut in pieces

1/2 cup butter

4 tablespoons olive oil

Salt to taste

1 1/2 cups dry white wine

1 large lemon, thinly sliced

18 ounces noodles

2 1/2 cups freshly grated Parmesan cheese

Parsley for decoration

Combine the tomatoes, chopped parsley, basil oregano, pepper and cloves in a mixing bowl. Set aside.

Dry pieces of chicken thoroughly. Melt butter with the oil in a large skillet. Sauté the chicken until lightly golden, salting lightly on each side if desired. Avoid crowding the pan thus allowing the chicken to brown evenly. Transfer chicken to a casserole. Drain off excess fat from skillet. Add the wine and boil over high heat, scraping to deglaze the pan. Stir the wine and scrapings into the tomato mixture. Pour this mixture over the chicken and top with the sliced lemons. Preheat oven to 325°. Cover the casserole and bake in the oven 1 hour. The chicken may be prepared to this point, cooled, and refrigerated until the following day.

Presentation: Boil the noodles in 4 quarts of lightly salted water. When tender, drain thoroughly in a colander. Remove the hot chicken to a large platter. (Now is the time to use a Thanksgiving platter, for this dish needs space.) Arrange the chicken in the center of the platter. Transfer the noodles into the juices of the casserole and add the Parmesan cheese. Over medium heat stir until the cheese is melted. Surround the chicken with the noodle-cheese mixture and decorate with parsley. Serve immediately. Serves 8 generously.

As my son Michael was thumbing through his big notebook of recipes he stopped. "Mother, here is one of your best chicken recipes and I will wager to say you haven't prepared it in a long time." I glanced at the ingredients and remembered the fantastic flavor. "A bit rich," I said, "but I suppose one could eat only two pieces instead of three." After remaking this crusty chicken, I knew it must be added to this collection of poultry recipes.

SESAME CHICKEN

COATING

2 cups flour

1 teaspoon salt

$^1/_2$ teaspoon nutmeg

$^1/_2$ teaspoon garlic powder

1 bottle (2 oz) sesame seeds

$^3/_4$ cup butter, melted

2 eggs, well beaten

$^1/_2$ cup milk

2 $^1/_2$ to 3 pound chicken, cut in pieces

Preheat oven to 350°. Combine the coating ingredients, mix well and place in a plastic bag. Pour the melted butter into a shallow dish or pan. Combine the eggs and milk in a shallow dish. This procedure will be a bit messy so have everything ready to keep the assembly line moving. Set a baking pan close by.

Dip pieces of chicken in the milk mixture. Shake in flour mixture, dip in the melted butter and shake again in the flour mixture. It is best to prepare two pieces of chicken at a time. Place in a baking pan and cover with aluminum foil. Bake 45 minutes, uncover and bake 30 to 35 minutes or until just a light golden color. The coating makes a thick paste over the chicken and does not brown as deeply in color as fried chicken. With the thick coating, the chicken is kept moist and tender. Serves 4.

Company coming? Poached chicken breasts take little time — and the finished meat may be used in many ways. Poach the chicken breasts according to the following recipe and you'll have the prime ingredient for a number of delectable dishes.

POACHED CHICKEN BREASTS

3 whole chicken breasts

4 small shallots, finely chopped

1 bouquet garni: 3 sprigs parsley, small piece celery, 1 bay leaf

$1/2$ teaspoon salt (optional)

8 whole peppercorns

$1/2$ teaspoon tarragon

2 cups dry white wine

Water to cover

It is best to use chicken breasts with the bone left in for they hold a shape better, making them easier to slice. Place the chicken in a skillet at least 2 inches deep and large enough for all to be on one layer. Add the shallots, bouquet garni, salt, peppercorns and tarragon. Pour wine over the chicken and add sufficient water to cover. Over moderate heat bring to a boil, then reduce heat until barely simmering, and cook 10 to 15 minutes. Remove from the burner, cover and allow to set for 30 minutes. If just barely simmered and allowed to finish cooking with no heat, the chicken breasts should be moist and tender. Remove chicken breasts to a dish to cool. Discard the skin and remove the bone. If not to be used right away, wrap securely in plastic wrap and refrigerate. To freeze the chicken, cover with the cooking liquid, to keep the meat from drying out. Otherwise, strain the cooking liquid into a container, cover, label and freeze to use again to poach or add to a soup.

CHICKEN SALAD WITH FRUIT

3 cups poached chicken breast, cut in bite size pieces

2 cups cantaloupe balls

1 cup seedless grapes, green or purple

$\frac{1}{2}$ cup toasted, slivered almonds

$\frac{1}{2}$ to $\frac{3}{4}$ cup homemade mayonnaise

Combine the chicken, cantaloupe, grapes and almonds together in a bowl. Add sufficient mayonnaise to bind all together. Cover and chill until ready to serve. If calories are of concern, mix half mayonnaise and half plain yogurt. Serves 4.

Another meal starring poached chicken is the club sandwich. This is not the three-layered sandwich filled with whatever a chef might have on hand, but a really yummy, moist club sandwich. I shall not give exact measurements except to suggest 3 pieces of bacon for each sandwich. Do use a good homemade white bread, for the ingredients just seem to blend better. When making several sandwiches, have all ingredients prepared and ready to put together as the bread is toasted.

A PERFECT CLUB SANDWICH

Grill bacon until crisp and free of fat. Drain on paper toweling, mopping more grease off with extra layers of paper. Keep warm in a very low oven. Drop tomatoes in boiling water for just a few seconds or hold over a gas flame until the skin loosens. Then, the skin will slide off easily. Slice as evenly as possible, discarding the stems and cutting out the core. Remove lettuce leaves from refrigerator and dry thoroughly. Slice poached chicken breasts the long way about ¼ inch thick. Toast the bread and have soft butter and mayonnaise at hand. Brush butter over the toasted bread, add a leaf or two of lettuce, a light film of mayonnaise, then sliced chicken breast, another film of mayonnaise, sliced tomatoes next, several strips of bacon and top with buttered slice of toasted bread. Slice diagonally and enjoy!

CHICKEN BREASTS WITH BROCCOLI

2 whole chicken breasts, poached

2 packages (10-ounces each) frozen broccoli

4 tablespoons butter

4 tablespoons all purpose flour

Salt to taste

Few grindings of white pepper

1 cup milk

1 cup chicken broth

1 cup sliced mushrooms

1 tablespoon butter

2 teaspoons lemon juice

2-ounce jar pimento, drained and diced

$\frac{3}{4}$ cup grated Swiss cheese or part skim Farmer's cheese

1 tablespoon chopped parsley

$\frac{1}{4}$ cup toasted sliced almonds

Poach chicken breasts, page 122. Remove from liquid and set aside. Cook the broccoli according to directions on the package, just until tender crisp. Drain and arrange the vegetable in a 7 x 11 inch baking dish. Top with the chicken breasts. Melt the butter in a saucepan and whisk in the flour until smooth. Add a sprinkling of salt and the white pepper. Whisk in the milk and broth until smooth and lightly simmering, stirring constantly. Sauté the mushrooms in a small skillet in the tablespoon of butter and add the lemon juice. Cook just until tender and add to the cream sauce with the pimento, cheese and parsley. Stir until the cheese is melted. Preheat oven to 350°. Pour the cheese sauce over the chicken breasts and sprinkle with almonds. Bake about 25 minutes or until hot and bubbling. Serves 6.

Note: To reduce calories, use a light margarine, reconstituted skim milk and a low-calorie cheese such as Farmer's or Borden's low cholesterol.

Everyone from my 104-year-old mother-in-law to my youngest grandchild adores chicken pot pie. There are many versions of this American favorite. I offer two concepts here that can be used to make individual pies for freezing as well as a large casserole. A suggestion: I have found that my youngest grandchildren prefer the vegetables cut in small pieces. Turkey may be substituted for the chicken.

CHICKEN POT PIE

9 cups chicken broth

2 cups scraped, sliced carrots

1 cup celery, cut in diagonal slices

5 cups cubed cooked chicken or turkey

$\frac{3}{4}$ cup butter

2 medium onions, coarsely chopped

1 cup all purpose flour

Grindings of black pepper

$\frac{1}{8}$ teaspoon nutmeg

$\frac{3}{4}$ cup finely chopped parsley

Salt to taste

2 cups blanched broccoli flowerettes

2 cups fresh or frozen peas

Measure 4 cups of the broth into a saucepan and add the carrots and celery. Bring to a simmer, cooking uncovered, until tender, 15 to 20 minutes. Transfer these vegetables with a slotted spoon into a very large mixing bowl. Add the chicken.

In a separate saucepan, melt the butter and sauté the onions until just golden, about 8 minutes. Whisk in the flour until smooth and allow to cook 5 minutes. Add all the broth, including that which was used for the vegetables. Whisk rapidly until smooth and simmering. Stir in the pepper, nutmeg, parsley and salt to taste. Let simmer 5 minutes. (Blanch broccoli flowerettes: place in saucepan and pour boiling water to cover and immediately drain in a sieve.) Add the peas and broccoli to the bowl with chicken and vegetables. Pour the thickened chicken broth over all and stir thoroughly. Taste again and adjust seasonings. The recipe will make about 16 cups. Transfer to a large casserole and if the pie is to be used right away, prepare biscuits (recipe following) and pop into a preheated 450° oven. Bake until biscuits are browned, about 15 to 20 minutes. Or, if using for a special dinner, let cool, cover thoroughly with aluminum foil, label and freeze. When ready to use, let stand at room temperature until thawed and then heat in a 400° oven until bubbling. Remove, add the biscuits and cook at 450° until golden. Or place the frozen pie loosely covered in a 350° oven for 45 minutes or until piping hot. Proceed as directed, topping with biscuits.

Individual ramekins: My favorite way to prepare chicken pot pie is using individual baking dishes, 4 to 5 inches in diameter and about 2 inches deep. I've given only general directions for ramekins for they certainly come in all sizes. For example, smaller pies are preferable for small children — even a custard cup will do very well. Fill each ramekin within $\frac{1}{4}$ inch of the top. Let cool for freezing; cover tightly with aluminum foil and label. The ramekins can be used as individual servings topped with biscuits or pastry (recipe follows). Now, lovely dinners are ready for just a single person or a family gathering. Delicious served with sautéed whole mushrooms and a fruit salad.

BUTTERMILK BISCUITS

2 1/2 cups all purpose flour

1/2 teaspoon salt

3 teaspoons baking powder

1/2 teaspoon baking soda

5 tablespoons butter or vegetable shortening

1 cup buttermilk

Melted butter

Preheat oven to 450°.

Sift flour, salt, baking powder and baking soda into a mixing bowl. Cut in the butter with a pastry blender until mixture resembles coarse cornmeal. Make a well in the center and add the buttermilk. Stir quickly with a rubber spatula until a dough is formed. Turn the dough out on a floured surface and knead lightly. Pat or roll the dough about 1/4 inch thick. Cut with a floured biscuit cutter and place on an ungreased baking sheet. Bake in a preheated oven 12 to 15 minutes.

When making biscuits for a large chicken pot pie, use a 1½-inch biscuit cutter. With the individual ramekins, choose either a very small size (1 inch) or cut one large biscuit, about 3 inches across. The remaining dough can be made into biscuits to be served with butter and preserves. Chicken pot pie must be heated first; when hot, remove from oven and top with the biscuits. Return to oven, bake as directed and serve immediately when biscuits are golden brown.

PASTRY FOR CHICKEN POT PIE

1/2 cup butter or margarine

2 1/4 cups unsifted all purpose flour

1 teaspoon salt

1/4 teaspoon baking powder

5 to 6 tablespoons ice water

Cut the butter into pieces and place in a shallow mixing bowl. Sift the flour, salt and baking powder over the butter. Cut together with a pastry blender, or add all the ingredients to a food processor fitted with a steel blade and pulse until well blended. To the flour mixture, add cold water, mixing quickly with a fork until mixture forms a ball. With food processor, pulse constantly adding water just until a ball of dough forms, then stop. Gather dough together, kneading lightly if necessary to pick up the little pieces of dough, round into a ball and cover with plastic wrap. Refrigerate until pies are cooled. Cut pastry in half for ease of handling and roll one portion on a floured counter or pastry cloth about ¼ inch thick. Cut in rounds to fit individual ramekins. Place on top of each dish and press to sides for sealing. Pierce the pastry with a fork. At this point the pies may be wrapped and frozen. What a relief to have an excellent dinner, for unexpected guests or at the end of a frustrating day.

If cooking unfrozen, preheat oven to 425°. Bake pies 10 minutes, lower heat to 350° and continue baking 25 to 30 minutes or until pastry is golden and pie is bubbling.

If the pies are frozen, remove from freezer and unwrap. Preheat oven to 425°. Place pies in oven and bake about 40 minutes or until the crust is golden and the pie is bubbling.

At the age of eighteen my eldest son Nick took a year between high school and college to hitchhike around the world on foot, by bicycle, student boat and freighter. When his boat docked in Pakistan, half way around the world, he faced a traumatic confrontation with a foreign culture as swarms of people, a constant din and strange aromas greeted his ship. Thirty minutes passed before he summoned enough guts to disembark.

Nick survived Pakistan, and sailed around India to Calcutta. He could find no decent lodging there within his budget of five dollars a day, but he possessed a promising telephone number. He got in line with several men waiting to use a public telephone. Soon he found himself in conversation with a young man about ten years older than himself and wound up accepting this man's offer to be his house guest for two weeks. The Indian was married to a Chinese woman and thus was out of caste. Each evening the couple separated to eat dinner with their own families. Nick joined his host, thirteen siblings and the parents. There was one light globe suspended form the ceiling over the evening meal which was always a curry, each time hot enough to make Nick break into a sweat. Nick was certain the meat in one stew was dog.

When Nick returned home he helped me in devising a hot sauce to give a final finish to a curry dinner I had been working on for several years. He assured me that my efforts were strictly *pukha sahb*, the very tops in an exotic Indian dinner. I had learned that in the Dutch East Indies, the Hollanders took their curries quite seriously. At the same time, they were jolly and loved to turn a meal into a complete ceremony with rice, curry and condiments carried in by young sarong-clad boys bearing aromatic dishes on huge platters. Thus, they called the featured curry dish "Fourteen Boy Curry." Both the English who adore the spicy curry and the Dutch preceded these dinners with gin slings and accompanied the meal with chilled beer. The Dutch called such a meal Ristafel; in London the many Indian restaurants provide a delicious relief from the average, bland English cuisine.

The following recipe can be doubled to serve 20 people. No centerpiece is needed for the condiments placed in colorful bowls and arranged in an oval, a heaping platter of rice and big dish of curry create an intriguing and inviting dinner party.

Explain to guests that the rice topped with the curry may be placed in the center of a plate and surrounded by the condiments. Or each condiment may be placed atop the curry ending with a little hot sauce so that one has a veritable volcano with an enchanting aroma.

Although this is a turkey curry, chicken or shrimp may be substituted. For a large dinner party, turkey has always been my favorite, for I could have a family dinner with roast turkey one evening and use the remaining boned turkey for the curry. After boning the turkey, the bones and skin can be simmered with water to cover, a few spices to make a broth for the curry.

A FOURTEEN BOY CURRY

¼ pound butter

I tablespoon curry powder

3 cups turkey or chicken broth

¾ cup flour

2½ cups milk

¾ Coconut milk*

8 cups diced cooked turkey

Salt to taste

Melt the butter in a large skillet. With a wooden spoon (metal imparts an unpleasant taste to curry) stir in the curry powder. While this is lightly bubbling, mix the turkey broth and flour in a blender at high speed.

Gradually add the flour mixture to the curry stirring constantly. Add the milk and coconut milk. Bring to a light simmer and stir until thickened. The mixture should be similar to a very light gravy. The sauce must not be too thick for it should be a consistency to drench the prepared hot rice. Add the turkey, bring to a simmer until the meat is thoroughly hot. The curry is ready to serve or can be cooled, covered and refrigerated overnight. If preferred cool, cover and freeze.

*Coconut milk: fresh coconut milk is the best, but if not available, heat 1 cup of milk and pour over ¾ cup canned coconut and allow to steep several hours. Strain through cheesecloth, pressing out all the milk from the coconut. There will be about ¾ cup of coconut milk.

CONDIMENTS AND FINAL PREPARATION

Grated egg whites

Grated egg yolks

Crisp bacon, broken in pieces

Sautéed bananas

Green peppers, coarsely chopped

Eggplant, cubed and sautéed

Green onion, coarsely chopped

Fresh pineapple, cut in pieces

Ground mixed nuts

Mandarin oranges

Kumquats, optional

Chutney

Dark raisins

Coconut

Eggs: Hard-boil six eggs and cool. Peel and then grate the whites and the yolks into separate bowls. This may be done the day ahead; cover with plastic wrap, refrigerate and remove at least three hours before serving to become room temperature.

Bacon: Slowly sauté 2 pounds of bacon until brown and crisp. Drain on paper toweling and crumble into a bowl. Prepare bacon on the day to be served.

Bananas: Select 6 to 8 semi-ripe bananas. Peel and slice thickly, about ½ inch. Brush lime juice over the bananas and sauté lightly in butter. Place in a bowl — these should be prepared the day they're to be served.

Green pepper: Chop three peppers or enough to fill selected bowl, place in water and refrigerate. The next day, drain and place in serving bowl.

Eggplant: Remove skin from a large eggplant and cut into small cubes. Drop the cubes into a bowl of milk, then into a pan of flour and sauté in olive oil. Add grindings of black pepper and a light salting. Drain on paper toweling and place in an ovenproof dish so that just before serving, the eggplant can be reheated in the oven and then placed in serving bowl.

Pineapple: Peel and remove the core of a ripe pineapple. Slice in sections, cut in small pieces, place in a serving bowl and top with light sprinkling of cinnamon if desired. Cover with plastic wrap and refrigerate overnight. Remove three hours before serving.

Mixed nuts: Whirl two cups of mixed nuts (salted or unsalted) in a food processor. This can be accomplished several days before serving. Place the ground nuts in a serving bowl, cover and set aside.

Mandarin oranges: It would be wonderful to have fresh mandarin oranges, but if not, use the canned, drained thoroughly; or use sectioned fresh oranges. Place oranges in serving bowl, cover, refrigerate and remove three hours before serving.

Kumquats: Drain a bottle of kumquats and place in serving bowl. These little fruits add piquancy that melds with the curry, but they are optional.

Chutney: Purchase the very best available. Many brands are named Major Grey, but use the chutney made in India. An excellent chutney is most important, for the pungent, spicy flavor gives an authentic touch to a curry dinner. A good chutney can be expensive, but because of its aromatic flavor only a spoonful is needed for each serving.

Dark raisins: Pour boiling water over 2 cups of raisins in a sieve. Drain and place on paper toweling to dry. The raisins are now plumped and ready for the serving bowl.

Coconut: A moist coconut is best. Some frozen brands are too sweet; canned is preferable unless you have the time and patience to grate fresh coconut! Fill a bowl with coconut and cover until ready to use.

Green onions: Coarsely chop 3 to 4 bunches of green onions using a portion of green for color. Cover and refrigerate until three hours before serving.

Hot s auce: Melt 4 tablespoons of butter in a small sauce pan. With a wooden spoon stir in 6 tablespoons of curry. Continue stirring until the curry is dissolved and the mixture lightly bubbling. Add 2 cups of chicken broth, bring to a simmer and remove from the burner. Serve in a gravy or sauce boat but do warn guests of the contents suggesting only a sprinkling over the curry. More can always be added.

Rice: Add 2 cups of rice to 4 cups of boiling water. Add 2 tablespoons of butter, reduce heat, cover and simmer about 15 minutes or until all the water is absorbed and the rice is tender. Salt may be added to the water if desired.

Presentation: For a buffet, first present the large bowl of rice, then the turkey curry. Arrange the condiments in this order: egg whites, egg yolks, bacon, bananas, green pepper, eggplant, pineapple, green onions, nuts, oranges, kumquats, raisins, chutney, coconut and finally the hot sauce. A buffet is simpler, however a seated dinner presents a fun challenge, for passing all the condiments can become hilarious with the comments about what is coming and going and where to place it all. Serve a fresh fruit salad and the Indian bread called chapata if available. If not use toasted pita bread as a great substitute.

Like curry, roast turkey is the centerpiece of a long food tradition and is served with appropriate pomp and ceremony. Anticipation grows as the mingled aromas from the kitchen invade the house. As my family grew I soon learned that turkey was a delight other than just holidays, for there could be three days of feasting and no one was picky about those meals! I prefer to bake a turkey without the stuffing which was always arranged in separate casseroles with a little turkey broth spooned over the top. The paste used to top my turkey results in a luscious golden crusty bird.

CLASSIC ROAST TURKEY

15-pound turkey

½ cup soft butter

10 tablespoons all purpose flour, approximately

4 tablespoons lemon juice

Salt

If the bird is frozen, place in refrigerator to thaw in original wrapping for two days. To speed thawing, place turkey under cold running water. Or follow directions on the wrapper for thawing. If possible, purchase a fresh turkey simply because the flavor is much better. Avoid a self-basting turkey for with the following directions, this is not necessary. Rinse the bird, remove the giblets from the neck cavity and pat the turkey dry with paper toweling. Place the butter in small bowl of an electric mixer and add sufficient flour and lemon juice to make a thick creamy paste. When the turkey is dry, rub the inside with salt, if desired. Tuck the wings under and rub the paste all over the turkey. If any paste is left, rub it on the inside. With a fresh turkey, the paste can be applied the night before and the turkey refrigerated with a light covering. If not, make the paste preparation as early as possible the day of baking. Tie the legs together to present a well formed bird. If a thermometer is used, insert in center of the inside thick muscle adjoining the cavity. Preheat oven to 325°. Place the turkey, breast side up, in a roaster large enough that the bird does not touch the sides, or use a large shallow baking pan. Cover loosely with aluminum foil tucking at the ends of the roaster but do not let it touch the top of the bird. If possible, have the turkey at room temperature before baking; otherwise cooking time will be lengthened. (When you arise in the morning, before you brush your teeth, take the turkey out of the refrigerator!) A 15-pound turkey will take about 4½ hours to roast. A 20 pound bird will roast in 6 to 7 hours. If the turkey is stuffed, it will take a little longer to cook.

Place the neck and giblets in a large saucepan and cover well with water. Simmer until tender, removing the liver within 30 minutes. Use 1½ cups of this broth with ¼ cup melted butter to baste the turkey every 30 minutes. The remainder of the broth will be used for gravy. Forty-five minutes before the turkey is done, remove the foil and cut the string holding the legs so the complete bird will brown. When the legs move easily, the meat feels soft, and the skin is a lovely golden brown, the turkey is done. A meat thermometer will register 195° when finished.

Remove the turkey to a large platter and let it stand 20 minutes before carving. Pour off a portion of the fat from the roaster, leaving about 1 cup. Or pour all the liquids into a jar and remove as much fat as possible, returning the rest to the roaster. For a smooth, creamy gravy sprinkle ½ cup flour over the bubbling liquids at medium high heat. Whisk rapidly until smooth. Add 1 cup of turkey broth and 1 cup milk. Keep stirring and add sufficiently more milk or broth until the gravy is the thickness you prefer. Sprinkle with salt and grindings of black pepper; taste and adjust. Turn the heat very low. Have a warm gravy boat ready but let the gravy barely simmer while the turkey is carved and all the other goodies are passed. This takes time and it is best to keep the gravy hot or otherwise it will begin to congeal, which is most unappetizing. The gravy will be hot and ready for the dressing and whipped potatoes. Have a wonderful dinner!

QUAIL AND PHEASANT WITH WILD RICE

2 pheasants

6 to 8 quail

I small ginger root, grated

2 teaspoons thyme

I teaspoon rosemary

Grindings of black pepper

I teaspoon salt

½ to I cup Basic Vinaigrette Dressing, page 56

Melted butter

Dry sherry

Fresh parsley

Wild rice and mushrooms*

Wash the pheasants and quail, drying thoroughly. Combine the ginger, thyme, rosemary, pepper and salt. Rub over the pheasant and quail. Place the birds in a large bowl and cover each with the vinaigrette dressing rubbing over all quite thoroughly. Cover and marinate overnight, refrigerated. Preheat oven to 350°. Remove the birds from the marinade and brush each with melted butter and place in a roaster. Bake the pheasants for 1 hour, covered. Uncover and bake until tender, about 45 minutes. The quail should cook 45 minutes covered and 30 minutes uncovered. Remove from oven. Have the wild rice finished and placed on a large platter. Center pheasants and bury the quail in the rice around the larger birds. Decorate with sprigs of parsley. Serves 6 to 8.

WILD RICE AND MUSHROOMS

Wash 2 cups wild rice thoroughly in a sieve under running water, stirring to clean thoroughly. Combine the rice with 4 cups of water and 1 teaspoon salt. Bring to a boil, lower heat, cover and simmer 45 minutes to 1 hour or until tender. Taste for salt and adjust. While the rice is cooking, slice 1 pound of mushrooms and sauté in 3 tablespoons of butter until tender and liquid. Sprinkle with a few drops of lemon juice. Add to the finished wild rice and arrange on a platter to receive the birds.

When the season arrives for fresh, small quail, buy two per person, marinating for a short time and broil until golden in color. To enjoy this delicacy, tear it apart with your hands—it is the only way. Just provide plenty of napkins and offer warm, wet terrycloth towels afterwards. One-half a quail may be offered as a first course, served hot or chilled.

BROILED QUAIL

4 small quail

Lemon juice

2 tablespoons Dijon-type mustard

1 1/2 tablespoons dry white wine

1/2 teaspoon each basil and tarragon

Salt, optional

With kitchen shears, split the quail down the back. Rub with lemon juice. Combine the mustard, wine, herbs and salt. Mix well and with fingers rub all over the quail. Place in a baking sheet, skin side down, and set aside to reach room temperature. Preheat oven to broil. Grill 6 to 8 inches from the element 8 to 10 minutes on each side or until the birds are brown and crisp. Serve two birds per person. Serves 2.

Since duck is a rich bird, the cooking method is a bit different than for a chicken. Remove all visible fat and add no additional oil or butter of any kind. A duck is self-basting so do not prick the skin. As the fat gathers in the roaster during the cooking process, siphon off several times with a bulb baster. A 5-pound duck will be done in 2 hours, but not well done. If a crisper bird is preferred, bake another 30 minutes. The French prefer duck that is medium rare. If this is your preference, roast less than the 2 hours.

DUCK WITH ORANGES

5 to 6 pound duck

Salt

Grindings of black pepper

2 large oranges

1 small onion

3 teaspoons potato flour

1 1/2 cups orange juice

1/2 cup dry red wine

1 tablespoon red currant jelly

Preheat oven to 350°. Season the duck lightly with salt and pepper. Quarter one orange and stuff inside the duck with the onion. Tie the legs together. Place in a baking pan and roast in the preheated oven for 2 to 2½ hours. Whether the bird is room temperature or cold will make a difference in cooking time. Keep siphoning off the fat until there are only 2-3 tablespoons left when the bird is finished. With a vegetable peeler, cut off thin slices of peel from the remaining orange and cut in julienne strips. Cover with cold water in a saucepan and bring to a boil. Drain immediately. Remove any remaining white skin from the orange and divide in sections. Remove the duck and discard the stuffing. Place the duck on a warm platter and keep warm in a 150° oven. Blend the potato flour into the pan juices with a whisk. Stir in the orange juice and wine, stirring until the mixture boils. Add the currant jelly and orange rind. Taste for seasoning. Simmer 5 minutes. Ladle into a sauceboat and add the orange sections. Spoon a bit of the sauce over the duck and serve the remaining sauce separately. One duck will serve 4.

Fish and Seafood

As I have collected recipes and ideas for food preparation over the years throughout our travels, I have especially enjoyed the fruits of the sea as they are prepared in seacoast cities throughout the world. However, we have made our home mostly in places a long way from the ocean. Still, when it is possible to obtain beautiful fish from American rivers or seafood from the American coasts that is fine and fresh, this chapter suggests some delicious ways they can be served.

Janet and Bill Loring, my niece and nephew, have lived in Colorado most of their forty years of marriage and often mailed me gorgeous fresh rainbow trout. Janet shared her favorite trout recipe with me. I have loved this recipe, for it is easy to prepare and results in trout that are perfectly cooked and handsome.

Trout, fillet sole, orange roughy, all may be prepared in the following simple, but classic method that takes only a few minutes to produce the finest in fish cookery.

TROUT MEUNIERE

4 fillets of boned trout

Cold milk

Flour

Sprinkling of salt

Grindings of black pepper

1/2 cup butter or margarine

Juice of 2 lemons

1 tablespoon chopped parsley

6 ounces toasted sliced almonds, optional

Dip the fillets in the milk and sprinkle lightly with flour shaking off any excess. Season lightly with salt and pepper. Set aside on a plate. In a heavy skillet melt the butter and sauté the fillets slowly until lightly brown on both sides. Remove fish to a warm platter. To the butter in the skillet add the lemon juice and parsley. Let simmer two or three minutes. Sprinkle almonds over the fish and pour over the lemon butter. Serve immediately. Serves 4.

BAKED TROUT WITH MUSHROOMS

4 trout, $\frac{1}{2}$ to $\frac{3}{4}$ pounds each

Freshly ground pepper

Salt

Flour

6 tablespoons butter

4 tablespoons olive oil

$\frac{3}{4}$ pound fresh mushrooms, thinly sliced

2 tablespoons lemon juice

$\frac{3}{4}$ cup thinly sliced scallions

$\frac{1}{4}$ cup fresh white bread crumbs

Parsley for decoration

Wash the trout inside and out and pat dry with paper toweling. Season the fish lightly with pepper and salt and roll in flour, shaking off any excess. In a heavy skillet (10 to 12 inches, large enough for the fish) melt 2 tablespoons of the butter with the olive oil over medium high heat. When the foam subsides, add the trout. Do not crowd; cook only two at a time if necessary. Cook them for 5 minutes on each side until golden brown. Transfer the trout to a plate.

Preheat oven to 450°. In a clean skillet melt two tablespoons of the butter over moderate heat. Add the sliced mushrooms, stirring so they are well coated, and sprinkle with the lemon juice. Cook 3 to 4 minutes until they just soften slightly. With a slotted spoon remove mushrooms and spread them over the bottom of a buttered oven proof baking dish, large enough to hold the fish in one layer. Melt the remaining 2 tablespoons of butter in the skillet and add the scallions, stirring and cooking 2 minutes. Transfer to a bowl. In the same skillet, lightly brown the bread crumbs. Add another tablespoon of butter if needed.

Arrange the trout atop the mushrooms in the baking dish. Any juices left on the trout dish should be added to the main casserole. Sprinkle the fish with the crisped bread crumbs and spread the scallions on top. Bake on the middle shelf of preheated oven for 10 to 15 minutes or until the crumbs and scallions are browned. Serve with beautiful fresh parsley tucked around the heads. Serves 4.

Red snapper is a beautiful iridescent fish with red highlights. It is almost always available. Its mild flavor and tender texture pleases even the pickiest eaters.

BAKED RED SNAPPER

3 pounds red snapper

1-2 teaspoons lemon juice

Salt and freshly ground black pepper

1/2 cup olive oil

2 medium onions, chopped

3 medium tomatoes, peeled, seeded

1/4 cup finely chopped parsley

4 cloves garlic, minced

1 teaspoon oregano

1/2 teaspoon thyme

1/2 cup dry white wine

2-3 teaspoons soft bread crumbs

Lemon wedges

Black Greek olives (optional)

Preheat oven to 350°. Brush a shallow baking dish with a little of the oil. A white oval fish casserole is perfect for baking and serving.

Wash the fish well under running water. Drain and dry thoroughly with paper toweling. Rub fish with the lemon juice and sprinkle lightly with salt and pepper. Mix together the oil, onions, tomatoes, parsley, garlic, oregano and thyme. Spread half the mixture over the bottom of a baking dish and lay the fish on top. Cover with the remaining vegetable mixture. Pour the wine over all and sprinkle top with bread crumbs. Bake in preheated oven 45 to 50 minutes basting occasionally. Decorate with lemon wedges and optional olives. Serves 6 to 8.

During the summers when my eldest grandsons would fly from Colorado to stay a few weeks, poached salmon was first on their list of food for Grandma to cook. The day before arrival I prepared the fish so that it would be chilled and ready to consume. The boys preferred the salmon unadorned but Grandpa and I loved the traditional sauces, such as the Sauce Verte included with this recipe.

POACHED SALMON WITH SAUCE VERTE

Court bouillon for poaching

2 cups dry white wine

4 quarts water

1 onion, sliced

3 stalks celery, sliced with leaves

1 carrot, sliced

4 sprigs parsley

1 teaspoon dried thyme

2 bay leaves

6-8 peppercorns

3 lemon slices

3 garlic cloves

1 salmon, 4 to 5 pounds

Cheesecloth

Combine all ingredients for the court bouillon in a fish poacher with a rack. Bring to a boil, lower heat and simmer 30 minutes. Strain the poaching liquid, discarding the vegetables. Return the strained liquid to the poacher and cool to lukewarm.

Wrap the fish carefully in cheesecloth and tie with string. (Do not have the fish boned or it will fall apart.) Place the fish on the rack and into the cooled court bouillon. If there is not sufficient bouillon to cover the fish, add more wine and water. Bring slowly to just a simmer over moderate heat and cook gently 20 minutes. Remove poacher from the burner, cover and let fish cool in the liquid.

Transfer the fish to a platter and remove the cheesecloth and skin. Cover with plastic wrap and refrigerate until chilled. Serves two hungry boys several days, or is excellent on a buffet table or a dinner for eight served with boiled potatoes, English style.

3 cups chopped parsley

2 cups fresh tarragon or 1 teaspoon dried

10 medium spinach leaves

4 large leaves of chives or 2 tablespoons of frozen, chopped

10 to 12 sprigs watercress

2 cups mayonnaise, homemade please (Mayonnaise, page 233)

Chop all herbs and spinach coarsely, place in a bowl and add boiling water to cover. Let steep 3 minutes. Drain, run cold water over the mixture and squeeze dry. Place in a food processor and pulse until well chopped. Add the mayonnaise to the processor and whirl several times until very well mixed. Pour the sauce in a china or glass bowl for serving with the salmon.

During a seven weeks' journey winding through Quebec, New Brunswick, Nova Scotia and south into New England following the fall colors, I relished gorging on superb salmon, lobster and New England pies of wondrous variety. Indeed it is a wonder I did not gain twenty pounds. Although we live in the middle of our nation with no ocean front, we find that amazingly fine salmon is often available, even in Oklahoma. The following preparation, long a favorite, has two serving suggestions, one with just fresh lemon and the other with basil butter.

GRILLED SALMON STEAKS WITH BASIL BUTTER

6 salmon steaks, 1 inch thick

$^3/_4$ cup dry white wine

$^3/_4$ cup olive oil

$1^1/_2$ tablespoons lemon juice

$^3/_4$ teaspoon salt (optional)

Freshly ground black pepper

1 teaspoon dried basil

$^1/_2$ teaspoon dried thyme

$^1/_2$ teaspoon dried rosemary

$^1/_2$ teaspoon dried savory

1 tablespoon minced parsley

Fresh lemon or Basil Butter*

Arrange steaks in a single layer in a shallow dish. Combine the wine, oil, lemon juice, salt, pepper and herbs and stir until well mixed. Pour over the fish and allow to marinate at least four hours, turning the steaks several times.

Preheat the broiler. With four hours of marinating the salmon should be room temperature and will cook quickly. Place the steaks in a broiling pan, reserving the marinade. Broil, 6 inches from the element, about 5 minutes on each side. When the steaks are turned, brush with marinade and continue broiling. Total time of broiling should take no more than ten minutes. Check one steak for doneness by pricking with a fork. Salmon steaks grilled over a charcoal burner are superb — especially on a lovely fall evening.

Serve each portion with half a lemon covered with a muslin cap (available in culinary shops) or topped with basil butter. Any leftover salmon is a treat for lunch the following day. Serves 6.

BASIL BUTTER

Combine ½ cup of soft butter (or margarine) with ½ cup finely chopped fresh basil and 2 teaspoons Dijon-type mustard. Refrigerate until just congealed. With a melon scoop make balls of all the mixture and place on waxed paper. Freeze and then place in a plastic container, cover tightly, label and keep in the freezer. When preparing salmon steak, allow one ball per steak to become room temperature. Use the ball of basil butter immediately when the steaks are removed from the oven and placed on a plate. With a fork rub the butter over the steak, allowing it to melt. This mixture is excellent on other broiled or baked fish, steaks, lamb and veal chops.

After my first visit to France many years ago, I was determined to prepare quenelles and to my delight found that freezing did not harm the texture. For many years salmon or pike quenelles reposed in my freezer ready for very special dinners. At one such dinner, eight guests were seated at my table, which was festive and gleaming with an embroidered tablecloth from Damascus, china from England, crystal from Ireland, with a low, lovely centerpiece banked by candles. The first course was salmon quenelles, one per person, served in a shell comfortably anchored in a white damask napkin that had been folded just to fit the serving plate. A gentleman on my right looked quizzically, but with a twinkle in his eye, at the most elegant dish and asked, "Mary, do I eat the napkin?"

SALMON QUENELLES IN SHRIMP SAUCE

THE PANADE

$1/2$ cup hot water

$1/2$ cup milk

8 tablespoons butter

I cup all purpose flour

I teaspoon salt

$1/2$ teaspoon nutmeg

4 medium eggs

Combine the water and milk in a saucepan and bring to a boil. Add the butter, stirring until melted. Rapidly whisk in the flour all at once. Keep stirring until the panade forms a ball. Remove from the burner and add the salt, nutmeg and the eggs one at a time beating thoroughly until the mixture is smooth and satiny. The beating may be accomplished in a food processor fitted with the steel blade. Refrigerate the panade until chilled.

THE QUENELLES

2 pounds fresh salmon or pike

$1/4$ teaspoon white pepper

$1/2$ teaspoon salt

$1/2$ teaspoon nutmeg

3 unbeaten egg whites

$1/4$ - $1/2$ cup heavy cream

Check the fish carefully, removing bones and skin. Be especially careful with pike which has fine, tiny bones. If frozen fish is used, defrost and dry thoroughly with paper toweling. Cut the fish in pieces; this also assists in finding any hidden bones. Place all the fish in a food processor with steel blade in place. Whirl the fish several times. Add the white pepper, salt and nutmeg and egg whites, pulsing until well blended. Add the cooled panade and whirl until well mixed. Keep the processor running and slowly add sufficient cream to create a soft consistency that will not fall apart. Test a teaspoonful in simmering water to check how well it holds together. Chill the quenelle mixture for easier handling. Brush a large skillet with melted butter. Add water until skillet is half full. Bring to a simmer. Shape the quenelles with 2 tablespoons (egg shape) and drop each into the simmering water. When the skillet is filled but not crowded, gently turn the quenelles over. Let simmer no more than 5 minutes on each side. Remove with a slotted spoon to drain on paper toweling. Repeat with remaining quenelle mixture. When cooled, the quenelles may be frozen in plastic containers with waxed paper between layers, or you may proceed with the final preparation.

SHRIMP SAUCE

3 tablespoons butter

3 tablespoons flour

1 $\frac{1}{4}$ cups fish stock or clam juice

Salt to taste

Grindings of white pepper

Lemon juice

$\frac{1}{2}$ cup heavy cream

$\frac{3}{4}$ cup coarsely chopped cooked shrimp

Grated Gruyère cheese

Melt butter in a saucepan and whisk in the flour stirring 2 to 3 minutes. Blend in the fish stock and continue to stir over medium to low heat until mixture thickens. Add salt to taste and a few grindings of white pepper. Stir in several drops of lemon juice; taste for flavor. Remove from heat and add the cream. Return to a low burner and heat just until very warm; do not allow to boil. Add the shrimp and continue to cook until thoroughly heated.

Individual servings: Place a teaspoon of sauce in bottom of a small cooking shell. Top with one quenelle and cover with sauce. Sprinkle with the grated cheese. This amount of shrimp sauce is sufficient for 6 to 8 quenelles. Preheat oven to 350°. Place all the shells on a baking sheet and into the oven until the cheese is melted and sauce is bubbling. Place each shell atop a folded napkin on a plate and serve while hot.

Casserole: Lightly butter a shallow baking dish and pour in a small amount of sauce just to cover the bottom. Arrange eight quenelles in the casserole and cover with remaining sauce. Sprinkle grated cheese over the quenelles and bake in a 350° oven until hot and bubbling. These may be served on hot, fluffy rice, one or two per person.

Napkin folding: Fold a damask napkin lengthwise a bit wider than the cooking shell. Take each end and fold under until the creases meet in the middle. Placing the shell in the center provides an anchor, making it easy for a guest to handle while eating. Arrange on an 8-inch plate.

Either sole or flounder fillets may be used in this delightfully easy main entree that can be prepared in 15 to 20 minutes and baked in 30.

BAKED SOLE

3 shallots or 4 scallions

5 sprigs of parsley, finely chopped

3 large chives blades

$\frac{1}{4}$ pound mushrooms, chopped

1 tablespoon flour, approximately

Bread crumbs, whole wheat or white

6 small fillets of sole or flounder

Salt

Grindings of black pepper

$\frac{1}{2}$ cup dry white wine

$\frac{1}{2}$ cup chicken broth

Grated Parmesan cheese

Preheat oven to 350°. Brush an oval fish casserole with butter and set aside.

Combine the shallots, parsley, chives and mushrooms in a bowl, mixing well. Sprinkle one-half this mixture over the buttered baking dish and sprinkle lightly with flour — more than 1 tablespoon may be needed. Top with a sprinkling of bread crumbs. Place the fish on top of this mixture. Salt lightly and add the pepper. Cover the fish with the remaining mixture. Over all this pour the wine and chicken broth. Dust again with bread crumbs and sprinkle with grated cheese. Bake 25 to 30 minutes or until the fish is tender and the liquids are simmering. Serve immediately.

Note: If the fish is frozen, allow to thaw and blot away as much moisture as possible with paper toweling.

It was our great pleasure to enjoy a Swedish student for a year during our son

Mike's senior year of high school. Over the Christmas holidays we drove to Florida to show him a portion of the United States, returning through New Orleans at New Year's when the annual big football game was played. We spent one evening in the French Quarter where the streets had been roped off, allowing no cars within the area that was patrolled by policemen on horseback. The Quarter was chaotic with thousands of people having an uproarious time anticipating tomorrow's game. We stopped at Pat O'Brien's and let the boys have one of their tall fancy drinks (including the tall curved glass) and as we wandered the streets peeking in at the bawdy houses, Svante became very excited and wished to know if there was anyplace else like this in the United States. I assured him this was totally unique. Svante was enchanted with the Creole food. Shrimp Creole can be enjoyed mildly spiced or strong with more pepper. Although preparation of fresh shrimp can be a bit tedious, it is worth the effort, for too often commercially cooked shrimp can be much too well done and tough.

SHRIMP CREOLE

$\frac{1}{3}$ cup canola or olive oil

I cup coarsely chopped green pepper

2 cups coarsely chopped onion

I cup chopped celery

2 cloves garlic, peeled and minced

3 $\frac{1}{2}$ cups canned tomatoes

$\frac{1}{2}$ teaspoon paprika

$\frac{1}{4}$ teaspoon black pepper

$\frac{1}{4}$ teaspoon white pepper

$\frac{1}{4}$ teaspoon cayenne pepper

$\frac{1}{2}$ teaspoon dried thyme

I teaspoon salt

I large bay leaf

2 cups water

2 pounds fresh shrimp, peeled and deveined

Hot fluffy rice

Heat the oil in a large skillet. Sauté the green pepper, onion, celery and garlic until tender stirring occasionally, about 10 to 12 minutes. Blend in the tomatoes and stir in the paprika, the three peppers, thyme, salt, bay leaf and water. Bring to a simmer and cook for 30 minutes or until the sauce thickens slightly. Stir in the shrimp, cover and let cook only 5 minutes, just until the shrimp are pink. Cook no longer or the shrimp will become tough.

Place a serving of rice in center of each plate and top with a generous serving of Shrimp Creole. Serves 6 to 8.

My husband seated me at an outside table in Constitution Square, the center of Athens, ordered drinks and explained he would be gone only a few minutes to check with American Express. I was dressed for dinner in my favorite yellow dress with shoes to match, very obviously American from tip to toe. No sooner had Gene disappeared from view than a man sat down at the next table and began looking at a newspaper, but with his black eyes flashing over the edge. I looked to the left and there was another Greek gentleman snapping those engaging black eyes. To my great consternation a third settled at another table and I was surrounded. I could only look up at the sky or down at my melting drink. Finally my husband appeared, looked down at me, and smilingly asked, "How many propositions have you had?" I grimaced at him but realized that all those black inviting eyes had disappeared. To our delight, a young Greek girl, Maria Stini, a former AFS student in Tulsa, joined us, along with her mother. They brought a huge bouquet of red roses and then escorted us to a large taverna with a Greek band and singers. Mrs. Stini could speak no English but two of our sons, Mike and Peter, had hitchhiked to their home in Corfu so she kept grabbing my hand repeating, "Mike, Mike." Both boys had related that in the Stini home, the mother had polished their shoes, run their bath water and piled their plates with wonderful Greek food and tiny fresh strawberries. Maria ordered an exotic variety of Greek food which began to appear at our table on enormous platters. Walking back to our hotel later, a full moon shone brightly on the Acropolis, a truly magnificent climax to our final evening in Greece. The following spicy, pungent yet light casserole is reminiscent of the flavors produced in the wonderfully relaxed Greek tavernas.

GREEK SHRIMP

2 garlic cloves, peeled and minced

1 medium onion, peeled and finely chopped

4 tablespoons olive oil

1 28-ounce can tomatoes and juice

$\frac{1}{2}$ cup dry white wine

$\frac{1}{4}$ cup minced fresh basil or 1 teaspoon dried

1 teaspoon dried oregano

2 tablespoons butter

2 tablespoons olive oil

2 pounds fresh shrimp, shelled and deveined

$\frac{1}{4}$ cup cognac

Grindings of black pepper

$\frac{1}{8}$ teaspoon red pepper flakes

$\frac{1}{4}$ to $\frac{1}{2}$ pound Feta cheese

3 cups fluffy cooked rice

Sauté the garlic and onion in the 4 tablespoons of oil in a heavy skillet until lightly golden, about 10 minutes. Do not allow to burn. Add the tomatoes, wine, basil and oregano. Stir well and simmer uncovered until the sauce thickens, 15 to 20 minutes. Set aside.

Preheat oven to 400°. In a separate skillet heat the 2 tablespoons each of butter and oil. Sauté the shrimp over medium high heat just until pink. Do not overcook. Sprinkle with cognac and flame shaking the skillet until the flame subsides. Sprinkle with the black pepper and red pepper flakes, mixing well. If a spicier flavor is desired, add another $\frac{1}{8}$ teaspoon of red pepper flakes to the shrimp. Transfer the shrimp to a casserole and top with the sauce. Crumble the feta cheese and sprinkle over the sauce. Bake 15 to 20 minutes or until the feta has melted and the sauce is bubbling lightly. Serve over the hot rice. The recipe will serve six, doubles easily and may also be frozen.

Another delightful preparation for shrimp pairs it with light and fluffy soufflé. Made with the shrimp or the alternative spinach filling, this is a superb dish for a luncheon or light supper, affording pleasure in both texture and beauty. Even though this is basically a soufflé, I have found that men as well as women thoroughly enjoy this entree. One of my male tasters left a message on my answering machine with the challenge that I could not top this one!

SOUFFLÉ ROLL WITH SHRIMP FILLING

THE SOUFFLÉ

4 tablespoons butter

$\frac{1}{2}$ cup all purpose flour

2 cups milk

1/2 teaspoon salt

2 dashes cayenne pepper

4 beaten egg yolks

4 egg whites

1/8 teaspoon cream of tartar

Preheat oven to 325°. Brush a baking sheet, 10 x 15 inches, with melted butter. Line the pan with waxed or parchment paper. Brush again with melted butter and dust lightly with flour. If preferred, use a vegetable spray which works as well as butter.

In a 2-quart saucepan melt the butter and whisk in the flour. Stir and cook one or two minutes with a whisk and add the milk, stirring constantly until thick and creamy. Add the salt and cayenne pepper, adding more pepper if you like a spicier flavor. Transfer the sauce to a mixing bowl for easier handling and beat in the egg yolks. Beat the egg whites and cream of tartar until softly stiff. Fold the beaten egg whites into the sauce carefully but thoroughly. Spread the soufflé mixture evenly in the prepared baking sheet. Bake in preheated oven 40 to 45 minutes or until a light golden brown—it will be puffed and spring back when lightly pressed. Loosen the edges of the soufflé and turn out on a clean, thin tea towel. Peel off the paper and discard. Have the filling ready and spread evenly over the soufflé. Roll lengthwise, jelly roll fashion using the cloth to assist, holding tightly and turning the soufflé seam side down. Unroll the tea towel and, since the soufflé is warm and soft, slide, with assistance of the tea towel, onto a long platter, seam side down. The roll can be kept warm in a 150° oven for 20 to 30 minutes. Serves 8 generously.

SHRIMP FILLING

1 pound cooked shrimp

2 tablespoons butter

1 cup finely chopped celery

1/3 cup finely chopped green onions

3/4 cup toasted almonds, coarsely chopped

1 tablespoon lemon juice

3-ounce package cream cheese, softened

1/2 cup plain yogurt plus 2 tablespoons

¼ cup grated Swiss cheese

Chopped parsley for garnish

Coarsely chop the shrimp and set aside. Melt the butter in a skillet and sauté the celery and onions until soft. Add the almonds, shrimp and lemon juice, stirring until well combined and the mixture is hot. Combine the cream cheese and yogurt, adding to the shrimp mixture. Stir to mix well and allow to cook slowly a few minutes until hot. There will be more shrimp filling than spinach; the shrimp filling may be added to the soufflé a bit differently. Place one-half the shrimp filling over half the soufflé. Roll as directed with the spinach filling. Place on a long platter, seam side down and spread the remaining filling over the top of the soufflé. Top with the grated Swiss cheese and garnish with parsley. Serves 8 to 10.

SPINACH FILLING (A VARIATION)

2 packages frozen spinach (10 ounces each), cooked and drained

1 cup finely chopped ham

2 tablespoons butter

¼ cup chopped green onions

1 tablespoon Dijon mustard

3-ounce package cream cheese, softened

½ cup plain yogurt plus 2 tablespoons at room temperature

When the spinach has drained, squeeze dry and chop finely. Chop the ham and set aside. Melt butter in a skillet and sauté onions until soft. Add the spinach, ham and mustard, stirring until mixture is warm. Combine the cream cheese and yogurt and add to the spinach mixture. Continue to heat several minutes until warm and well mixed. The spinach mixture is now ready to spread over the warm soufflé.

Kebabs are extremely versatile. In various places in the world I have enjoyed them made with beef, lamb, or vegetables. Here is a divine and marvelously easy kebab made with scallops that can be prepared and cooked in fifteen to twenty minutes. Try serving these delicate mollusks with Rice and Wheat Pilaf (page 168) for a different and delightful combination.

SCALLOP KEBABS WITH MUSHROOMS

$\frac{1}{2}$ pound large mushrooms

Olive oil

Lemon juice

1 pound large scallops

$\frac{1}{2}$ cup melted butter

1 cup dry bread crumbs

$\frac{1}{2}$ cup finely chopped parsley

$\frac{1}{2}$ teaspoon marjoram

Grated rind 1 lemon

Freshly ground black pepper

Slices of lemon

Clean the mushrooms with a damp cloth. Leave the stem in but trim any rough edges. Place in a mixing bowl and sprinkle just enough oil and lemon juice to impregnate the mushrooms with flavor. Set aside.

Place the scallops in a sieve and pat dry with paper toweling. Melt the butter and place in a small bowl. Combine the bread crumbs in a separate bowl with the parsley, marjoram and lemon rind. Season with freshly ground black pepper. (I have added no salt as the end result simply did not need any, but you may add a little with the pepper.) Dip the dried scallops into the melted butter and then the bread crumb mixture. Arrange the scallops, lengthwise on four long skewers, keeping a space in between each scallop. Slide the mushrooms through the stem on two skewers. Coat a baking sheet with a vegetable spray. Preheat oven to broil, placing the rack about six inches from the element. Broil 3 or 4 minutes on each side or until the bread crumb mixture becomes golden. When turning the skewers, if some of the scallops do not revolve, use a fork to gently turn them over. Serve with slices of lemon. The recipe serves 4 generously.

Combining delicate scallops with the extraordinarily flavorful Italian Arborio rice results in a memorable dinner or luncheon. Neither the scallops nor the rice are at all difficult to prepare. Arborio rice is available in fine supermarkets and specialty stores.

SCALLOPS WITH ARBORIO RICE

¼ cup butter

6 tablespoons chopped scallions

I cup Arborio rice

⅔ cup dry white wine

1¼ cup chicken broth

3 tablespoons butter

I cup julienne strips of leek, white part only

½ large sweet red pepper, cut in julienne strips

I pound large scallops

Salt to taste

Grindings of black pepper

⅓ cup dry white wine

3 tablespoons grated Parmesan cheese

Melt the ¼ cup of butter in a saucepan and sauté the scallions just until soft. Add the rice, cooking and stirring until transparent. Add the ⅔ cup of wine and bring to a boil. Add the broth and simmer gently for about 15 minutes, adding more stock if necessary. Simmer until the liquid has been absorbed and the rice is tender.

Melt the 3 tablespoons of butter in a skillet; add the leek and red pepper stirring for 4 minutes or until just tender. With a slotted spoon remove to a plate. The scallops should be drained in a sieve and if frozen, patted dry. If the scallops are very large, they may be sliced in half lengthwise. Add the scallops to the skillet and sauté quickly on both sides until just opaque. Do not overcook as they will become tough. Season lightly with salt and pepper. Add the ⅓ cup of wine and simmer gently 2 minutes. Stir in the cheese. Arrange the rice on a serving platter and top with the leek, red pepper and scallops. Serves 4.

Seafood makes a luxurious buffet dish when served with rice or noodles. This recipe can easily be doubled and will then serve 25 people.

BRANDIED SEAFOOD WITH MORNAY SAUCE

2 cups scallops

1 1/2 cups dry white wine

3 shallots, finely chopped

4 tablespoons butter

2 cups medium shrimp, cooked

1 pound fresh or frozen crabmeat

Mornay sauce*

Salt to taste

Grindings of white pepper

2 dashes of paprika

3 tablespoons heavy cream

1/3 cup brandy

Fresh lemon juice

Nutmeg

Parmesan cheese, freshly grated

Tiny bay scallops are preferable, but if not available, slice large scallops in several pieces. Combine the scallops, wine and shallots in a skillet. Bring just to a simmer and poach gently 3 minutes. Add 1 tablespoon of the butter, the shrimp and crabmeat. Do not use the fake crabmeat. If the real thing is not available, use lobster, cooked and cut in pieces.) If the crabmeat is frozen, thaw before adding to the scallops. Simmer lightly just until the seafood is hot. With a slotted spoon remove the seafood from the liquid to a clean bowl.

Boil the wine rapidly until reduced to 5 tablespoons. Stir in the Mornay sauce (recipe follows), season lightly with salt, white pepper and paprika. Let mixture come to a simmer and strain the sauce into a bowl. Beat the cream with a whisk until fluffy and fold into the sauce.

In a clean skillet, sauté drained seafood in remaining 3 tablespoons butter 3 minutes. Flame with the brandy. Add the Mornay sauce and season to taste with drops of lemon juice and gratings of nutmeg. Again adjust for salt and pepper. Preheat broiler in oven. Pour the Brandied Seafood in a buttered baking dish and sprinkle generously with Parmesan cheese. Place under broiler until light and bubbling. For a buffet, serve in a chafing dish.

4 tablespoons butter

4 tablespoons all purpose flour

2 cups hot milk

Salt

White pepper

$1/2$ cup grated Swiss cheese, packed

Over moderate heat melt the butter in a saucepan. Add the flour and whisk until smooth and bubbly. Remove from burner and add the hot milk all at once, stirring vigorously with the whisk until smooth. Return to burner, add salt to taste and a few gratings of white pepper. Reduce heat and let simmer lightly 5 minutes, stirring constantly. Blend in the cheese until melted. Serves 12.

Vegetables

The ancient Greeks and Romans learned to love asparagus which grew wild in the Mediterranean countries. They began to cultivate it around Rome in the latter days of the empire. With the advent of the Visigoths, asparagus was totally scorned, but it kept growing wild and still does today in the Provence. Centuries passed and as the Muslims appeared so did asparagus. From Spain it spread into France. In Spain it is called *espárrago*, in Germany, *spargel*, in Italy, *asparago* and in France, *asperge*. The first colonists of North America brought asparagus crowns in their baggage and introduced asparagus to the New World.

The cooking of green asparagus is quickly accomplished but white asparagus has a different texture and must be peeled and cooked for an extended time before it becomes tender. White asparagus is picked just as soon as a spear pierces the ground; if left alone, it grows taller and turns green. If the green asparagus is left to grow, it will become quite feathery and florists enjoying using these lovely feathers as a filler for bouquets.

BAKED FRESH ASPARAGUS

1 1/4 pounds fresh green asparagus

3 tablespoons finely chopped parsley

1/4 cup olive oil

Salt, optional

Grindings of black pepper

Preheat oven to 400°. Wash asparagus and cut off tough ends. Arrange the asparagus in a baking pan close together and sprinkle with the parsley and olive oil. Add optional salt and a few grindings of black pepper. Cover with aluminum foil and bake until asparagus is done, about 15 minutes. Serves 4 to 6.

When my eldest son was hitchhiking in Europe, he approached Paris only to find the hotels filled because of an International Automobile show. That first night he slept under a steam shovel. The next morning he contacted a Parisian family, the Minards, whose address I had mailed him. A beautiful glass elevator encased in wrought iron whisked him to the Minards' elegant apartment. The family took this wet, bedraggled American boy in and let him stay two weeks. Each of my sons in turn stayed with the Minards and soon fell in love with elegant French cuisine, for Mme. Minard is an exquisite cook. Asparagus Vinaigrette was a favorite of theirs, and soon became mine, and one son gave me asparagus plates which I love using.

ASPARAGUS VINAIGRETTE

2 to 3 pounds fresh green asparagus
Basic Vinaigrette Dressing with Dijon mustard, page 56

The delightful flavor and simplicity of preparation of this dish captured me. Wash asparagus under running water, and break or cut off the tough ends. If the asparagus stalks are thin, no peeling is necessary. When the stalks become larger, I do prefer to peel with a vegetable peeler, for this can be a quick, simple process. Place in a skillet, cover with water, bring to a boil and cook rapidly until just tender-crisp, no more than 5 minutes. Pour off the hot water and run cool tap water over the vegetable to stop the cooking. The asparagus can be served hot, warm or cooled. Place in individual asparagus plates and pour a little vinaigrette dressing over each. This should be eaten with fingers — not a fork! Serves 6 to 8.

ASPARAGUS WITH LEMON BUTTER

3 pounds asparagus
$\frac{1}{2}$ cup butter
2 tablespoons lemon juice
$\frac{1}{2}$ teaspoon salt
Dash cayenne pepper
2 tablespoons chopped parsley or chives

Break asparagus at the point where the stalks snap easily. Trim with a sharp knife. Wash under running water and peel with a vegetable peeler. Place in a skillet so the stalks lie flat. Cover with water and bring to a boil. When

asparagus is peeled the cooking time is short (5 minutes) and the vegetable
should be tender crisp. Pour off the water. Melt the butter and add the
lemon juice, salt and pepper. Pour over the asparagus and turn so that each
stalk is covered. Place in a serving bowl and sprinkle with parsley. Serves 6
to 8.

ASPARAGUS WITH HOLLANDAISE SAUCE

3 pounds asparagus
Blender Hollandaise Sauce, page 231

Prepare and cook the asparagus as described in Asparagus with Lemon
Butter. When the asparagus is just tender, drain and place individual serv-
ings in asparagus plates. Top with 2 tablespoons of Blender Hollandaise
Sauce. Serves 6 to 8.

A most expensive vegetable in our country, white asparagus is available in only
a few areas. I first prepared it in St. Louis and the asparagus came from Illinois just
across the Mississippi River.

WHITE ASPARAGUS

2 to 3 pounds white asparagus
Basic Vinaigrette Dressing, page 56
Lemon butter

Preparation of white asparagus is not difficult but the cooking process
requires a longer time. All worth the effort for the delicate flavor is quite
delightful.

White asparagus must be peeled. Wash under running water, trim off the
tough ends and reserve. Peel with a vegetable peeler and save the peelings.
Place the asparagus in a skillet, cover with water and bring to a boil. Let
boil at moderate rate for about 30 minutes. White asparagus has a different
texture requiring longer cooking. Test for doneness, pour off the hot water
into a saucepan and place the cooked vegetable in a serving bowl or individual plates. Serve either with the Basic Vinaigrette dressing or lemon butter
as described in Asparagus with Lemon Butter, (page 155). To the reserved
water, add the peelings and tough ends. Boil until the water begins to taste
strongly of asparagus. Strain the liquid and then make a cream soup. Make

your favorite cream sauce, about two cups, and add the asparagus liquid. I created this idea the first time I handled this beautiful vegetable and since it is so rare and expensive, I just did not want to waste any of the asparagus. Try it—delicious. The whole asparagus will serve 6.

When asparagus is not in season and you long for a delicious green vegetable, there are many ways of serving green beans. French-style green beans are perfect for the combination that follows. The frozen vegetable is most satisfying and much easier than slicing a pound of fresh beans. Follow directions carefully on the package of green beans to avoid overcooking.

GREEN BEANS WITH ALMONDS

I pound frozen French-style green beans

⅓ cup butter

4 tablespoons water

I teaspoon lemon juice

Salt to taste

⅛ to ¼ teaspoon cayenne pepper

I cup slivered almonds

I teaspoon finely chopped garlic

Pour boiling water over the frozen beans in a saucepan and drain immediately into a sieve. In the same saucepan melt ½ of the butter and add the 4 tablespoons of water, lemon juice, a small amount of salt and cayenne pepper (if a spicy flavor is desired, use the full ¼ teaspoon). Add the beans, cover and cook over a moderate burner until tender, 5 to 8 minutes. In a saucepan or small skillet melt the remaining butter and add the almonds. Stir constantly until a golden color. Blend in the chopped garlic. Place the beans in a warm serving dish and pour the almond mixture atop the beans. Serves 6 to 8.

Fresh young beets are transformed with just a touch of orange zest. The combination of orange with beets has long been a favorite in more elaborate recipes. Sometimes the simplest preparation is the best. When small fresh beets arrive in the spring, to boil them and add sweet butter with a bit of orange rind is sublime.

BEETS WITH ORANGE ZEST

2-3 pounds spring beets, tops removed

Boiling water, salted to taste

4 tablespoons butter

Grated rind 1 large orange

Scrub the beets with a brush. Drop into boiling water and cook uncovered until tender, about 30 minutes. Be certain the vegetables are well covered with boiling water. When tender, remove from burner and pour off the hot water. Turn into a colander and run water over the beets to cool. When the beets are cool enough to handle, peel off the skin with a sharp knife — the skin will almost slip off. Cut off the ends. Slice in ¼ inch pieces and place in saucepan with the butter over a moderate burner. Add the orange zest and stir gently. Add more butter if necessary. Continue to heat and shake the pan to keep beets from burning. Serve while hot. Usually I save the very smallest of the beets and tuck into a plastic bag with a vinaigrette sauce to enhance a green salad. Serves 6 to 8.

BROCCOLI

Select broccoli with flowerettes all bright dark green. Any yellow means the broccoli is old and will be tough. Wash 2 pounds broccoli and with a sharp knife peel the stalks and trim the ends. For this amount of broccoli have a large saucepan or soup kettle with plenty of boiling water. Drop the broccoli in and allow to boil just until tender crisp, no more than five minutes. Drain thoroughly. Dress the broccoli with any of the following:

Basic Vinaigrette, page 56

Hollandaise Sauce, page 231

Herbed Cheese Sauce, page 45

Sweet butter

Here are two favorite ways to dress the estimable carrot. The first gives a little different twist to a vegetable that is always with us. The orange of the carrots with red grapes give a visual contrast on a dinner plate and now with grapes arriving from both California and South America, the cost is never prohibitive. For ease in eating, slice the grapes in half.

BABY CARROTS WITH RED GRAPES

2 pounds whole baby carrots, scraped and cleaned

3 tablespoons butter

2 tablespoons granulated sugar

$\frac{1}{2}$ pound red grapes

3 tablespoons chopped fresh parsley

Place the carrots in a saucepan, cover with water, bring to a boil over moderately high heat and cook until just tender. Drain off the water. Add the butter and sugar, and sauté 5 minutes, stirring to avoid burning. Slice the grapes in half, add to the carrots and sauté 2 minutes, just until the grapes are heated through. Sprinkle parsley over the combination in a warm bowl. Serves 8.

GLAZED CARROTS

24 baby carrots

1 teaspoon salt

2 tablespoons sugar

$\frac{1}{4}$ pound butter or margarine

1 tablespoon minced parsley

Trim the ends of the carrots and scrape clean. Place the carrots in a 4-quart heavy saucepan with water to cover. Add the salt, sugar and butter. Bring to a boil, lower heat and simmer approximately 30 minutes or until the water has evaporated. The carrots will become glazed with a thick buttery syrup. Toss the pan gently several times toward the end of cooking to coat all the carrots evenly. Transfer to a serving dish and sprinkle with parsley. Serves 6.

Steaming: Cook the carrots in a steamer until tender. Remove the pan and drain off the water. Transfer carrots into the bottom pan. Add the sugar, salt and butter. Cook tossing until coated and piping hot. Garnish with chopped parsley.

Sometimes we forget how fragrant and delicious celery can be when cooked. Everyone does love crisp, green celery to munch on or to add in salad. This can be a delightful vegetable when you are looking for something just a bit different.

BRAISED CELERY

4 hearts of celery

1 large onion, peeled and sliced

2 carrots, scraped and sliced

3 to 4 cups chicken broth

2 tablespoons butter

Trim the tops and bottom of the celery. Discard any discolored outer stalks. Wash thoroughly in running water. Place in a large saucepan, pour boiling water over the celery and simmer for 6 minutes to remove any sand that might have been missed. Drain and run cool water over the vegetable to stop the cooking and allow handling. Halve the bunches lengthwise.

Place the onion and carrots in a baking dish that will hold the celery in one layer. Arrange the celery cut side down over the carrots and onions. Add sufficient broth to almost cover the celery and dot with pieces of butter. Preheat oven to 375°. Cover the celery dish with aluminum foil and bake about 1 hour or until tender. Remove from the oven and serve while warm. No salt is needed for both the celery and chicken broth will have enough. Serves 4 to 6.

CORN ON THE COB ON THE QUEEN MARY

One enterprising friend, Jeanne Earlougher, often brought hot corn on the cob to our weekend gatherings at the lake. She had a large, wide-mouthed thermos jug. Jeanne shucked and cleaned enough corn to fit into the thermos. Boiling water was poured into the thermos to the top and then capped tightly. All this was prepared at home and by the time she and her husband and teenagers arrived and dinner was served in the middle of the afternoon after much skiing and swimming, the corn was extracted, butter, salt and pepper were handy and everyone loved having hot corn on the cob out in the middle of the lake.

I learned to make corn pudding during a brief stay in Vicksburg, Mississippi. Southerners throughout the region love evening barbecues and corn pudding blends exceedingly well with spicy meats. The flavor for this pudding derives mainly from the creamed corn with little to obstruct the taste. In Vicksburg the dish is pronounced "cawn puddin."

CORN PUDDING

16 ounce can cream-style corn

1 tablespoon sugar

1 teaspoon salt

3 tablespoons melted butter

5 medium eggs, well beaten

3 cups whole milk

1 tablespoon cornstarch

1 tablespoon water

Preheat oven to 325°. Brush a 7 x 12" glass dish with butter and set aside. In a mixing bowl combine the corn, sugar, salt, butter, eggs and milk stirring to mix well. In a small bowl combine the cornstarch and water stirring with a fork until dissolved. Add to the corn mixture. Stir the mixture very well and pour into the prepared baking dish.

Bake for one hour or until the custard is set. Serve hot or warm in the baking dish. Serves 8.

I enjoyed sweet onions cooked in the following manner in both south Texas and later in New Jersey. I tried both the Vidalia and the Texas sweet onions for comparison and, frankly, I was happy with both. An easy vegetable to prepare that most people will enjoy.

BAKED SLICED ONIONS

3 large sliced Vidalia or Texas onions

Salt and grindings of black pepper

Melted butter or margarine

Grated Swiss or cheddar cheese

Preheat oven to 350°. Brush a baking dish that has a cover with soft butter.

Peel and slice the onions. Arrange one layer of onions in prepared baking dish and dust lightly with salt and pepper. Swirl melted butter over the layer of onions. Continue making layers of onions and butter. Cover and bake in preheated oven 45 minutes. Remove and sprinkle with a layer of grated cheese. Return to oven, uncovered, until the cheese is melted and just beginning to brown. Serves 6 to 8.

PARSNIPS

Choose parsnips that are small and fresh. If ends are split and the roots are quite large, they will be tough. Clean very much like carrots. Trim the tops and ends and scrape with vegetable peeler. Cut in slices, place in saucepan and cover with water. Bring to a boil and cook until tender, about 10 minutes. Drain the water off thoroughly and add two tablespoons of butter to one pound of parsnips. Stir and cook in the butter until the vegetable glistens.

BAKED SLIVERS OF POTATOES

For one large baking potato: Scrub thoroughly under water with a brush. Dry completely. Slice the potato in half, then in fourths and finally in eighths. Place the pieces on a baking sheet and bake in a preheated 400° oven about 30 minutes or until a golden brown. If desired the potatoes may be sprinkled lightly with salt before cooking.

This make a marvelous hors d'oeuvre and may be served with any meat. They are fun to eat with your fingers. Delightfully mealy and crisp and a wonderful way to eat potatoes with no calories added!

NEW POTATOES WITH VINAIGRETTE DRESSING

A quick, easy addition for a summer dinner that may be done with any desired number of potatoes. Medium size or smaller potatoes will be best. Boil scrubbed new potatoes in water to cover until fork tender.

 Drain thoroughly. Slice each potato in half while hot and place in a serving bowl. Swirl any vinaigrette (pages 56-58) over the potatoes and sprinkle with chopped green onions and fresh chives. Serve about 2 potatoes per person unless very small.

The aromas of the Provence in France will waft through the house when this earthy combination of vegetables is simmering. Even though preparation of all the ingredients may be a bit of trouble, the result can be served as a hot vegetable or a cold hors d'oeuvre and may be made several days in advance, for ratatouille keeps well for several days when refrigerated.

RATATOUILLE

1 medium eggplant

2 large onions, peeled and sliced

2 green or red sweet peppers, diced

$\frac{1}{2}$ cup olive oil

4 medium tomatoes, peeled, seeded and coarsely chopped

2 zucchini, cut in $\frac{1}{2}$-inch pieces

Salt to taste

Grindings of black pepper

$\frac{1}{2}$ teaspoon marjoram

$\frac{1}{2}$ teaspoon basil

2 tablespoons chopped parsley

1 clove garlic, peeled and minced

Peel the eggplant and cut in ½ inch slices. Salt the slices and stack together, placing a weight on top and let stand 30 minutes. In a large skillet, over a low burner, sauté the onions and peppers in the oil. When the vegetables begin to soften, add the tomatoes and the eggplant sliced in cubes. Stir in the zucchini, a sprinkling of salt, pepper and the marjoram, basil and parsley. Stir very well until all ingredients are mixed. Let simmer approximately 45 minutes, uncovered. The vegetables should be soft, the liquid reduced but the mixture should not look like a puree. Fifteen minutes before the end of cooking time, add the garlic and taste for salt and pepper. Adjust. Serves 6 to 8 as a hot vegetable or more as a cold appetizer.

Acorn squash is a vegetable of which I was totally unaware until I married. It was another food I found my young husband enjoyed. With the generous assistance of my mother-in-law, I learned to make it his favorite way. My biggest difficulty was slicing the squash in half. I stuck a knife in the squash and lifted it up in the air and whammed it on the table. It worked!

BAKED ACORN SQUASH

2 acorn squash

Brown sugar

Cinnamon

Butter or margarine

Preheat oven to 350°. Coat a baking sheet with vegetable spray.

Wipe the squash clean and slice each in half from the stem to the bottom. Clean out the seeds and place the squash cut side down on the baking sheet. Bake in preheated oven 45 minutes or until tender. Turn the squash over with a spatula and to each half add a heaping teaspoon of brown sugar. Sprinkle cinnamon on top and add bits of butter or use a liquid margarine to swirl over the inside. Return to the oven and bake until the center ingredients are bubbling, about 5 to 8 minutes. Serve immediately. Serves 4.

Thanksgiving with the Washington Gubsers brings together a fascinating mix of nationalities and delectable food. Armenian, Hungarian, Scotch, Irish, English, Swiss, German and Lebanese guests surround the table. Amazingly, my Princeton grandson Steven fell in love with a very American dish and he spoke to me several times about the sweet potatoes made by Ildiko Yeni-Komshian, a lovely Hungarian by birth, married to an Armenian. Now there are more sweet potato casseroles than nationalities at this dinner but I, too, thought this special dish one of the best. Here is the recipe, thanks to Ildiko's generosity and Steven's prompting.

SWEET POTATO CASSEROLE

2 pounds cooked sweet potatoes

4 tablespoons butter, melted

$1/3$ cup orange juice

6 tablespoons brown sugar, divided

3 tablespoons bourbon

$1/2$ teaspoon salt

$1/2$ teaspoon cinnamon

$1/4$ teaspoon nutmeg

2 tangerines, peeled and sectioned

$1/2$ cup chopped pecans

1 tangerine, peeled and sectioned

6 whole pecan meats

Preheat oven to 375°. Brush a 2-quart casserole with melted butter and set aside. Combine the sweet potatoes, butter, orange juice, 3 tablespoons of sugar, bourbon, salt, cinnamon and nutmeg in a large mixing bowl. Whip together with a flat beater on a heavy mixer or by hand with a whisk. When the potato mixture is thoroughly blended, fold in the tangerine sections and the chopped nuts. Turn mixture into the buttered casserole and top with remaining tangerine sections interspersed with the whole pecan meats. Sprinkle the remaining 3 tablespoons of sugar over the fruit and nuts. Bake for 30 minutes until bubbling hot.

Note: When peeling the tangerines, scrape off excess white pith and remove seeds. If fresh tangerines are not available, use one 11 oz can of mandarin oranges, drained and divided in half.

The best time to enjoy baked tomatoes is in the summer when the large beefsteak tomatoes arrive in the market. In the winter watch for hot house tomatoes. Occasionally a few from Mexico will be surprisingly good — some even smell like tomatoes. Fresh herbs have become available most of the year and in the summer in abundance. Annie Gubser , my Washington daughter-in-law, who is always trying to devise quick methods for flavorful food, bakes cherry tomatoes with a delightful result. She is an expert with marinades and this fast vegetable is a result of her love for those marinades.

BAKED HERBED TOMATOES

3 large tomatoes

¾ cup bread crumbs

2 tablespoons chopped fresh basil or 1½ teaspoon dried

3 tablespoons chopped parsley

2 to 3 tablespoons melted butter

Preheat oven to 350°. Rub a baking sheet, 10 x 17, lightly with oil. Core tomatoes and slice each in half. The slices should be about ¾ inches thick. Combine the bread crumbs, basil and parsley. With a fork stir in the melted butter until well mixed. Sprinkle the crumb mixture on top the tomatoes. Bake, uncovered in preheated oven for 20 to 25 minutes. Serves 6.

BAKED CHERRY TOMATOES

2 pints cherry tomatoes

½ teaspoon each basil, oregano, thyme

½ cup olive oil

2 tablespoons red wine vinegar

1 tablespoon lemon juice

1 clove garlic, peeled and minced

1 1/2 teaspoons Dijon mustard

1/4 cup capers, drained

Place the tomatoes in a baking dish large enough to hold them in one layer. Sprinkle with the basil, oregano and thyme. Combine the oil, vinegar, lemon juice, garlic and mustard stirring with a fork until creamy. Pour over the tomatoes mixing to cover each tomato. Sprinkle the capers over the tomatoes. Bake in a preheated 350° oven 10 to 15 minutes. Transfer to a bowl and serve with a slotted spoon. Serves 6 to 8.

ZUCCHINI AND CHERRY TOMATOES

4 small zucchini

2 tablespoons butter or olive oil

1 teaspoon dried thyme

1 teaspoon dried basil

Sprinkling of salt, optional

Grindings of black pepper

1 cup cherry tomatoes

1 1/2 tablespoons toasted sesame seeds, optional

2 tablespoons fresh parsley

Wash zucchini, cut off the ends and slice on the bias. Place butter or oil in a skillet over medium high heat. Add the zucchini, stir and season with the thyme, basil, salt and pepper. Continue to stir until the vegetable is tender crisp. Add the tomatoes and stir, continuing to cook about 1-2 minutes. Add the sesame seeds and parsley. Transfer to a warm serving bowl.
Serves 4 to 6.

Grains

Bulgur Wheat

Bulgur is whole grain wheat parboiled, sun dried and cracked between rollers (the ancients used rocks). It is a staple in the cuisines of Armenia, Lebanon, Syria, Jordan, Georgia, Iran and some areas of Russia. The spelling can be bulghur, burgul, or bulgur, but they are all the same wheat. In a health food store or import store, bulgur wheat may be found in three sizes, fine for kibbeh, medium for taboulie, and coarse for pilafs. With pre-prepared wheat the cooking time is less than regular wheat, making it popular with health food devotees for little vitamin content is lost. Where there are beautiful mountain streams, there still will be the old mills in operation. Two in the Ozark Mountains not too far from my home in Tulsa, are the Hodgens Mill and War Eagle, both producing excellent bulgur wheat. One combines the wheat with stoneground grits which makes a mighty fine pilaf. Check sources of supply.

Bulgur wheat can be coarse and crunchy or light and fluffy, depending on the size of grain purchased. Regardless of texture the resulting dish will be a savory, agreeable substitute for potatoes, rice or pasta. One cannot help but feel a health benefit while enjoying such a food, for little of the vitamin content is lost. I shall give several ideas for pilafs using bulgur wheat. I found years ago, while my sons were teenagers, that they and their friends loved my first attempt combining wheat and mushrooms. There is no doubt that this versatile and ancient grain has delighted civilization for thousands of years.

BULGUR WHEAT PILAF

¾ cup onion, finely chopped

2 tablespoons butter or oil

1 cup bulgur wheat

¼ cup dark raisins, optional

2 cups chicken broth

Salt and black pepper to taste

⅓ cup pine nuts, lightly toasted

½ cup finely chopped parsley

In a saucepan, sauté the onion in the butter or oil until soft, 5 to 8 minutes. Stir in the wheat and cook several minutes stirring constantly until the bulgur just begins to turn golden. Add the broth and raisins. If canned broth is used, little salt will be needed. Bring to a boil, lower heat to simmer and cover. Cook approximately 15 minutes or until the liquid is absorbed. If the pilaf becomes dry, add more broth. A coarsely ground wheat may take longer to cook than a more finely ground grain. When ready to serve, add the pine nuts and parsley. Stir and fluff the pilaf. One recipe will serve 6 but can easily be doubled.

Note: The addition of 1 tablespoon of grated orange rind with the broth and raisins will give the pilaf a flavor popular in ancient Persia. The ancients loved pilafs to be on the aromatic sweet side.

This is a very gratifying grain and rice casserole incorporating a quick rice and bulgur wheat. In the past I have opposed quick grains and potatoes but when I tried quick brown rice, my taste buds readily accepted this newer version of a long-cooking rice.

RICE AND WHEAT PILAF

¾ cup pine nuts

½ cup butter or margarine

1 cup quick-cooking brown rice

1 cup bulgur wheat

3½ to 4 cups chicken broth

1 teaspoon Italian mixed herbs, page ??

1 large clove garlic, minced

¾ cup finely chopped parsley

Preheat oven to 325°. Place the nuts in a cake pan and toast until lightly colored, about 5 to 8 minutes. Shake the pan several times, as pine nuts do burn easily and become bitter. Set aside.

Over medium high heat, melt the butter in a saucepan. Stir in the rice and bulgur, stirring until well coated. Continue to stir until the rice begins to brown lightly. Add the chicken broth with the Italian herbs and garlic. Transfer to a casserole, stir well, cover and place in a preheated 350° oven. Bake 30 minutes or until the liquid has been absorbed. Add more broth if needed. Remove from the oven and stir in the parsley and pine nuts. Serves 8.

A combination of two favorite foods, rich grains of wheat and luscious eggplant, that can supply enough healthful ingredients to satisfy a true vegetarian. This could serve as a main entree accompanied with a bountiful salad, baked tomatoes and an oatmeal bread.

WHEAT AND EGGPLANT

¼ cup butter

2 cups bulgur wheat

2 cups water

1 teaspoon salt or to taste

Grindings of black pepper

1 large or 2 small eggplant

¾ cup chopped onion

¼ cup olive oil

2 cups chicken broth

Melt the butter in a saucepan and add the wheat, stirring constantly for 5 minutes. Add the water, stir and let simmer lightly until the wheat is tender, about 20 to 25 minutes. Season with salt and pepper.

Peel and cube the eggplant. In a large skillet sauté the onion in olive oil until just limp, about 5 minutes. Season with salt and pepper.

Add the eggplant stirring to coat with the oil and onions. Add more oil if necessary. Cover and cook about 10 minutes until the eggplant becomes tender. Combine the eggplant with the wheat mixture and add 1 cup of chicken broth. At this point, if desired, the wheat pilaf may be placed in a casserole to bake at 350° until liquid is absorbed. Otherwise, stir and cook in the saucepan until all is well mixed and tender. Taste again for salt and pepper. Add more broth if necessary for wheat does absorb a great deal of liquid. The pilaf will keep well, refrigerated, for several days and can be frozen for future use. Serves 8 generously.

During the 1960s and 70s when my three sons were struggling through their teenage years, we had a huge houseboat built, forty-four feet long. Ten could sleep on the front deck, four inside and any number with enough courage atop the boat. Often I fed twenty to thirty teenagers (and parents) for they loved the ambiance of this big, cumbersome boat and showing off their skiing skills as we all floated around the lake. So much activity demanded lots of food and amazingly all these young people loved the cracked wheat with mushrooms. It is best made with a coarse Bulgur or cracked wheat cereal. My recipe served 6 to 8, depending on how hungry those kids were, but then I always doubled the recipe. I often made it.

CRACKED WHEAT WITH MUSHROOMS

1 1/2 cups sliced mushrooms

1/2 cup finely chopped onion

1/4 cup butter or light oil

1 1/2 cups cracked wheat

3 1/2 to 4 cups chicken broth

Grindings of black pepper

Salt to taste

In a large saucepan sauté the mushrooms and onion in the butter until tender, about 5 minutes. Add the cracked wheat and continue to sauté stirring constantly 5 to 8 minutes or until the wheat just becomes a light golden color. Do not allow to burn. Add the chicken broth and pepper. Blend well and reduce heat until mixture simmers. Cover and cook 30 minutes.

Check to see if the mixture has become too dry and add more broth if necessary. Or the wheat pilaf may be placed on a casserole and baked in a 350° oven 30 to 40 minutes.

Stir several times and add more broth if necessary. Taste for salt content and adjust. If a canned broth is used, little salt will be needed. This freezes very well.

Barley, Rice, and Millet

One of the most ancient of grains, barley was harvested extensively in the Tigris and Euphrates valley with millet and wheat to make a flat bread. It was cooked as a cereal long before the Egyptians came into power. Barley is superb in a casserole that replaces potatoes or rice, and it is an excellent addition to soups.

BARLEY CASSEROLE

$1/2$ cup pine nuts or slivered almonds

$1/3$ cup butter

1 cup finely chopped onion

1 cup pearl barley*

1 cup finely chopped parsley

Grindings of black pepper

6 cups beef or chicken broth

Salt to taste

In a saucepan sauté the pine nuts in the butter about 5 minutes stirring constantly. Do not allow to burn or the nuts will become bitter. With a slotted spoon remove the nuts to paper toweling and add the onion to the saucepan, sautéing until soft and golden, about 8 minutes. Add barley to the onion and continue to cook 6 to 7 minutes stirring constantly. Blend in the parsley, pepper, broth and pinenuts. Stir very well, taste and add salt if necessary. Transfer the mixture to a 2-quart casserole and bake in a preheated 350° oven for one hour, stirring twice. If the mixture becomes a bit dry, add a little more broth. Test and taste the barley to check for flavor and tenderness. If necessary, bake another 15 minutes. Serves 6 to 8.

*Pearl barley is available at most supermarkets and health food stores. Instant barley can be used, and if so, the cooking time will be less.

Every culture in the world has developed its own way of cooking rice to suit its particular foods. When I was a child, we doused it with butter and sprinkled it with sugar. As an adult I fell in love with Middle Eastern rice for it is a beautiful accompaniment for many entrees.

MIDDLE EASTERN RICE

¹/₄ cup butter or margarine

3 tablespoons minced onion

I cup rice

2 ¹/₂ cups chicken broth

¹/₂ cup toasted pine nuts

¹/₄ cup chopped parsley

Salt to taste

Grindings of black pepper

Melt the butter in a saucepan and sauté the onion for about 4 minutes or until just soft. Add the rice and sauté, stirring constantly, until it just begins to become golden. Pour in the chicken broth, bring to a boil, lower heat to simmer and cover. Let simmer about 15 minutes until the liquid is consumed. Add the pine nuts and parsley. Season to taste with salt and pepper. Serves 6.

Note: Toast the pine nuts in a pie plate for about 8 minutes in a 325° oven. Watch carefully as the nuts do burn easily — they should just be lightly golden.

Some of the worry about burning rice is avoided when baking it in the oven. I love this method, particularly for brown rice since its cooking time is long. Brown rice is earthy, healthful and delicious and especially good with poultry and fish.

BAKED BROWN RICE

2 tablespoons butter

I clove garlic, peeled and minced

I cup brown rice

2 ¹/₂ cups chicken broth

2 tablespoons chopped parsley

¹/₄ teaspoon thyme

¹/₂ bay leaf

2-3 dashes cayenne pepper

¹/₂ teaspoon salt

Preheat oven to 350°. Melt the butter in a baking dish that can be used on a burner. Sauté the garlic 3 minutes, stirring with a wooden spoon. Add the rice and continue to stir for several minutes until each grain is well coated. Add the broth, parsley, thyme, bay leaf, cayenne and salt. Cover and place in the oven. Bake approximately 1 hour. Check for dryness, adding more broth if necessary. Taste for salt content. Remove bay leaf and serve. The recipe makes about 3 cups.

This superb grain grown in northern Italy with its unusual melt-in-the-mouth texture make a flavorful addition to a collection of rice recipes. Look for Arborio rice in fine supermarkets and specialty shops, for it is expensive and not available in many stores. During the cooking process, which should be slow, allowing the rice to absorb flavor, this grain will become a tender mass, quite different from American or Chinese rice. Arborio rice is equally good with a baked chicken or a more complicated Osso Bucco.

ARBORIO RICE

1/2 cup butter or margarine

1 medium size onion, finely chopped (about 1 cup)

2 cups Arborio rice

1 cup dry white wine

4 cups hot chicken broth

1/2 cup grated Parmesan cheese

Salt to taste

Melt butter in a large saucepan over medium heat. Add the onions and sauté 5 to 8 minutes, stirring to keep from burning. Add the rice and continue to stir until each grain is coated. Pour in the wine and 2 cups of the broth. Bring to a simmer, cover and cook until most of the liquid has been absorbed. Continue to simmer covered and add remaining broth 1/2 cup at a time letting each addition become absorbed. Slow cooking gives Arborio rice its unusual lush flavor and texture. The complete cooking time should take about 30 minutes. The rice will be bound in a mass but each grain tender and separate. Stir in the cheese until melted. Taste for salt content but with both the broth and cheese, little salt is necessary. Serves 8 to 10.

Wild rice is not a rice at all but an aquatic cereal grain with the biological name of Zizania Aquatica. After hundreds of years wild rice is still harvested in the traditional Indian way. Canoes glide through the lakes and rivers, a person bends the grasses over the canoe and beats off the kernels. Not all ripen at the same time so the process is repeated during several weeks as the kernels ripen. The grains are then heated carefully, pounded to loosen the chaff and the rice is thrown in the air from a sheet of birch bark or blanket, preferably on a windy day, to blow the chaff away. Not only has wild rice been an important food for the Indians, but many aquatic birds stuff themselves on the grains before flying south. The first French explorers called wild rice "wild oats" but it is a unique food, barely related to any other. Minnesota, northern Wisconsin, Michigan and Ontario have a monopoly on wild rice which has now become a luxury food in other countries besides Canada and the United States. Wild rice is naturally wonderful with wild game and fish, and is also wonderful served with beef and chicken. When cooking it has an intense musky, earthy aroma like no other grain.

WILD RICE

General directions for cooking wild rice: Wash 1 cup of wild rice thoroughly by placing in a sieve and let water run over the grains. Bring 4 cups of lightly salted water to a rapid boil. Slowly add the rice, being certain the water does not stop boiling. Lower heat and simmer, covered, for about 30 minutes. Test for tenderness and cook longer if necessary. Drain thoroughly in a sieve. The rice may be returned to a saucepan and any of the following suggestions may be added. Serves 6 to 8.

$\frac{1}{2}$ cup toasted almonds with 2 tablespoons of butter

$\frac{1}{2}$ cup toasted pine nuts with 2 tablespoons of butter

1 cup sliced mushrooms, sautéed in a tablespoon of butter with a few drops of lemon juice just until soft

$\frac{1}{2}$ cup each of chopped celery and onions sautéed in 2 tablespoons of butter until just tender.

One of the most ancient of grains, millet has been found in archeological digs thousands of years old. Used in breads and as a cereal, it is filled with good quality protein and no fat. During the final testing my assistant leaned over the skillet, stirring and sniffing, raised her head with a big grin and said, "Oh, it smells like popcorn!"

MILLET

I cup whole millet

2 cups hot chicken broth

2 tablespoons butter

Salt to taste

Grindings of black pepper

3 tablespoons Parmesan cheese

Place the millet in a heavy, dry skillet over a medium burner. Stir and toast until the millet becomes golden and produces an earthy, savory aroma. Add the hot broth and butter with a light sprinkling of salt and grindings of black pepper. Lower heat to a simmer, cover and cook about 30 minutes or until the broth has been absorbed and the millet is fluffy. Transfer to a serving dish and fluff with a fork. Sprinkle with the Parmesan cheese and serve while hot. Serves 4 to 6.

Orzo and Quinoa

Orzo is a delightful super-easy side dish that I love for its flavor and simplicity to prepare. If orzo pasta is not available in your supermarket, look in specialty shops and health food stores.

GARLIC FLAVORED ORZO

I cup orzo (rice-shaped pasta)

2 tablespoons butter

I clove garlic, peeled and minced

Salt and grindings of black pepper

Parsley for garnish, if desired

Cook the orzo in a saucepan of boiling water and until tender. (Should still be a bit chewy.) Drain well in a sieve and place back in the saucepan. Melt the butter in a small saucepan and add the minced garlic. Bring to a simmer and let cook 2 or 3 minutes. Stir into the cooked orzo thoroughly. Season with salt and pepper. Serve with a sprinkling of parsley on top. Serves 4.

Pronounced keen-wa, this highly nutritious grain was at one time a staple for the ancient Incas, although it disappeared when the Spanish invaded. Now it is being grown on the highlands of Colorado, but most quinoa comes from Peru and can be found in health food stores. Quinoa is extremely high in protein and many other nutrients. The grain is easily and quickly cooked and can be used in place of rice or potatoes. The nut-like flavor is unique—do try quinoa for something different that is certainly healthful.

QUINOA

2 cups warm water or chicken broth

I cup quinoa

Salt to taste

Grindings of black pepper, optional

Quinoa must be washed first using a strainer to let water run over the grains. This washes away the natural, bitter tasting saponins, a soap-like substance on the outside of the grains believed to be there for the protection of the grains. Combine the warm liquid and quinoa in a saucepan and bring to a boil. Lower heat and simmer 10 to 15 minutes uncovered until the water is absorbed. This usually only takes about ten minutes and the grains will be translucent. Serve with a little butter or just plain. Serves 6.

Note: Try sautéing 2 tablespoons of finely chopped onion in a tablespoon of butter or oil for 3 minutes. Add to the quinoa and the warm liquid. Cook as described above.

SAVORING THE MEMORY

Desserts

Cake-The Family Favorite

After two days of carefully watching our Intourist guides on our first journey to the Soviet Union, I decided to approach the leader, whom we called "the little Colonel," concerning a small problem. I explained to her that by the time we reached Kiev in two weeks, my husband would have a birthday. Would it be possible to have the hotel provide a birthday cake? I, of course, would be happy to pay for the cake. She assured me this would be no problem and was most pleasant about the request. Off we flew to the Black Sea, Georgia, Armenia, Azerbaijan and finally to Kiev. Through all these days there were many adventures. We soon learned that within the Soviet Union there was little communication between countries, except by soldiers standing around. Good food was somewhat scarce. For instance, the only place we could obtain decent juice to drink was in the foreign bar of a hotel where the four teenagers in our group found delicious canned Greek orange juice. After all the poorly equipped airplanes, hard beds, cucumbers at every meal, and hard-boiled eggs for breakfast, we finally arrived in Kiev, which is quite a lovely city. As we were milling around the lobby of our hotel waiting for the sorting of our passports, I reminded the Little Colonel about the birthday cake. In about 30 minutes she appeared and explained this would not be possible, for there was a change of shift, or something. I asked if it would be possible to buy one for we were right in the center of the city. She wrote "birthday cake" on my little notebook, I grabbed my husband and explained we were going exploring to find this cake. I was determined. We walked down one of the main thoroughfares, finding an occasional small bakery, but no cake. We were stopped in an underpass by a quick rain shower when a pleasant looking man began chatting with me. My husband kept pulling me away—I think he thought the man was KGB. Finally, I showed the man the words "birthday cake" and he said it was not possible.

Disappointed, we returned to our hotel and as we freshened up for the evening, I had another idea. We would go out in Kiev and have Chicken Kiev with no birthday cake. Downstairs we inquired about private restaurants when the "Little Colonel" appeared. I explained we would not be with the group that evening, as we wanted Chicken Kiev. She look at me and said, "What about the cake?" Startled, I retorted, "What cake?" "Oh, it has all been arranged." We gave up trying to find Chicken Kiev in Kiev, and trying to understand Russia; we settled for dinner in our hotel, which actually was one of our better meals. And, then, in came a big waitress bearing the cake with lighted candles. I was stunned. The cake looked a bit odd, but we accepted gracefully. Gene blew out the candles as we all sang "Happy Birthday." I gave him his birthday present, a gold mustache brush (which almost made the "Little Colonel" flip) and then we cut the cake. It was composed of a thick canned yellow pudding with vanilla wafers running through the whole thing. Cloyingly sweet. But, the four teenagers ate it all with relish. And there was no bill.

As a bride I soon discovered my husband's favorite cake was angel food. I looked askance at a recipe, but fortunately had inherited an electric mixer from my mother-in-law which made the prospect of cake making much brighter. One Saturday afternoon the two of us bravely mixed all the ingredients and to our surprise a cake emerged. My young husband was elated and began eating as soon as he could separate the cake from the pan (which is an entirely different problem).

My husband preferred the cake plain, but through the years I experimented with several ideas. Eliminate the suggested flavorings and use the grated rind of two fresh limes and juice. The freshness of the lime with the sweetness of the cake is a superb taste. Or try grated rind of one large orange and its juice, substituting for the flavors in the original cake. The same may also be done with two fresh lemons, grating the rind and using the juice as flavoring. Another idea that is fun: punch holes all over the cake with an ice pick and carefully pour in Crème de Menthe or a favorite liqueur.

MARY'S ANGEL FOOD CAKE

1 cup sifted cake flour

1 1/2 cups sifted confectioner's sugar

2 cups egg whites, room temperature

1 1/2 teaspoons cream of tartar

1/4 teaspoon salt

1 teaspoon vanilla flavoring

1/2 teaspoon almond flavoring

1 teaspoon lemon juice

1 cup granulated sugar

Preheat oven to 375°. You will need an angel food cake pan, ungreased.

Resift the cake flour and confectioner's sugar three times on waxed paper. If the egg whites are cold, place them in a mixing bowl and set in a pan of warm water to remove the chill. When using a heavy mixer, pour the eggs whites into the bowl and insert the wire whip. If using a regular mixer, use the large bowl. To the egg whites add the cream of tartar, salt and three flavorings. Beat at medium speed to "break" the egg whites, then turn speed to high. Continue beating until the egg whites are stiff but not dry. When they're dry you have gone too far and the flour mixture will not fold in as smoothly. Continue the beating, adding the granulated sugar. Feel the mixture and when there is no gritty feeling of sugar, stop. Transfer the mixture to a very large bowl.

Using a large rubber spatula, begin folding in the flour mixture by sifting over the egg whites four times. Fold, do not stir, until completed. Folding inserts air into the batter. When all the flour mixture is incorporated into the egg whites, pour the batter into the ungreased cake pan. With a silver knife cut through the batter several times to break any bubbles. Smooth over the cuts. Place in oven and bake 30 to 35 minutes until the top becomes golden. Cool cake by turning on top of a bottle that will fit the hole in the pan. When cooled, loosen cake by running a knife around the edge and center and shake the cake loose on a wire rack or cake plate. The cake will serve 10 to 12.

The one time I created an elaborate cake was on my husband's birthday. He was inordinately fond of bitter chocolate so in combination with a puffy white icing I created quite a taste thrill. Since angel food cake was a favorite of my husband I began preparing a special creation for his birthday and our anniversary. Soon I learned the technique of making a boiled, fluffy icing and later adorning it with the shadow chocolate topping. When my eldest son was five, he stood on a chair beside me eagerly watching while I spread soft boiled icing over the cake, for he knew the empty bowl would be his to lick. Licking came sooner than he thought for just as I finished, his foot slipped and his face fell flat on top of the cake. He raised his head in great consternation, looked at me through white eyelashes with icing up his nose, on his cheeks and around his mouth. I took one look, burst into laughter and cried, "start licking." He gave a sugary grin and licked while I scraped his face and smoothed out the cake.

WHITE FLUFFY ICING WITH SHADOW FROSTING

2 cups granulated sugar

2 tablespoons white corn syrup

²/₃ cup water

2 egg whites

Pinch of salt

1 teaspoon vanilla flavoring

In a saucepan combine the sugar, syrup and water. Place on moderate high heat and stir until sugar is dissolved. Cover and cook until the syrup boils rapidly and crystals on sides of pan are dissolved. Place the egg whites in bowl of heavy mixer and using the wire whip beat for 2 minutes. When syrup is boiling rapidly remove the cover and add five tablespoons to the beating egg whites. Continue to beat the egg whites and return syrup to burner now turned to high heat. Cook the syrup to a soft ball stage, 238°— no further! While this process is evolving, use a silver spoon and dip into the boiling syrup, then hold the spoon high to watch for a thread to form. Continue doing this until a long thread forms and flies off — this should match the 238°. Gradually add the hot syrup to the beating egg whites.

Continue to beat until the icing is cool and a spreading consistency that will hold its shape on the cake. During the beating process add a pinch of salt if desired to cut any blandness of flavor and measure in the teaspoon of vanilla flavoring. Spread the icing over the cake, starting with the sides and finishing on top. Any excess icing can be poured into the center hole of the angel food cake.

THE SHADOW

Melt 4 squares of unsweetened chocolate in top of a double boiler. If desired use 2 squares of unsweetened chocolate and 2 squares of semi-sweetened chocolate. When the chocolate is melted and smooth — and the cake icing is totally cooled — pour the chocolate over the top of cake allowing it to run down the sides. Allow the cake to sit now until the chocolate congeals. All this is most effective with the black chocolate atop the very white icing, striking in appearance and a divine indulgence! Purchase a candle that plays Happy Birthday and guests will indeed celebrate.

For chocolate lovers: a light angel food cake low in cholesterol that is delectable even with no icing. But for splurging, admittedly the cocoa frosting imbued with rum does literally melt in the mouth. Do use a fine flavored cocoa for the best in flavor.

CHOCOLATE ANGEL FOOD CAKE WITH RUM ICING

$\frac{3}{4}$ cup sifted cake flour

$\frac{1}{3}$ cup cocoa

1 $\frac{1}{2}$ cups confectioner's sugar, sifted

2 cups egg whites, room temperature

1 $\frac{1}{2}$ teaspoons cream of tartar

$\frac{1}{2}$ teaspoon salt

1 teaspoon vanilla flavoring

1 tablespoon Amaretto liqueur

1 cup granulated sugar

Preheat oven to 375°. One ungreased angel food cake pan will be needed.

Resift the cake flour with the cocoa and the confectioner's sugar on a sheet of waxed paper. Place the egg whites in large bowl of a heavy electric mixer. Add the cream of tartar, salt, vanilla flavoring and Amaretto. Beat at medium speed to "break" the egg whites, then increase to high speed continuing to beat until the egg whites are creamy, stiff and make sharp peaks. Gradually add the granulated sugar, continuing to beat. Feel the mixture (with your fingers) and when there is no grainy feeling, stop the beating. Transfer the egg whites to a large mixing bowl. Sift ¼ of the flour mixture over the egg whites and with a large rubber spatula fold in carefully. Sift and fold in the remaining flour mixture.

Pour the batter into the ungreased cake pan and with a knife cut through the batter to release air bubbles. Smooth the top and bake in preheated oven 30 to 35 minutes. Remove from oven and turn the pan upside down on a slender neck bottle to cool. When cooled, turn out on a cake stand for frosting.

COCOA AND RUM ICING

$\frac{3}{4}$ cup cocoa

4 cups confectioner's sugar

$\frac{1}{4}$ pound butter or margarine

3 tablespoons light rum

$^1\!/_2$ cup evaporated milk

Combine the cocoa and sugar in a mixing bowl, blending thoroughly. In bowl of an electric mixer, cream the butter and beat in one-half the cocoa mixture. Add the rum and one-third of the milk. Beat until creamy and add remaining cocoa mixture and milk. Continue beating several minutes until creamy. Stop and scrape down the side and bottom of the bowl. This is sufficient frosting for one angel food cake.

During my prolific cake baking days, I acquired a 14-year-old nephew for a summer, making a total of five very active males to feed. I decided to keep an account of the number of cakes and pies produced for two months. After two weeks, I discovered feeding such hearty appetites left no time for counting. I threw the notebook away and just had fun cooking. Orange cake is my own favorite that I loved for my birthday. One time in Florida I had a cake very similar to mine, still warm from the oven and made with fresh orange juice. After many years I can still remember the soft texture and light, lovely flavor.

ORANGE CAKE

2 $^1\!/_4$ cups sifted cake flour

3 $^1\!/_2$ teaspoons baking powder

$^1\!/_2$ teaspoon salt

$^3\!/_4$ cup softened butter or margarine

1 $^1\!/_2$ cups granulated sugar

3 egg yolks

1 cup orange juice

grated rind of 1 orange

3 stiffly beaten egg whites

Preheat oven to 350°. Brush three 8-inch cake tins with melted butter or coat with a vegetable spray.

Resift the flour with baking powder and salt. Set aside. Combine the butter and sugar in the bowl of an electric mixer beating until light and creamy. Add the egg yolks one at a time, beating well after each addition. Begin beating in the flour mixture and orange juice alternately, starting and ending with the flour mixture. Stir in the grated rind. Remove bowl from the mixer and with a rubber spatula, fold in the beaten egg whites until well mixed. Divide batter equally among the prepared pans, spreading batter toward the rim of the cake pans. Bake in preheated oven 20 to 25 minutes or until a cake tester comes out clean and the cake begins to separate from the edges. Turn out on wire racks to cool.

ORANGE FILLING

1/4 cup cornstarch

1 cup sugar

1/2 teaspoon salt

1 1/2 tablespoons lemon juice

2 tablespoons grated orange rind

2 tablespoons butter

Combine the cornstarch, sugar, salt, lemon juice and grated rind in top of double boiler. Mix until smooth and cook over lightly boiling water until thick, stirring constantly. When creamy and thick, remove from burner and add the butter, mixing well. Set aside to cool before spreading on the cake.

ORANGE FROSTING

1/4 cup butter or margarine

2 cups confectioner's sugar

2 egg yolks, optional

2 tablespoons orange juice, approximately

Cream the butter and sugar in a small bowl of an electric mixer until well mixed. Stir in the egg yolks, beating until creamy. Add sufficient orange juice until frosting is thick, smooth and spreadable.

Place one cake layer on a cake stand and trim any rough edges. Spread half the orange filling over the top. Trim the second layer and place on top of the first. Spread remaining orange filling over the top. Trim the third layer and place atop the second cake and press lightly so the three adhere.

With a silver knife or small spatula spread the Orange Frosting over the sides of the cake. Then frost the top ending with two or three swirls. Note: Egg yolks may be omitted in the frosting and more orange juice added if necessary.

3/4 cup sugar

2 tablespoons cornstarch

3/4 cup cool tap water

2 egg yolks, lightly beaten

3 1/2 tablespoons fresh or frozen lemon juice

1 tablespoon butter

Combine the sugar and cornstarch in a saucepan, blending well. Stirring constantly, gradually add the water. Blend in the egg yolks and lemon juice. Place pan on medium heat and continue to stir until mixture is thickened. Let bubble one minute. Remove from heat and stir the butter. Set aside to cool — do not stir. The result will be a lovely, thick filling that spreads easily over two layers of cake. Using the lemon filling in conjunction with the butter frosting gives a professional touch to a luscious cake.

Note: For an orange filling, substitute ¾ cup of orange juice for the water and omit the lemon juice.

It was a stormy night as we coasted the Queen Mary into a protected cover. Fifteen were on board to spend the night and I was concerned about the canvas awning across the front deck preventing rain from slithering down the necks of those sleeping outside. Of more concern were the dark clouds about fifteen miles away, traveling rapidly southwest to northwest. That means tornadoes. As we all watched vivid streaks of lightning, tornado funnels began to form. As the lightning flashes illuminated the night sky, we counted six black funnels. Scary. But as we watched, we all knew the storm was moving away from us, and, fortunately, the funnels stayed in the clouds. Sure enough, the storm moved off and we were safe on the Queen Mary.

With a sigh of relief, I turned to my mini-kitchen and brought out the rum cake — the favorite of the teenagers — that erased all cares and worries about a dark and stormy night.

RUM CAKE

2 cups sifted cake flour

1/2 teaspoon baking powder

1 cup butter

1¾ cups sugar

5 large eggs

1 teaspoon vanilla flavoring

2 tablespoons dark rum

Preheat oven to 325°. Brush a bundt pan with melted butter or coat with a vegetable spray.

Resift the flour with the baking powder and set aside. Cream the butter and sugar in the large bowl of an electric mixer until light and fluffy. Add the eggs one at a time beating well after each addition. Stir in the vanilla flavoring and rum. Gradually beat in the flour mixture. Scrape down the sides of the bowl and continue beating until creamy and smooth. Pour the batter into the prepared bundt pan, spreading evenly. Bake in preheated oven 1 hour. When cake tester indicates it is done remove from oven and cool in the pan 20 minutes on a wire rack. Place a cake plate over the cake and invert immediately. While cake is warm, drip with the following sauce:

RUM SAUCE

As soon as you pop the cake in the oven, prepare the sauce. Combine 1 cup of sugar with ½ cup water. Bring to a boil, stir to remove crystals on side of the pan and let boil one minute. Remove from burner and allow to become room temperature. Add 2 tablespoons dark rum. Punch the cake with a cake tester all over the top. Drip the sauce by using either a bulb baster or a spoon. This should be done gradually to allow the sauce to completely absorb into the cake.

With a pound of each basic ingredient, pound cake becomes a wondrous big cake ready for a variety of occasions. No doubt this is the reason Thomas Jefferson and George Washington often had it prepared, for both enjoyed entertaining many guests — both for evening meals and breakfast. Sliced thickly and toasted, pound cake is a treat served for breakfast with fresh fruits or homemade preserves. Sliced thinly and it becomes perfect for an afternoon tea and then can be transformed into a lovely evening dessert topped with strawberries, whipped cream and even a custard sauce.

The cake is at its best when made with all ingredients at room temperature. Then it becomes a high, golden cake, beautiful in texture. Frankly, my reason for enjoying pound cake was that it just might survive two or even three meals with my three sons.

CLASSIC POUND CAKE

2 cups soft butter

2 $\frac{1}{4}$ cups sugar

9 large eggs

4 cups sifted cake flour

$\frac{1}{2}$ teaspoon salt

$\frac{1}{2}$ teaspoon mace

1 teaspoon cream of tartar

Grated rind 1 large lemon

2 tablespoons fresh lemon juice or 2 tablespoons brandy

Preheat oven to 325°. Spray a 10 inch cake mold (angel food cake pan) with a vegetable spray.

In the large bowl of an electric mixer, preferably a heavy machine, beat the butter and sugar until light and creamy. (I feel certain that in Mr. Jefferson's kitchen, the strongest of cooks undertook the preparation of this cake sitting on a bench with a big wooden mixing bowl in her lap.)

Stir the eggs in one at a time. Resift the cake flour with the salt, mace and cream of tartar. Beat in the flour mixture ½ cup at a time. (Be patient!) Add the grated rind, lemon juice or brandy. Continue to beat until very light and creamy. Stop the motor and scrape down the sides and bottom of the bowl with a rubber spatula. Beat again until well mixed and creamy.

Pour the batter into the prepared cake pan spreading the batter evenly. Bake 60 to 70 minutes and test for doneness. When finished, turn the cake out on a wire rack to cool. The cake may be sliced into 15 or 25 pieces according to the occasion.

Labne is yogurt that has been placed in cheese cloth or a coarse cotton bag and left to hang overnight to drip dry, removing the whey. Labne has a soft creamy texture and can be purchased in many Middle Eastern stores. If not available, the process is quite easy using a good yogurt— not one containing gelatin. Enjoy a melt-in-the-mouth healthful dessert!

LABNE CHEESE CAKE WITH CHERRY TOPPING

GRAHAM CRACKER CRUST

1½ cups crushed graham crackers

¼ cup sugar

¼ teaspoon cinnamon

⅛ teaspoon nutmeg

Dash allspice

¼ cup melted butter

Preheat oven to 375°. Use with a pie plate or a 9-inch springform with removable sides. Blend all the ingredients in a mixing bowl with a fork. Press mixture evenly on the bottom and side of the pan. Bake 8 minutes. Remove from oven and cool on a wire rack.

THE CAKE

1½ cups labne, room temperature

15-ounce can sweetened condensed milk

⅓ cup lemon juice

1 teaspoon vanilla flavoring

Place the labne in a bowl of an electric mixer and whip until fluffy. Gradually add the milk continuing to beat until well mixed. Add the lemon juice and vanilla flavoring, blending well. (If a tarter taste is desired, add more lemon juice.) Pour the mixture into the baked crust. Refrigerate for at least three hours until the filling has set. Garnish with cherry glaze.

CHERRY GLAZE

14-ounce can sour cherries

2 tablespoons sugar

2 tablespoons cornstarch

Drain the cherries. Blend the juice with the sugar and cornstarch in a saucepan. Cook over moderate heat, stirring constantly, until thick and clear. Add the cherries. Remove from burner and cool. When cooled pour over the chilled cheesecake and return to refrigerator for about one hour. Or top each individual serving with cherry glaze. Strawberries, fresh peaches or blueberries may be used in place of cherries.

Forty years ago I met a lovely young woman and we quickly became great friends, exchanging many confidences about the differences in our religions and cuisine. (She's Jewish, while I grew up in a Methodist parsonage.) Her generosity overwhelmed me, for one day she gave me her cheese cake recipe and the baking pan for it which I still treasure. Not a high, dry cake for the consistency of this cheese cake is creamy and charmingly seductive. The texture literally dissolves in your mouth. The secret is its simplicity and good, hard beating.

CLASSIC CHEESE CAKE

2 cups crushed graham crackers (approximately 27 single crackers)

2 tablespoons sugar

$\frac{1}{2}$ cup melted butter

$1\frac{1}{2}$ pounds cream cheese, room temperature

4 large eggs

I cup sugar

2 teaspoons vanilla flavoring

3 tablespoons lemon juice

The graham crackers may be whirled in a food processor or crushed with a rolling pin. Combine the crushed crackers and 2 tablespoons of sugar in a bowl. Blend in the melted butter stirring with a fork until well mixed. Transfer to a springform cake pan (with removable sides). Press and smooth mixture over the bottom and up the sides of the pan (about halfway). Set aside.

Preheat oven to 350°. In the large bowl of an electric mixer, beat the cream cheese until smooth. Add the eggs, one at a time, beating constantly. Blend in the remaining ingredients and continue beating and scraping down the sides with a rubber spatula to avoid any lumps. Clean beater with a knife and resume beating at a moderate speed for 10 minutes. The mixture will be light, fluffy and increased in volume. Pour cheese mixture into prepared cake pan smoothing toward the sides. Bake in preheated oven 40 minutes. Remove cake and allow to cool in the pan on a rack. The cake is ready for a topping or cooled, covered and frozen for future use. Serves 10 to 15.

Sour Cream Topping: To be used when the cake has finished baking and is still warm. Combine and mix well 1 cup sour cream, 2 teaspoons sugar and ½ teaspoon vanilla flavoring. Spread on the cake and place in a preheated

425° oven 5 minutes — just enough time to "set." Remove and sprinkle lightly with cinnamon.

STRAWBERRY TOPPING

1 quart fresh strawberries
$\frac{1}{2}$ cup currant or strawberry jelly
2 teaspoons Kirsch

This topping is to be prepared after the cake has cooled. Arrange strawberries on top of the cake—they may be left whole or sliced. Melt the jelly over low heat; cool slightly. Stir in the Kirsch. Brush the glaze over the strawberries. Refrigerate at least 2 hours before serving.

BLUEBERRY TOPPING

2 cups fresh blueberries
$\frac{1}{3}$ cup water
$\frac{1}{2}$ cup sugar
2 tablespoons cornstarch
3 tablespoons water
1 tablespoon lemon juice
$\frac{1}{2}$ cup heavy cream (optional)

Heat ½ cup of the blueberries and ⅓ cup of water in a saucepan to boiling. Reduce heat and simmer uncovered for 5 minutes. Mix sugar and cornstarch and stir in the 3 tablespoons of water. Add sugar mixture to the cooked berries and heat to boiling stirring constantly. Boil and stir until thickened and clear, about 2 minutes. Remove from burner and cool to room temperature. Stir in the remaining blueberries and lemon juice. Spread over the cooled cheesecake. Refrigerate. If desired, whip the cream and decorate with rosettes or any design of your choice. Keep refrigerated until ready to serve.

Deep in the beautiful ranch country south and west of Austin, Texas, not too far from the famous LBJ compound, lives a charming family who relish excellent food other than the well known southwestern barbecue. My hostess was, as with most Texas women, delighted to share the recipe for this very special dark, rich chocolate cake tinged with lovely raspberry. The original cake was in the shape of a heart for Valentine's Day with fresh red raspberries on top—luscious and elegant!

$^1/_2$ cup unsweetened cocoa powder

1 cup boiling water

$^1/_2$ cup butter

2 cups sifted all purpose flour

2 cups sugar

1 $^1/_2$ teaspoons baking soda

$^1/_2$ teaspoon salt

2 large eggs

$^1/_2$ cup sour cream

1 teaspoon vanilla flavoring

Raspberry liqueur (Chambord)

Raspberry preserves (seedless)

9 ounces semi-sweet chocolate

1 cup heavy cream

Preheat oven to 350°. Prepare a 9-inch springform pan by coating with a vegetable spray and dusting with a small amount of flour or use a heart shape pan or a 9-inch tube pan.

In the large bowl of an electric mixer combine the cocoa powder with boiling water and butter. Stir until the butter is melted and set aside to cool. Resift the flour with the sugar, baking soda and salt. Add the flour mixture slowly to the cooled cocoa mixture, stirring constantly to avoid spattering; as the mixture thickens, increase speed to medium high. Stir in the eggs one at a time incorporating each completely. Add the sour cream and vanilla flavoring. Scrape down the sides of the bowl and continue stirring until the batter is smooth. Pour into the prepared pan and bake about 45 minutes. Test for doneness with a cake tester and if not done, bake 5 to 10 more minutes. Remove cake from oven and cool in a wire rack removing sides of spring form pan.

When the cake is cooled slice into 3 layers. Measure the depth of the cake and place toothpicks around the cake to assist in making the layers even when slicing. Brush each layer with raspberry liqueur quite thoroughly — it is best to use a feather brush. Spread the raspberry preserves or jam over the layers. Top each layer with the Chocolate Ganache as they are stacked.

CHOCOLATE GANACHE

Combine the 9 ounces of semi-sweet chocolate (chips are fine) with 1 cup of hot cream. When heating the cream, stir constantly until hot, add the chocolate chips and blend until melted. Remove from burner and let cool, stirring occasionally. Spread over each layer as they are stacked and then frost the complete cake. Place in refrigerator until ready to serve. If fresh raspberries are available, top the cake with these luscious little berries.

Among the odds and ends that I inherited as a bride in the middle of the Great Depression was a skillet about nine inches in diameter. It had a small iron handle, making it ideal for baking Upside Down Cake. I loved that old skillet, slightly bent but sturdy, which like many items ultimately ended up on the Queen Mary. Here it gave long service and finally disappeared when we abandoned the ship. Upside down cake was very special to my sons for they loved the melted brown sugar and butter dissolving into the cake batter.

UPSIDE DOWN CAKE

¹⁄₂ cup butter

1 cup brown sugar

8 slices canned pineapple, drained

Red candied cherries

Pecans or walnuts

THE CAKE

1 ¹⁄₂ cups sifted all purpose flour

¹⁄₂ cup granulated sugar

1 ¹⁄₂ teaspoons baking powder

¹⁄₂ teaspoon salt

¹⁄₂ cup milk

2 large eggs

¹⁄₂ teaspoon vanilla flavoring

Preheat oven to 350°

Melt ¼ cup of the butter in a 9-inch skillet that can be used in the oven. Another type of utensil may be used if it can be placed on a burner and in the oven and is 9 inches wide and 2 inches deep. Add the brown sugar, stirring until melted. Remove from the burner and arrange the drained pineapple slices on top of the melted sugar and butter. Decorating can be accomplished by placing a cherry in the center of each pineapple or a whole nut. Then, sprinkle nuts around the slices of fruit. Set aside.

Sift together the flour, sugar, baking powder and salt. In a mixing bowl beat together the milk, eggs and vanilla flavoring. Gradually add the egg mixture, beating until smooth. Pour the batter over the pineapple slices spreading evenly. Bake in preheated oven approximately 40 minutes until a golden brown.

The melted brown sugar will be bubbling; let the cake settle for about 5 minutes. Turn out on a serving tray. My family loved it warm from the oven. The cake may also be served at room temperature with a touch of whipped cream. Serves 8 easily.

AMERICAN PIE CRUST

FOR A TWO-CRUST PIE

2 cups unsifted all purpose flour

$^1\!/_2$ teaspoon salt

$^2\!/_3$ cup plus 2 tablespoons chilled vegetable shortening

4-6 tablespoons cold water

Combine the flour and salt together in a shallow mixing bowl. The shortening may be mixed into the dry ingredients in several methods. One method is cutting quickly with two knives or a pastry blender. Another method is through use of hands, picking up flour and shortening and crumbling until well mixed. Or, if preferred, combine flour, salt and shortening in a food processor fitted with steel blade, pulsing just until the shortening is crumbled into the flour. Each method must be performed quickly. Add only half the amount of water suggested and then more additions until the mixture forms into an easily handled dough — and not too wet. As with bread making, when water is introduced into flour, this action develops the gluten. In pastry making the dough must be handled swiftly or it will become tough. The pastry may be wrapped in plastic and refrigerated until a more convenient time but no longer than two days.

When finished and ready to make a pie, divide the dough in half, covering the half not being used. For best results use a pastry cloth and a stockinette over the rolling pin. Using quick light strokes roll away from you, making pastry larger than the pie pan. With a dough scraper, carefully lift the pastry and fit carefully into the pan. Or roll pastry over the rolling pin and lay across the pan. Press down gently and either cut off the excess dough or tuck underneath the edge making a thicker layer for crimping. Prepare the pie filling and cover with the second ball of pastry that has been rolled to fit the pan. Any extra pastry can be cut into pastry leaves and adhered to the edge of pie crust with a bit of water or egg white. Crimp edges of pastry either with a fork or fingers. Bake a double crust pie in a preheated 425° oven 10 to 15 minutes, then reduce heat to 350° and finish baking according to directions in selected recipe. The filling of a fruit pie tends to bubble over; place aluminum foil underneath the pie to protect the oven floor and avoid a mess for you to clean.

Note: Butter or margarine may be used to replace the vegetable shortening. Both should be thoroughly chilled before using. Butter makes a richer but a more flavorful pie crust. Actually leaf lard is the best — this I used a very long time ago and the pie crust was marvelous, but only used half the quantity, because it is so rich. That was long before cholesterol was born!

Single Pie Crust: Follow the directions above, using one-half the ingredients specified. When using a cooked filling, then the crust must be baked alone. Pierce bottom of pie crust with a fork. Cut a round of wax paper and carefully fit into the pastry. Place a layer of white beans or special weights available in culinary shops. Bake the crust at 425° for 10 minutes. Remove the paper and weights (storing for another time) and bake another 5 or 8 minutes until the pastry is lightly golden.

Years ago when my sons were small I decided to prepare my first lemon meringue pie. Carefully I constructed a beautiful pie with much interest from my three young sons. I piled the meringue on top and explained that it only had to cook a few minutes and the pie would be finished. All three boys watched as I opened the oven door and there stood this gorgeous pie with a fluffy meringue just tinged with gold. I began to remove the pie when disaster struck! Somehow, something slipped and the pie tumbled to the floor, meringue side down. Dead silence. Quickly I grabbed a spatula, scooped up the pie with my hand on the pan, turned it over, smoothed the mess out and assured the boys that the meringue pudding would be just fine for dinner. We ate every bite.

LEMON MERINGUE PIE

1 baked 9-inch pastry crust, page 192

½ cup cornstarch

3 tablespoons all purpose flour

1½ cups sugar

¼ teaspoon salt

1¾ cups water

4 egg yolks, lightly beaten

2 tablespoons butter

1 tablespoon grated lemon rind

½ cup fresh lemon juice

4 egg whites

¼ teaspoon cream of tartar

½ cup sugar

Prepare the pastry crust and set aside to cool. Blend the cornstarch, flour, 1½ cups of sugar and salt in a saucepan. Gradually stir in the water. Place over medium heat and stir constantly until mixture comes to a boil. Boil 1 minute. For stirring, use a whisk at the beginning to avoid any lumping and change to a rubber spatula. Stir one-half the mixture slowly into the egg yolks and transfer to the saucepan stirring all thoroughly. Return to burner and cook, stirring, for 2 minutes. The mixture should be smooth and very thick. Remove from heat and add the butter, lemon rind and juice. Cool about 10 minutes. Pour the lemon mixture into the baked pie shell.

Preheat oven to 350°. Beat the egg whites and cream of tartar until foamy and beginning to take shape. While still beating, add the ½ cup of sugar gradually. Continue beating until the meringue forms stiff, glossy peaks. Spread atop the pie filling, being certain the meringue touches all around. Swirl the top around and be sure there are little peaks —fun and pretty when tinged with a little golden brown. Bake for approximately 15 minutes or until tipped with brown. Be certain to check for it may take a bit longer. Set the pie on a wire rack to cool. Six generous servings.

If my publisher would grant me the space, I could devote a complete chapter to Lynn Davis's adventures atop Aspen Mountain in a log cabin her husband has built on an old mining claim. Originally there was no running water but the cabin did contain a big wood-burning cookstove which was a totally new experience to this very modern, young but expert cook. Through a suggestion, they finally located a thermostat in Wisconsin, the origin of the stove. With the assistance of a professional cook from Argentina, Lynn learned how and when to bake a pie — and a whole Thanksgiving dinner. But, first, they had to import water. After running up and down this mountain on snowmobiles, they invested in a snowcat and then a second snowcat, so that one Thanksgiving they transported four people in a snowcat and four more people plus seven dogs in the second one. By this time running water was available, for each year Lynn and Stony transport 2800 gallons of water into a crawl space under the basement added to the original cabin. Lynn has given me a vivid description of baking this pie: how she stoked the stove, and kept it going, but learned to slow the stoking or the oven would be 600°—and there goes the pie! The cooktop on the stove has hot, very hot and even hotter areas, so pots and pans can just be moved around to fit the occasion. There is even a small ledge to place a saucepan to melt butter—Great-grandma never had it so good! These are healthy, vigorous people who adore outdoor sports from riding horseback to cross-country skiing. Let's follow Lynn while she bakes this luscious pie, as she accomplishes this feat on her wood stove and on an ordinary gas or electric stove. I baked two of her pies at 700 feet above sea level with perfect success. One I ate and one is in the freezer.

LYNN'S STRAWBERRY-RHUBARB PIE

Pastry for two-crust pie, page 192

2 cups all purpose flour

1/2 teaspoon salt

2/3 cup shortening plus 2 tablespoons

4-6 tablespoons cool water

Combine the flour and salt in a mixing bowl. Cut shortening into the flour with a pastry cutter, then stir and finish with your hands. With a fork add 4 tablespoons of the water and the remaining 2 tablespoons as needed to blend and adhere ingredients together. Form pastry into a ball and cut in half. On a lightly floured pastry cloth roll one-half the pastry in a circle larger than a 9-inch pie pan. Fold over and lift carefully with a dough scraper into the pie pan. Gently press the pastry to fit into the pan. Cover lightly with a tea cloth while preparing the top pastry and filling. Roll the second half into a rectangle. With a pastry cutter, cut 10 lattice strips, each about 1 inch wide. Lynn states fat strips look better than thin.

THE FILLING

1 1/2 cups sugar

1/8 teaspoon salt

1/3 cup all purpose flour

2 cups fresh strawberries, clean with damp cloth, cut large ones in half

2 cups fresh rhubarb, rinsed, dried and trimmed of surface strings

2 tablespoons butter

1 tablespoon sugar

Combine the sugar, salt and flour mixing well. Cut large strawberries in half, leave small ones whole. Slice rhubarb in pieces. Arrange half the berries and rhubarb in the pastry lined pan. Sprinkle with half the sugar mixture. Repeat with remaining fruit and sugar mixture. Dot with butter. Place the lattice strips on top, weaving in and out. Tuck any excess pastry underneath the edge and flute the edges. The pie can sit on a counter, covered with a tea towel to prevent drying, for 2 hours before baking. Preheat oven to 425°. Just before baking, brush top of pie with cold water and sprinkle with the tablespoon of sugar. Bake at 425° for 25 minutes until crust is lightly brown — but check. Reduce heat to 350° for 30 minutes.

Lynn chose strawberry-rhubarb pie recipe to give me, for this pie has now become synonymous with the cabin. Rhubarb grows along the road up Aspen Mountain to about 10,000 feet in the month of August. A wood stove cooks very fast; Lynn places the pie in the oven when the new thermostat registers 300° and checks it every 5 to 10 minutes for browning. As soon as the crust is browned, she covers the pie with foil and bakes it for another hour or until the juices are bubbling strongly. Because of this high altitude the pie cooks for about 1½ hours then is cooled and placed in a warming shelf. After either cross country skiing, or summer climbing and hiking, I can just imagine how delicious that warm pie would taste. Can't you imagine wood stove pumpkin and pecan pies for Thanksgiving?

Never shall I forget the first time our family drove to the tip of Florida. In all my journeys within the United States, the highway from Miami to Key West is one of the most stunning ocean drives filled with entrancingly beautiful colors of the sea, tropical plants on the Keys and evidence of man's ability to build long bridges across vast expanses of water. There, for the first time, we indulged in turtle steak, stone crab and Key Lime Pie. There are many versions of this distinctive pie, but in Florida the original is made with sweetened condensed milk. I shall give a choice of pastry or graham cracker crust and a choice of toppings, both are lovely and disarmingly delicious.

KEY LIME PIE

One crust pastry, page 192 or

GRAHAM CRACKER CRUST

1½ cups crushed graham crackers

2 tablespoons sugar

¼ cup melted butter

THE PIE FILLING

4 egg yolks

14 ounce can sweetened condensed milk

½ cup fresh lime juice

1 egg white

Whipped Cream Topping:

1 cup heavy cream

2 tablespoons sugar

Tiny twists of lime peel

Meringue Topping:

3 egg whites

½ teaspoon cream of tartar

6 tablespoons sugar

If preparing the pastry crust, bake and then cool. If making the graham cracker crust, combine the crushed graham crackers (crushed quickly in a food processor), the 2 tablespoons of sugar and melted butter. Work together with a fork and then press into the bottom and sides of a 9-inch pie tin. Bake in a preheated 375° oven for 8 minutes. Remove and cool.

Stir together the egg yolks and condensed milk. Add the lime juice stirring until smooth. Beat one egg white until softly stiff. Fold into the lime mixture thoroughly. Pour into choice of crust, smoothing to the sides. Cover lightly and chill for 3 to 4 hours.

Choice of topping: Beat the cup of heavy cream until stiff adding the 2 tablespoons of sugar. Spread over the lime filling and decorate with tiny twists of lime peel. Or whip the 3 egg whites with the cream of tartar and gradually add the 6 tablespoons of sugar. Spread over the pie filling and bake in a preheated 350° oven until the meringue is golden with touches of brown. Remove from the oven and when cooled, serve. Serves 6.

Following the idea of Key Lime Pie, is pie combining lemon, lime and orange has the same texture but a richer and more tart flavor. Serve small slices decorated simply with a twisted sliver of fresh lemon or lime rind.

TRIPLE CITRUS PIE

Graham cracker crust, Key Lime Pie, page 197

Zest of 1 lime, 1 lemon, 1 orange

4 egg yolks, unbeaten

14 ounce can sweetened condensed milk

$1/2$ cup mixed lime and lemon juice

2 tablespoons orange concentrate (thawed frozen orange juice)

Line a 9-inch pie tin with the graham cracker crust and bake at 375° for 8 minutes. Set aside to cool.

Grate the rind of the three citrus fruits (colored part only), mix together and set aside. To the unbeaten egg yolks add the condensed milk, the juice and the zest of the fruits. Stir until well mixed and pour into the cooled pie shell. Refrigerate for several hours until firm. Serve small slices, decorated with a sliver of rind that is slightly twisted. Serves 8 to 10 guests.

When July and August arrive with fresh peaches in abundance and at the peak of their flavor, there is just nothing better than a cobbler or a fresh peach pie — with fresh peach homemade ice cream. Big, juicy nectarines are also superb used in this pie.

BROWN SUGAR PEACH PIE

Pastry for two-crust pie, page 192

$1/2$ cup granulated sugar

$1/4$ cup brown sugar, packed

4 tablespoons all purpose flour

$1/2$ teaspoon cinnamon

6 cups peeled, sliced fresh peaches

1 tablespoon lemon juice

$1/4$ teaspoon almond extract

2 tablespoons butter, cut in pieces

Line a 9-inch pie pan with one-half the pastry as directed in master recipe. Combine the sugars, flour and cinnamon. Sprinkle the sliced peaches with the lemon juice and almond extract, mixing well. Arrange the peaches in the pastry lined pie pan and sprinkle the sugar mixture over as evenly as possible. Dot with pieces of butter.

Preheat oven to 425°. Roll out the second portion of pastry into an oblong. Cut into strips and lay them crisscrossed over the peaches. Crimp the edges. Bake in preheated oven for 15 minutes until just lightly browned. Lower heat to 350° and continue baking for 40 minutes or until the juices are bubbling and the crust is golden. If the edges become too brown, place strips of aluminum foil around the pie. Place foil underneath the pie to catch any drippings. Let pie cool on a wire rack 20 to 30 minutes before serving. Serves 6.

I used to watch with profound respect as my mother made this is old-fashioned pie. Although there were no measurements ever written or told to me, at the request of a food editor, I attempted making the pie. All the portions are quite simple and on my initial trial I succeeded, and the first bite was exactly as I remembered. Mother was raised on a farm in Red River County in northeast Texas where a dinner of black eyed peas, ham hock and cornbread dripping in real butter always ended with this pie. I thought it a perfect meal except for my father sprinkling hot pepper sauce all over the peas. At least he didn't pepper the pie!

MY MOTHER'S PEACH AND CUSTARD PIE

THE PIE CRUST (FOR A 9-INCH DEEP PIE PLATE)

$1 1/2$ cups all purpose flour

$1/4$ teaspoon salt

$1/3$ cup plus 2 tablespoons vegetable shortening

2 to 4 tablespoons ice water

Preheat oven to 450°.Combine the flour and salt in a shallow bowl and cut in the shortening with a pastry blender until the mixture is similar to very coarse cornmeal. Add the ice water, stirring rapidly with a fork until the mixture blends together. Round into a ball and place on a floured surface—a pastry cloth is perfect. Roll pastry out with a floured rolling pin and lift into the pie plate. Crimp the pastry around the edge to stand up and then prick the bottom with a fork. Bake the pastry in the hot oven 10 minutes. Remove; the partially baked pastry is now ready to receive the filling.

THE PEACHES

Place the contents of an 8 ounce package of dried peaches in a saucepan. Cover with cold water and bring to a simmer. Top with a lid and cook until tender, 15 to 20 minutes. Drain well and place the peaches in a food processor pulsing about three times. The peaches should not be absolutely smooth, but have texture. Set aside to cool while making the custard.

THE CUSTARD

3 eggs

½ cup sugar

2 cups milk

1 teaspoon vanilla flavoring

Nutmeg

Preheat oven to 450°. Whisk the eggs lightly and slowly add the sugar, beating constantly. Add the milk and vanilla blending well.

Spread the peaches over bottom of the prepared pie crust. Pour the custard over the peaches and dust lightly with nutmeg. Place the pie in the hot oven and lower heat immediately to 350°. Bake the pie until the custard is set, about 50 minutes. Check by slipping a knife into the custard. When the knife emerges clean, the pie is done. Cool on wire rack. The pie may be served warm, room temperature or even chilled. Serves 6 to 8.

Fresh lemon and lime are favorites of mine for desserts, fish entrees, enhancement of soups—actually there are unlimited uses. Fortunately, we are furnished with abundant crops of large limes from Florida and beautiful yellow lemons from California. My frozen lime pie provides a light, refreshing dessert and can be tucked in a freezer ready for any special occasion.

FROZEN LIME PIE

3 large eggs

$\frac{3}{4}$ cup sugar

Drops of green coloring

1 $\frac{1}{2}$ cups light cream

$\frac{1}{2}$ cup fresh lime juice

Grated rind of 1 large lime

GRAHAM CRACKER CRUST

2 cups crushed graham crackers

$\frac{1}{2}$ cup confectioner's sugar

Grated rind of 1 large lime

$\frac{1}{3}$ cup melted butter

3 cups vanilla ice cream

Beat eggs until thick and lemon colored. Gradually add the sugar and continue beating until mixture is light and fluffy. Add a few drops of green coloring to create a light summer shade. Blend in the cream, lime juice and grated rind. Mix well. Pour into a refrigerator tray and freeze until firm. Remove and break into chunks. Turn into a chilled bowl and beat with an electric mixer until smooth. Return to the tray and partially freeze.

In a mixing bowl, combine the crushed crackers with confectioner's sugar, grated lime rind and butter, stirring with a fork until well mixed. Reserve ¼ of the mixture for topping. Spread remaining cracker mixture in a deep 10-inch glass pie plate that can be used as a serving dish. Beat the vanilla ice cream until smooth and spread over the crust. Top with the half frozen lime mixture. Sprinkle the reserved crumbs over the top. Freeze until firm. Remove, cover tightly and label. Place back in the freezer until ready to serve. Serves 8 to 10.

Next to strawberry shortcake, my favorite dessert is pie — not just an ordinary pie, but one with beauty and dreamy elegance, filled with fresh ripe berries and slightly cooked fresh berries with just a touch of cream cheese.

Choose strawberries even in color with bright green stems. Do not wash or stem the berries until ready to use.

STRAWBERRY PIE

1 pre-baked pie shell, page 192

4 cups strawberries, clean and stemmed

²/₃ cup water

1 cup sugar

3 tablespoons cornstarch

¹/₃ cup water

3 ounces cream cheese

Cream or milk

Whipped cream, optional

Prepare the pie shell in a deep glass or pottery pie plate and set aside to cool. After the strawberries have been cleaned, save a few for decoration. In a saucepan combine the ⅔ cup of water with 1 cup of the berries. Bring to a simmer and cook 3 minutes. Combine the sugar and cornstarch and dissolve in the ⅓ cup of water. Blend into the berries, stir and boil rapidly 1 minute, stirring constantly. Cool the mixture in a pan of cold water.

In the small bowl of an electric mixer combine the cream cheese with a small amount of cream or milk and beat until a creamy spreading consistency. Spread the cheese on bottom of the pie crust. Slice the uncooked berries and spread over the cheese. Pour the cooled berry mixture over the fresh berries. Refrigerate at least 2 hours.

For decoration, use sweetened whipped cream and garnish with the reserved whole berries. If calories are important, omit the whipped cream and serve the pie topped with a few whole berries.

Quick Stawberry Sorbet is not a true sorbet but the final result has a sorbet texture. The preparation is simple, fast and delicious. The idea was sent by my good friend, Judy Bell of Portland, Oregon, a superb cook who is willing to attempt a variety of cuisines. She relates this is particularly gratifying after an Italian dinner.

QUICK STRAWBERRY SORBET

1 pound frozen strawberries, unsweetened

3 tablespoons orange juice

3 tablespoons Cointreau

3 tablespoons sugar

Whole fresh strawberries or candied violets for garnish

Place the frozen strawberries in a food processor fitted with a steel blade and add the orange juice, Cointreau and sugar. Let stand for 15 minutes. Process to start breaking up the frozen berries; there will be an earth-shaking noise at first. Again let the mixture stand a few minutes, scraping down the sides and stirring. Pulse again and continue to pulse until the mixture becomes a creamy mass much like a true sorbet. Taste and add more sugar or Cointreau if necessary. Serve in a footed sherbet dishes that have been chilled in the refrigerator. Garnish the top with a strawberry or candied violet and serve on dessert plates either alone or with a favorite cookie.

During my life on a small farm, I loved the local farmer's market where I could purchase a crate of red raspberries for eight dollars or a crate of strawberries for five. I chose the best of the strawberries for shortcake. I piled the strawberries high and then poured thick yellow Jersey cream all over the whole thing. My family ate every bite blissfully. One never thought about calories on a farm, and certainly the word cholesterol had not yet appeared. A true strawberry shortcake is a noble triumph of the culinary art. Ignore all these little plastic covered cakes hovering around the strawberry counter. A classic shortcake can give one a whole new look at life, and this is the way it should be done.

STRAWBERRY SHORTCAKE

1 quart fresh strawberries

1 cup sugar

2 cups all purpose flour

$1/3$ cup sugar

4 teaspoons baking powder

$1/2$ teaspoon salt

$1/8$ teaspoon nutmeg

$1/2$ cup butter

1 egg, well beaten

$1/3$ cup milk

Soft butter

Whipped cream

Clean and hull the strawberries. Slice and place in a bowl. Add the cup of sugar and mix well. With a pastry blender partially crush the berries and set aside.

Preheat oven to 450°. Brush a 9-inch skillet or cake tin with melted butter or coat with vegetable spray. Sift together the flour, sugar, baking powder, salt and nutmeg into a mixing bowl. With a pastry blender cut in the ½ cup of butter until mixture resembles coarse cornmeal. Add the beaten egg and milk, stirring until well blended. For a large cake, place dough in the 9-inch pan pressing to fit into the bottom. Or divide the dough in 4 portions and form into round patties placing on a buttered baking sheet. Bake in preheated oven approximately 15 minutes. Remove from oven and while hot, split the cake and brush each cut side with soft butter.

Place a layer of cake on a serving plate and cover with crushed strawberries. Top with the second layer of shortcake and remaining strawberries. Swirl sweetened whipped cream over and decorate with an extra strawberry. Individual cakes may be prepared in a similar manner and served on dessert plates.

Surely no one would ever tire of strawberry shortcake but should this be possible, I have the solution with a few delightfully light desserts when the very best strawberries arrive.

ZABAGLIONE WITH STRAWBERRIES

5 egg yolks

¾ cup sugar

1 cup cream sherry

4 cups strawberries

Sugar to taste

1 cup heavy cream, optional

Beat the egg yolks in the top of a double boiler until very light and lemony in color. Stir in the ¾ cup of sugar until the mixture is thick. Place the pan over just simmering water and add the sherry a little at a time, beating constantly. All this may be done with an electric mixer in the beginning and then switch to a whisk when the pan is placed over hot water. Continue to stir until the mixture becomes quite thick—it will foam up high and then settle down to become similar to a custard. Remove pan and set aside to cool. Stem and wash strawberries; allow to drain. Crush about one-third of the berries and combine with the whole berries. Add sugar to taste. Divide the strawberries among 6 or 8 stemmed sherbet compotes. I love to pour the Zabaglione immediately after cooking over the berries and serve. But, if desired, whip the cup of heavy cream and fold into the cooled Zabaglione. Pour this over the strawberries and enjoy!

STRAWBERRY FLUFF

4 cups strawberries

2 egg whites

I cup sugar

I teaspoon lemon juice

Wash and stem the strawberries and allow to drain. Slice each berry in several pieces and set aside. Place the egg whites in the large bowl of an electric mixer using the wire whip (if a heavy mixer) and beat until frothy. Add strawberries, a few at a time until they are mixed with the egg whites. Whip in the sugar, ¼ cup at a time, continuing to beat. Add the lemon juice. Keep beating until the mixture is stiff. Stop several times and scoop up any berries at bottom of the bowl. Continue to beat several minutes. Pile into tall sherbet glasses and top with a big fat strawberry. The amount of fluff will be about 6 cups.

STRAWBERRIES WITH POWDERED SUGAR AND LIQUEUR

Being a bit partial to my grandchildren, I soon found this to be one of their favorite strawberry desserts as they grew older. So simple to wash juicy, ripe strawberries leaving the stems on. After they have drained, arrange the berries in a circle on a round serving plate. In the center place a small bowl of powdered sugar and there you are —the children love it.

For a more sophisticated offering: wash strawberries, leaving the stems on and place in a lovely crystal bowl. Beside the bowl have two small crystal bowls, one with powdered sugar and the other with a favorite liqueur, such as kirsch, Amaretto or Grand Marnier. The technique is first to dip the berries into the liqueur and then the powdered sugar. And that, truly is ambrosia with each bite. Marvelous for a buffet table.

A light, lovely and quite simple custard-type ice cream I have devised is creamy and yet made with just whole milk. (Cream can be substituted for a portion of the milk but that is not necessary.) Frozen strawberries and peaches that have been tucked in the freezer, may be thawed briefly, whirled in a food processor and added to the ice cream.

Each ice cream freezer will have directions for freezing ice cream. Here are general directions for an electric freezer, using ice and salt. Pour the milk mixture into the container, insert the dasher and carefully place into the freezer. Cover with the lid. Pack the sides alternately with ice and ice cream salt to the top of the container. Plug in the freezer and allow to turn until the signal is given by the machine that the ice cream is ready. The same directions can be used for a freezer turned by hand except that certainly someone will sit on the freezer to keep it from turning and the person turning will surely be able to tell when the ice cream has begun to freeze. Wipe off the top, remove the lid and remove the dasher. (By all means taste. Be sure someone is on hand to finish cleaning the dasher over the sink!) Return the lid and pack with more ice, cover with a rug or thick towel until time to serve; the ice cream is ready.

MARY'S ICE CREAM

2 quarts of whole milk*

1 cup sugar

6 tablespoons flour

$1/2$ teaspoon salt, optional

6 tablespoons milk

2 large eggs, beaten

$1/2$ cup sugar

1 tablespoon vanilla flavoring

Scald the milk in a heavy saucepan or double boiler. In a mixing bowl combine the 1 cup of sugar, flour and salt. Add the 6 tablespoons of milk and stir well. Whisk the flour mixture into the hot milk and continue to stir with a wooden spoon until the mixture becomes thickened much like a thin white sauce. Beat the eggs and add the ½ cup of sugar. Blend in a small portion of the milk mixture into the eggs. Stir the eggs into the milk mixture and continue to cook stirring constantly about 5 minutes or until it becomes a light smooth custard. Add the vanilla flavoring. Allow to cool and the custard is ready for the freezer.

*2 cups of light cream may be substituted for 2 cups of whole milk

Peel and slice 2 cups well ripened peaches. Mash thoroughly or whirl in a food processor fitted with the steel blade. Add 1 cup of sugar and a few drops of lemon juice. Whirl two times and then let stand 1 hour before adding to the ice cream mix.

FOR STRAWBERRY ICE CREAM

Wash and remove stems from 4 cups fresh, ripe strawberries. Mash berries or whirl in a food processor. Add 1 cup of sugar, whirl only to mix in the sugar and allow to stand 1 hour. Taste for sugar content for the amount of sugar will depend upon the ripeness of the strawberries. Add to the ice cream mix.

At some point during World War II, apple crisp appeared on the culinary scene and quickly became a favorite across every state for it is a delightfully easy way to make apple pie. And apple crisp is delicious, so it has stayed with us, becoming a small American classic.

APPLE CRISP

   6 cups Granny Smith apples, peeled, cored and sliced

   1-2 tablespoons lemon juice

   1 cup all purpose flour

   $\frac{1}{2}$ cup brown sugar

   $\frac{1}{2}$ cup granulated sugar

   1 teaspoon cinnamon

   $\frac{1}{2}$ teaspoon nutmeg

   $\frac{1}{2}$ cup butter or margarine

   $\frac{1}{2}$ cup chopped pecans or walnuts

   Vanilla ice cream

Preheat oven to 350°.

Tart apples such as Granny Smith are the best for an apple crisp. Prepare the apples and place in a 10x7″ baking dish about 1½ inches deep. Sprinkle with lemon juice. Separately in a mixing bowl, combine the flour, sugars and spices. Cut in the butter with a pastry blender until very well mixed. Stir in the nuts. Sprinkle over the apples spreading evenly. Cover with aluminum foil and bake in preheated oven 25 minutes. Remove the foil and bake 35 minutes. The crisp is marvelous served warm, topped with vanilla ice cream. Serves 8 to 10.

The problem with fresh fruit crisp is stopping at one serving. Combining a lovely variety of beautiful fresh summer fruits is not only delectable and luscious, but delightfully easy for the process is similar to apple crisp but with a totally different flavor. A perfect summer dessert to offer for a dinner party.

FRESH FRUIT CRISP

8 to 9 cups mixed fresh fruits: blueberries, strawberries, peaches, nectarines, apricots, plums, raspberries

2 tablespoons apricot brandy

1 teaspoon lemon juice

1½ cups all purpose flour

½ cup granulated sugar

⅔ cup brown sugar, packed

1 teaspoon cinnamon

½ cup plus 2 tablespoons butter

½ cup chopped pecans or walnuts

Vanilla ice cream, optional

Preheat oven to 350°.

Prepare choice of fruits by peeling and slicing. Stir in the brandy and lemon juice. Spread the fruits in a 9x14" baking dish or two smaller pans. Glass is fine, for then the dessert may be served at the table with a bowl of ice cream on the side.

Combine the flour, the two sugars and cinnamon. Add the butter sliced in pieces. Cut the butter into the flour mixture with a pastry blender until crumbly. Add the nuts. Spread the flour mixture atop the fruit, patting out evenly. Cover lightly with aluminum foil and bake 20 minutes.

Remove foil and bake 30 minutes until the top is crispy and fruit is bubbling. Serve warm or room temperature. The crisp is marvelous while warm, topped with vanilla ice cream, or try frozen peach yogurt for an enticing flavor. Serves 10 to 12.

Throughout the United States are beautiful valleys and low hillsides perfect for growing exquisite, rosy peaches, a favorite fruit of Americans. One such valley in the curve of the Arkansas River close to my city of Tulsa is the area surrounding the little town of Porter. When sharp icy weather sweeps across the western plains, everyone worries about the peach crop. Despite any weather difficulties there is always a gala Porter Peach festival where folks come from all over to enjoy fresh peach ice cream and pick their own peaches. Porter peaches are just as fine as those from Georgia and Michigan so in July and August I love baking several juicy cobblers to tuck in the freezer for winter enjoyment when the snow is flying.

PORTER PEACH COBBLER

THE PASTRY

1 $\frac{1}{2}$ cups all purpose flour

$\frac{1}{2}$ teaspoon salt

$\frac{1}{3}$ cup plus 2 tablespoons butter or margarine

Ice water

Blend the flour and salt in a shallow mixing bowl. Cut in the butter with a pastry blender or add all ingredients to a food processor fitted with the steel blade and pulse until similar to a coarse cornmeal. If making by hand, add just enough chilled water to hold the pastry together mixing quickly with a fork. The same may be accomplished with a food processor. Round the pastry into a ball and pat on a tiny bit of flour.

Cover with plastic wrap and set aside while preparing the peaches.

THE PEACHES

10 cups peeled and sliced peaches

2 tablespoons lemon juice

1 $\frac{1}{2}$ cups sugar

3 tablespoons all purpose flour

$\frac{1}{4}$ teaspoon cinnamon

$\frac{1}{8}$ teaspoon nutmeg

2 tablespoons butter, cut in pieces

Preheat oven to 450°.

When handling this quantity peaches, heat water in a large saucepan until boiling. Remove from burner. Place two or three peaches in a sieve with a handle and lower into the hot water 1 to 2 minutes. Remove and place remaining peaches in hot water as directed. The skin will slip off easily. Slice the peaches, removing the pits, into a bowl and sprinkle with the lemon juice stirring carefully. Spread the peaches in a 12x7x2" baking dish. Mix the sugar, flour and spices together. Sprinkle evenly over the peaches and dot with butter.

With a floured rolling pin, roll the pastry to fit top of baking dish, covering the peaches and dish with sufficient pastry to crimp around the edges. Pierce the top several times with a fork. Bake in preheated oven 10 minutes. Lower heat to 350° and bake 30 minutes or until the pastry is lightly golden and the peaches are bubbling. Delectably delicious when served warm with fresh peach ice cream! Serves 8 to 10.

A beautifully constructed English trifle is a very special dessert. This I know quite well for I have consumed a great variety, even one made with canned fruit in a modest English home. One journey to England was for the wedding of a son. After the ceremonies we took an automobile trip into northern England and Scotland. We soon learned that if we wanted trifle it must be ordered first, or there would be none left at the end of our meal. Once we stopped at a bakery to purchase items for a picnic the next day and found trifle in small paper cups. Having no spoons, we simply drank the trifle.

So many wonderful things can be done with a trifle. It can be flavored with jams and fruits, then decorated simply with whipped cream, adding fruits on top or more ornately, fresh flowers.

AN ENGLISH TRIFLE

THE CAKE

2 cups sifted cake flour

$1/2$ teaspoon baking powder

1 cup soft butter

$1\frac{3}{4}$ cup sugar

6 eggs

Grated rind of 1 large lemon

1 tablespoon lemon juice

Preheat oven to 325°. Brush a 10-inch tube pan (angel food cake pan) with melted butter or coat with a vegetable spray. Set aside.

Resift flour with baking powder. Cream the butter and sugar in the large bowl of an electric mixer until light and fluffy. Add the eggs, one at a time, beating well after each addition. Continue beating for several minutes until the batter is light, smooth, and creamy. Stop the motor occasionally and scrape down the sides of the bowl. Pour the batter into the prepared cake pan, spreading evenly. Bake in preheated oven for 1 hour, testing with cake tester for doneness. Turn cake out on a wire rack to cool.

THE CUSTARD

8 egg yolks

6 tablespoons sugar

6½ cups hot milk

I tablespoon vanilla flavoring

Beat the egg yolks in the small bowl of an electric mixer until pale yellow and thick. Slowly add the sugar, beating constantly. Continue beating until thick and creamy. Gradually add a small portion of the hot milk. Transfer the mixture to the top of a double boiler and add the remaining milk, stirring thoroughly. Place over lightly boiling water and stir constantly with a wooden spoon until the custard thickens and coats the spoon. Have patience as this takes a bit of time—I usually read the newspaper. Remove the custard and add the vanilla flavoring.

FINAL PREPARATION

I cup dry sherry or light rum

Strawberry or raspberry jam

Fresh strawberries or raspberries

Mixed fruits, optional

Whipping cream, optional

There are special trifle bowls, but any large, attractive glass bowl will be fine. Cut the cake in ½ inch slices. Line the bottom of the bowl with the cake and spread lightly with choice of jam. Cover this with another layer of cake and more jam. Continue the layers until an inch or two below top of the bowl. If there is cake left over, it can be frozen and used later for strawberry shortcake. Pour in sufficient sherry to thoroughly saturate the cake. If the one cup is not enough, add more! Now pour the custard over all the cake and let it seep down into the cracks and crannies. Cover top of the bowl with plastic wrap and refrigerate several hours or preferably overnight. The trifle can be served plain or decorated with fresh strawberries or raspberries and piped decoratively with whipped cream. Or, as servings are placed on individual plates, a melange of fresh fruits (peaches, strawberries, raspberries, apricots, grapes) can be served on the side. Serves 12.

On a wandering journey through Devon and Somerset in southern England, two nights in the Oakland Inn proved exceptional. In our huge, lavishly appointed bedroom, a brand new pink bathroom jutted out of one corner. There was a small problem, for if I filled the tub for a bath and brushed my teeth in the pink lavatory at the same time, the water ceased in the tub. The owner of this charming English inn with all its foibles doubled as bus boy, house boy and in the evening appeared dressed in a handsome velvet jacket to serve our dinner. The chef was superb and the rolling tray of desserts displayed such treasures that the young Englishman with us ate two each evening. I was intrigued with the chocolate trifle for this was indeed an innovation from the usual vanilla pudding. To my delight, I was given the recipe, not quite complete, but sufficiently so that I could reproduce this handsome dessert to my satisfaction.

OAKLAND'S CHOCOLATE TRIFLE WITH KIRSCH

THE CAKE

5 ounces bitter chocolate

4 eggs, separated

1 cup sugar

1 cup sifted all purpose flour

1 teaspoon baking powder

$\frac{1}{2}$ teaspoon salt

$\frac{1}{3}$ cup cold water

1 teaspoon vanilla flavoring

Preheat oven to 350°. Brush two 9-inch cake tins with soft butter.

Melt the chocolate in a double boiler and set aside. Beat the egg whites until softly peaked and gradually add ½ cup of the sugar. Set aside. Beat egg yolks and remaining sugar until light and creamy. Resift the flour with baking powder and salt. Into the egg mixture fold in the flour ingredients,

⅓ cup at a time, alternately with the cold water and vanilla flavoring and finally the melted chocolate. Gently fold in the beaten egg whites. Divide the batter between the two prepared cake tins spreading evenly. Bake in preheated oven 25 to 30 minutes. Remove cakes to wire racks for cooling.

ENGLISH CUSTARD CREAM

4 cups milk

1 3-inch piece vanilla bean or 2 teaspoons vanilla flavoring

8 egg yolks

1 cup sugar

2 teaspoons cornstarch (optional)

Heat the milk with vanilla bean in the top of a double boiler until a film forms on the milk. (If using vanilla flavoring, add later.) Beat the egg yolks in an electric mixer, gradually adding the sugar and optional cornstarch until light and creamy. Slowly add the hot milk beating with a wire whisk until well blended. Pour the mixture back into the double boiler, set over hot but not boiling water, and stir constantly with a wooden spoon until the custard thickens slightly and will coat the spoon. If the custard shows any tendency to curdle, it is cooking too fast. Lower heat and whisk until smooth. Strain the custard, reserving the vanilla bean for another dessert or, at this point, add the vanilla flavoring. Cool the custard in a bowl of ice water stirring now and then. Other flavorings that may be used in place of vanilla are 1 to 2 tablespoons of rum, brandy, kirsch or any of the orange liqueurs.

FINAL PREPARATION

6 ounces sugar (³⁄₄ cup plus 2 tablespoons)

³⁄₄ cups plus 2 tablespoons water

6-8 ounces black cherry jam

4 ounces kirsch

15 ounce tin black cherries

8 ounces grated bitter chocolate

1 cup whipping cream

CHOCOLATE CURLS

Prepare a sugar syrup with the 6 ounces of sugar and 7 ounces of water. Combine the two ingredients in a saucepan, bring to a boil and stir until the sugar is completely dissolved. Set aside to cool.

Split the two cakes. Spread the black cherry jam over the two portions and then sandwich the two cakes together. Slice the cake into thin fingers and lay in a trifle bowl or a large crystal compote. Sprinkle the cakes liberally with kirsch and the juice from the tin of cherries. The cake must be well soaked. Whisk the grated chocolate into the cooled syrup and pour over the sponge. Sprinkle with the cherries, leaving a few for decoration.

Cover all this glory with the custard. If there is custard left over, drink it with a bit of nutmeg sprinkled over the top. Cover the bowl with plastic wrap and refrigerate.

The trifle may be served without decoration but at the Oakland's it was lavishly beautiful. Whip one cup of heavy cream and spread a portion over the cake. Then pipe rosettes in a circle and one in the center.

Decorate with chocolate curls and a few whole, well drained cherries. This superb dessert will easily serve 10.

Josette Spehl is not only an elegant lady but a superb cook. From her home in Brussels, Belgium she has graciously described this delectable and classic dessert covered with an aromatic Pralin de Pattisier. The Belgians are masters of chocolate.

CHARLOTTE AUX LIQUEURS

PRALIN DE PATISSIER

$\frac{1}{2}$ cup finely ground almonds

$\frac{1}{2}$ cup granulated sugar

I egg white

The Charlotte:

$\frac{3}{4}$ cup sifted confectioner's sugar

$\frac{1}{2}$ cup butter

4 large eggs

$\frac{3}{4}$ cup finely ground almonds

$\frac{1}{4}$ cup milk

2 ounces cognac, curaçao or a favorite liqueur

Ladyfingers, about 6 ounces

In a heavy medium size skillet, combine the ½ cup ground almonds, ½ cup granulated sugar and the egg white. Over medium heat stir constantly with a wooden spoon until the mixture is dry and a light gold color. At first the ingredients will come together as a ball but slowly loosen and become dry, in about 15 to 20 minutes. The mixture may be stored in a covered jar and used to decorate various pastries or ice cream.

CHARLOTTE

Combine the confectioner's sugar and butter in an electric mixer bowl and beat to a fluffy butter cream. Add the 4 eggs one by one. Beat well after each addition until the mixture is smooth again. Add the ¾ cup of ground almonds. With a spatula stir in the milk and cognac. Mme. Spehl's husband loved to add 1 tablespoon of coffee and this, too, is quite delicious. When all the ingredients are well blended, prepare a 9-inch ring mold by coating with a vegetable spray. Pour a sufficient amount of the butter cream to cover bottom of the mold completely. Break the ladyfingers into ½ inch pieces. Cover the layer of butter cream with a layer of ladyfingers. Pour in the remaining butter cream and top completely with ladyfingers—this will be the bottom. Cover and store in refrigerator overnight. When ready to serve unmold the charlotte on a serving platter so that the first butter cream layer becomes the top of the cake. By running a sharp knife around the edge and inside tube of the mold and turning over on the platter, the charlotte will slip right out.

Decorate the top and sides with the Pralin de Pattisier by gently pressing on the molded charlotte. Crumbs will fall so sweep up with a pastry brush and either continue to press on the cake or store with the remaining Pralin in a closed jar. Refrigerate until ready to serve. Since the charlotte is quite rich, only small portions need be served. Add a colorful flower on the side or center and perhaps two or three succulent strawberries. The charlotte will serve 10 to 12.

An irresistibly magnificent dessert I have had the pleasure to teach many times and to serve as the finale of gala dinners. The recipe originated in Switzerland where I indulged in a small portion one afternoon in Geneva at the tea shop in the Richmond Hotel. The dessert is lined with a jelly roll similar to that made by my mother many years ago and then filled with a luscious Bavarian cream. This is my version of a dessert beautiful to behold, charming to eat and all prepared the day before a dinner party.

A RED RASPBERRY SWIRLING BAVARIAN

THE CAKE

Melted butter

3 egg yolks

3 eggs

³/₄ cup sugar

³/₄ cup sifted all purpose flour

3 egg whites

¹/₈ teaspoon cream of tartar

2 tablespoons sugar

Confectioner's sugar

10-ounce jar red raspberry jelly

Kirsch

THE BAVARIAN CREAM

2 cups milk

1 teaspoon vanilla flavoring

8 egg yolks

¹/₃ cup sugar

2 packages plain gelatin

¹/₄ cup kirsch

2 cups heavy cream

2 cups apricot jam, strained

Kirsch

2 packages (10 ounces each) frozen raspberries

2 tablespoons lemon juice or kirsch

Brush 2 cookie sheets (15x10 inches) with melted butter. Line the baking sheets with wax paper or parchment and brush again with butter. Set aside.

Place 2 large, soft tea cloths on a table and spread the center of each with confectioner's sugar — about the size of the baking sheets. Spread sugar with hands to be certain there are no lumps.

Preheat oven to 350°. Place the egg yolks and 3 eggs in a small bowl of an electric mixer. Beat until light and slowly add the sugar, beating constantly until mixture is tripled in volume. Transfer to a larger mixing bowl. Sift the flour over the batter three times, folding in each sifting with a rubber spatula. Beat the egg whites to soft peaks and add the cream of tartar and sugar gradually, beating constantly. Fold into the egg batter. Divide the batter between the baking sheets, spreading evenly. Bake in preheated oven about 12 minutes or until golden in color. If you are using only one oven, bake separately in center of oven. Turn the cakes out immediately on the powdered sugar, remove paper and discard. Allow cakes to cool completely.

Stir the jelly in a small bowl until smooth by adding a bit of kirsch; use a small whisk or fork. Spread the jelly over the two cakes with a brush or spatula. Allow cakes to sit 30 minutes. Roll one cake from the long side as tightly as possible. Turn the cake seam side down. Roll up in the cloth and press to tighten the roll. Repeat directions with second cake. The rolls may be refrigerated overnight making them easier to handle, or removed from the tea cloth, covered tightly with plastic wrap and frozen to use later.

Brush a 2-quart soufflé bowl with melted butter and chill in refrigerator. Remove tea cloths from the jelly rolls. With a sharp knife, cut in ¼ inch slices. Avoid squashing while slicing. Place 1 slice on bottom of soufflé dish and make a ring of slices around it, pressing together tightly. Cut 1 slice in tiny pieces to fill in gaps, for the bottom will ultimately become the top. Place 1 row of slices on the side pressing together tightly to sides of the bowl. Place a second row on top. By pressing together tightly the slices will adhere perfectly to the bowl. Fill in any gaps with pieces of jelly roll. The rows of jelly roll should come almost to the top of the bowl — if not cut several slices in half to finish the top. Cover with plastic wrap and refrigerate until the filling is ready.

The Bavarian Cream: Combine the milk and vanilla in a saucepan. Over moderate heat bring just to a boiling point, remove and set aside. Combine the egg yolks with the sugar in bowl of an electric mixer. Beat until light and pale yellow in color. Combine the gelatin with the ¼ cup of kirsch to soften. Slowly pour one cup of the warm milk into the egg yolk mixture. Transfer the yolk mixture into the saucepan or in a double boiler (the latter is best) with remaining cup of milk. Place on low heat and cook stirring constantly until mixture coats a spoon, about 10 to 12 minutes. If the mixture curdles, this means the heat is too high; whisk until smooth. Remove custard from burner and add the gelatin, stirring thoroughly until dissolved. Cool and place in refrigerator to thicken, setting timer for 15 minutes. Stir and set timer again. Continue in this fashion until the mixture thickens and mounds slightly on itself when stirred. Remove from refrigerator. Whip the cream until it forms soft peaks and add ½ cup of strained apricot jam. Fold the cream into the custard. Remove the prepared soufflé dish and pour in the Bavarian cream smoothing the top. Slice the remaining jelly roll and arrange on top of the custard. (Pieces do not have to be filled in here for this will be the bottom.) Cover with plastic wrap and place a plate on top with a weight—a small can of tomatoes is fine. Return to refrigerator to set at least a day or preferably overnight.

Presentation: Select a round serving plate; crystal or white china is lovely. Remove the Barvarian cream, unwrap and carefully loosen the sides of the cake with a thin knife. Place the serving dish on top and turn both over. Leave it alone! In less than 30 minutes, take a peek and by that time it will be loosened. Gently pull off the bowl. Add sufficient kirsch to the remaining jam so that it may be brushed over the complete dessert. Refrigerate until ready to serve. Whirl defrosted raspberries in a food processor and run through a sieve. Add lemon juice or kirsch. Serve a portion over each slice of Swirling Bavarian. An additional decoration: when fresh raspberries are available, make two rows of berries on top of the Bavarian cream in a circle. Serves 10 to 12.

A beautiful dessert that is a delight to the eye and most appealing to the appetite. A favorite of mine for many years to serve at dinner parties and in my classes. This is a dessert that may be brought to the table in a large tray with a cupped edge. Guests love watching with great anticipation as this dessert is served.

BRANDIED CHERRY MOUSSE

1 cup strong coffee

48 regular size marshmallows

2 cups heavy cream, whipped

2 cans dark sweet cherries (Bing cherries)

Juice from the cherries

3 ounces brandy

Prepare a decorative 2-quart ring mold by rinsing the mold in cold water. Shake out excess water and brush lightly with oil.

Heat the coffee in a saucepan and when bubbling add the marshmallows. Lower heat to a simmer and stir constantly until the marshmallows are melted and the mixture begins to set. Remove from burner and allow mixture to cool, stirring occasionally. When cooled, fold in the whipped cream until well blended. Turn into prepared ring mold and chill. Drain the liquid from the cherries. Transfer liquid to a saucepan and boil down to one-half its content. Place the cherries in a bowl and add the brandy. Cover and refrigerate overnight. Refrigerate the juice separately.

When ready to serve, combine the juice with the cherries. Unmold the mousse on a silver or crystal plate with a raised lip around the edge. To unmold: run a sharp knife around the edge of the mousse, place the selected plate over the mold and turn tray and mold over. The mousse should fall out easily, but if not, wet a cloth with warm water and hold on top of the mold two or three minutes. Pour the cherries and juice over the mousse. Serve from the table into crystal bowls. Serves 6 to 8.

Now there are as many recipes for chocolate mousse as there are for Italian minestrone. But the creation at the former Cellar Restaurant in Oklahoma City is simply superb. With the gracious consent of Frank Hightower, owner of the Cellar, I am delighted to present this magnificent dessert.

THE CELLAR'S CHOCOLATE MOUSSE

15 ounces German's sweet chocolate

¼ pound unsalted butter

1 cup sugar

⅔ cup corn syrup

¼ cup water

½ cup egg yolks

1 cup egg whites

1½ cups whipping cream

Chopped pistachio nuts, optional

Melt the chocolate and butter in the top of a double boiler over medium heat. Remove from burner and set aside to cool. In a saucepan, combine the sugar, corn syrup and water. Stir well and cook over high heat until the mixture spins a thread 8 inches long, (234 °). There should be ½ cup or more of syrup. Meanwhile beat the egg yolks in bowl of an electric mixer until thick and lemony. Slowly pour the hot syrup into the beaten egg yolks continuing to beat. Add the cooled, melted chocolate stirring until well mixed. Separately beat the egg whites to stiff peaks and fold into the chocolate mixture. Place in a stainless steel bowl, cover and refrigerate overnight. The chocolate mixture needs to be in a sturdy bowl for the beating it will receive the following day. The chocolate mixture will become quite stiff.

The next day whip one cup of the heavy cream until softly stiff. Add the whipped cream to the chocolate mixture and beat furiously until it becomes a fluffy creamy mass of chocolate. Place in a decorative bowl and garnish with the remaining ½ cup of cream, whipped to soft peaks. Garnish with pistachios if desired. Serves 10 to 12.

While spending several days in southern France close to the Basque country, we decided to drive across the border and have lunch in Pamplona, the city noted for the running of the bulls. The tiny customs house was vacant and dilapidated so we drove on through rough hills occasionally dotted with fascinating conical haystacks. The road was narrow and lonely and we met no one until we reached the outskirts of Pamplona, a magnificent city. To our delight we did have Spanish custard that should be considered a national treasure. Spanish flan is served over the world in various innovative forms. This Spanish custard is a delicate fusion with a lovely sherry that is light, elegant and most appropriate following a rather heavy dinner. Do choose a fine dry sherry for an exquisite flavor.

SPANISH CUSTARD

9 egg yolks

1 cup sugar

9 tablespoons all purpose flour

7 cups hot milk

3 tablespoons dry sherry

Grated rind of 1 large lemon

1 teaspoon vanilla flavoring

8 tablespoons melted butter

1 cup graham crackers

Sifted confectioner's sugar

Dry sherry

In the top of a double boiler beat the egg yolks with an electric mixer until light and fluffy and lemon colored. (Freeze the egg whites to use later for angel food cake) If preferred the beating may be done in a separate bowl and then transferred to the double boiler. Blend the flour and sugar together. Gradually add the flour mixture to the egg yolks beating constantly. Blend in the milk slowly, stirring until smooth with a wooden spoon. Add the 3 tablespoons of sherry, lemon rind and vanilla flavoring. Place over simmering water and cook, stirring constantly until the mixture thickens and coats the spoon. Stir in 3 tablespoons of the butter. Remove from hot water and set aside to cool. Spoon the custard into sherbet dishes, cover each with plastic wrap and refrigerate. This preparation may be done the day before a dinner.

Crush the graham crackers with a rolling pin, place in a bowl and blend in the remaining butter with a fork until well mixed and crumbly. Remove custards from refrigerator and discard the plastic wrap. Place each sherbet dish on a dessert plate. Top each custard with 1-2 tablespoons of buttered crumbs, a sprinkling of confectioner's sugar and add to each 1 tablespoon of sherry. Serve immediately. The recipe will make 12 servings.

Never shall I forget a luncheon with J. Paul Getty in his castle at Guildford, England. The dining table, 75 feet long, was decorated with huge bouquets of mixed flowers in exquisite vases with each chair an antique (and mine not too steady). The perfect butler, dressed in tails and stiff shirt, and whose face never changed expression, was in complete charge. Three courses were offered: a ramekin with baked eggs topped with slivers of ham, the main entree of Beef Wellington cooked to perfection in the lightest of puff pastries, and finally a lovely plate with arranged mixed fruits napped with a custard sauce Before I could stop him, the butler poured thick cream over the whole plate of fruits! I did try to stop him because by that time I was saturated with excellent food and superb wines. Small silver bowls on the table were filled with exotic fresh fruits. (The month, October.)

Through all this Mr. Getty ate an entirely different meal. I had been told he ate only one meal a day and watching I realized breakfast, lunch and dinner were served at one sitting for a half grapefruit came first, then shredded wheat with milk, followed by a pureed green vegetable and some sort of meat. He ate no dessert but enjoyed several of the fresh fruits offered. I relished every bite and listened to the conversation as Gene and Mr. Getty talked, reliving their shared experience during World War II, running Spartan Aircraft factory in Tulsa.

Children delight in drinking custard sauce and adults love it on cake and fresh fruits. Never freeze a custard. The sauce keeps well refrigerated three to four days.

AN ENGLISH CUSTARD SAUCE

2 cups milk

4 egg yolks

1/2 teaspoon salt

4 tablespoons sugar

1 teaspoon vanilla flavoring

Scald the milk in the top of a double boiler. Beat the egg yolks, salt and sugar in the small bowl of an electric mixer until thoroughly blended.

Add the hot milk slowly to the egg mixture continuing to stir slowly. Return to the double boiler and cook over boiling water, stirring with a wooden spoon until thickened and the custard coats the spoon.

Have patience, for a custard must not cook too fast or it will curdle. If this does happen, whisk the custard briskly. The recipe may be doubled.

A succulent dessert particularly adaptable for a spectacular dinner on a cold winter's night. The aroma of the bananas baking in red wine and other luscious ingredients and then carried to the table flaming will excite your guests and family.

FLAMING BANANAS

6 large ripe bananas

Fresh lemon juice

1/4 - 1/2 cup butter

1 cup dry red wine

1 cup brown sugar

½ teaspoon cinnamon

½ teaspoon nutmeg

¼ teaspoon cloves

Grated rind of 1 large orange

1 cup crushed macaroons

1 cup slivered, blanched almonds

3 tablespoons dark rum

Peel the bananas and split lengthwise, then cut each across once. Brush with the lemon juice. Melt the butter in a skillet and sauté the bananas lightly adding more butter if needed. Do not allow to brown or burn. Arrange the bananas in a single layer in a shallow buttered baking dish.

Preheat oven to 350°. Combine the wine, brown sugar, spices and orange rind in a saucepan. Bring to a boil and let bubble rapidly 5 minutes. Pour the wine syrup over the bananas. Combine the macaroons and almonds. Sprinkle this mixture atop the bananas. Place in preheated oven. Heat until bubbling and the nuts and macaroons are just beginning to brown. Remove from the oven. The baking can be accomplished during the dinner hour and then the dessert served piping hot. Or it can be baked earlier and served warm. Heat the dark rum in a small container, pour over the top of the dessert, set aflame, turn out the lights and carry to the table in blazing brilliance. Serves 8 to 10.

My husband avoided cooking, at my request, but he adored standing at the head of the dining table carving turkey, prime roast of beef, a crown roast of lamb—nothing phased him. But he could prepare one dessert, Bananas Foster, and here he was in his element, spooning hot syrup over the fruit and then flaming the ingredients. We went through a phase of Cherries Jubilee but fell in love with Bananas Foster after many trips to New Orleans. There, years ago, a waiter wrote the recipe for me on a postal card.

BANANAS FOSTER

6 bananas

Lemon juice

½ cup butter

1 cup brown sugar

4 tablespoons banana liqueur

Cinnamon

4 ounces rum

Vanilla ice cream

All ingredients must be prepared and at hand beside the chafing dish in front of the cook. Also needed are large sherbet dishes or compotes, a large dish ready to hold the ice cream and a spoon. Peel the bananas and cut in half lengthwise. Brush with lemon juice and place on a plate. To the chafing pan add the butter to melt and then the brown sugar, stirring until it, too, is melted. Slip the bananas into the sugar mixture and allow to cook until just beginning to soften. Pour the banana liqueur over the fruit and sprinkle with cinnamon. Have the rum slightly warm and flame over the bananas shaking the pan to mix well and keep the flame going. The ice cream should be dipped and waiting in dessert dishes (my part!) and then spoon the bananas and syrup over the ice cream. Serve immediately. Serves 6 to 8.

I really wanted to bestow a fancy name for this dessert but it is truly a light pudding that separates, creating a small layer of cake at the bottom. Each time I prepared this delectable pudding and carefully stored the bowl with contents in the refrigerator to await dinner, some mysterious invader dipped a huge spoonful right out of the center. The "invader" might as well have placed a sign, "Michael was here!" Obviously, this has been a favorite dessert for my three sons.

LEMON PUDDING

3 teaspoons butter

2 tablespoons flour

¾ cup sugar

¼ teaspoon salt

1 cup milk

2 tablespoons fresh lemon juice

2 egg yolks

2 egg whites

Preheat oven to 350°.

Combine the butter, flour, sugar and salt in a large bowl of an electric mixer. Cream these ingredients until thoroughly mixed. Add the milk, lemon juice and egg yolks, blending well. In a separate bowl, beat the egg whites until softly stiff. Fold into the lemon-butter mixture. Pour into a one-quart casserole. Bake in preheated oven until the custard is set, about 35 to 40 minutes. Test with a silver knife and when it emerges clean, the pudding is finished. One recipe fed our family of five with nothing left. The recipe doubles easily.

A family recipe from Janet Loring, my nephew's wife, who related that each time her mother produced this little masterpiece, the children all gave sighs of happiness. Not cluttered by eggs or cream, the blancmange gives the appearance of a lovely shimmering dark "jello." Dramatically white whipped cream may be added to the center giving a startling picture of contrast. Whole fresh strawberries dipped in chocolate is an additional ornament that I have suggested. Often such strawberries can be purchased in fine markets.

CHOCOLATE BLANCMANGE

3 $\frac{1}{2}$ cups milk plus $\frac{1}{2}$ cup

1 cup sugar

3 squares bitter chocolate

2 envelopes plain gelatin

1 tablespoon vanilla flavoring

1 cup heavy cream, whipped and sweetened

Whole fresh strawberries, dipped in chocolate

Prepare a 2-quart round mold by spraying lightly with a vegetable spray wiping any excess off with paper toweling.

In a large saucepan combine the 3½ cups milk, sugar and chocolate. Place over a medium burner until the chocolate is melted, stirring frequently. Dissolve the gelatin in the ½ cup of milk, stirring with a fork to combine. When the chocolate is melted, add the gelatin. Beat with an electric mixer until the mixture is smooth and looks like chocolate milk. If you do not have a hand mixer, place the saucepan on the stand of an electric mixer. Add the vanilla flavoring. Pour into the prepared mold and refrigerate for at least 4 hours or until set. Unmold on a round white serving plate. Fill the center with the sweetened whipped cream (Please do not use the fake canned variety for it soon weeps and sags.) with strawberries on the side. Serves 8 unless the children get into the dessert first.

At times in my travels yogurt has been a welcome mainstay. On my first journey into the Middle East I was not certain about foods but I soon found that wherever we traveled, into the Bekaa Valley, Amman, Jordan, Cairo, up the Nile River and even in our hotel in Beirut, yogurt was always available. I knew how yogurt was made and that it would be safe, for the milk is brought to the boiling point. Besides, I found people in the Middle East made superb yogurt — not any of these commercial boxes with gelatin and fruit, just wonderfully flavorful yogurt. Many wonderful things can be done with yogurt. For example — going on a picnic! Prepare this simple yogurt dessert with green grapes, place in a fruit jar and tuck into an ice chest. With a sack of favorite cookies, dessert is ready. The quantities given are minimum but from this basic recipe increase to any amount needed.

A QUICK YOGURT DESSERT

$^1/_2$ cup plain yogurt

$^1/_2$ cup green grapes

1 tablespoon Galliano, Crème de cacao, kirsch or Grand Marnier

Combine all ingredients, stir well and place in a bowl, jar or container that can be covered. Refrigerate until ready to serve. I have given suggestions for several liqueurs but try any favorite. Be certain the yogurt purchased is plain with neither sugar nor vanilla flavoring added.

SUMMER FRUIT DESSERT

When all the delectable berries from Oregon, California, and Michigan and local fruit arrive in the summer months, try combining several and top with a raspberry sauce — light and seductive to the last bite.

10-ounce box frozen raspberries, sweetened

2 tablespoons kirsch

4 cups mixed fruits: blueberries, raspberries, strawberries, peaches, blackberries

4 tablespoons kirsch

Light sprinkling of sugar

Plain yogurt, optional

Defrost the raspberries and whirl in a food processor fitted with the steel blade. Let drain through a strainer to eliminate the seeds. Add the 2 table-spoons of Kirsch and transfer to a jar with a lid and refrigerate. In a mixing bowl combine choice of fruits and add the 4 tablespoons of Kirsch and a light sprinkling of sugar. Stir to mix lightly. Refrigerate until chilled. Spoon the mixed fruit into stemmed sherbet compotes and pour raspberry sauce over each. This amount will serve four generously. An optional embellish-ment: add about ½ cup plain yogurt in the bottom of each compote. Top with the berries and then the raspberry sauce. I assure you it is all as deli-cious as ice cream. A favorite cookie could be added on the side. Serves 6.

FRESH FRUIT WITH LEMON AND SHERRY

Glorious and simple in the summer but most adaptable for winter using frozen fruits with available fresh fruits. I've made this in large quantities so frequently that I shall give measurements for serving 25 people. This big bowl of fresh fruits became a favorite with teenagers during the days of our houseboat, the Queen Mary.

> 6 quarts of fresh fruit
>
> Juice of 2 lemons
>
> An equal amount of dry sherry
>
> 4 tablespoons sugar, optional

Prepare any of the following fruits: peaches, apricots, plums, orange sec-tions (or Mandarin oranges), strawberries, blueberries, apples, pears and an assortment of melons such as cantaloupe, casaba, crenshaw, Christmas, Persian, Maya and honeydew. Avoid watermelon and bananas. Cut the fruits in large bite-size pieces and place in a large glass or ceramic bowl. Combine the lemon juice and sherry with optional sugar, stirring well. Pour over the fruits and stir carefully — preferably with your hands. Cover the bowl with plastic wrap and chill. All this may be prepared and refrigerated overnight. To enhance the beauty with a glass bowl, peel and slice kiwi fruit and simply adhere to the inside of the bowl at the top. The texture of the kiwi makes a perfect glue easily sticking to the glass—lovely for a buffet brunch.

The recipe can easily be cut in half for a small group or enlarged to any amount desired. Use plenty of the suggested melons for they make up the body of this dish which can be used as a dessert, salad or for a brunch.

BAKED RHUBARB WITH STRAWBERRIES

3 cups cleaned, sliced rhubarb

1 cup sliced strawberries

Blueberries, optional

2 teaspoons lemon juice

1 1/2 cups sugar

Preheat oven to 325°. Arrange prepared rhubarb in a buttered baking dish. Top with the strawberries and a few blueberries, if desired. Sprinkle with the lemon juice and then the sugar. Cover and bake about 30 minutes or until tender, hot and bubbling. Excellent served hot with plain yogurt. Serves 6.

CANTALOUPE WITH FRESH FRUIT

During the summer and fall when cantaloupe is best, try my idea for either a first course at a seated brunch or a light summer and fall dessert. Slice a cantaloupe in half the long way. Cut off a small portion on the bottom of each half so that the melon will stay level. Choose a melange of fruits such as a variety of grapes, strawberries, raspberries, blackberries, peaches, plums and apricots. Slice the larger fruits in small pieces and fill each half of the cantaloupe. This, of course, can be accomplished with as many melons as you wish. For a brunch, just sprinkle the mixed fruits with lemon juice. But for a dessert, add a wine to cover the fruit, red, pink or even a port. Cover with plastic wrap and refrigerate until time to serve the dessert. This is most refreshing before or after a heavy meal. In ancient Rome the name for peach was persica, for the first to be shipped to the Romans came from Persia. The true origin is China so for centuries, peaches, their seeds and the trees have traveled over the world. Never shall I forget the movie, The Good Earth, when the Chinese bridegroom stalked home munching a peach. When he finished, the pit was tossed aside. His small bride following behind carefully picked it up and upon arrival in her new home planted the seed. When peaches must be shipped, they are never picked fully ripe. In choosing a peach, check that there are no bruises and no juice oozing from any portion. If the peaches are hard, leave them in a paper sack until they just begin to ripen and then place on a counter to finish. Any that are fully ripe should be eaten or refrigerated.

POACHED FRESH PEACHES

In August when freestone peaches are in abundance and fresh red raspberries are available, prepare and relish this sublime desert.

1 ½ cups sugar

4 cups water

½ vanilla bean

2 slivers lemon zest ½ inches wide

8 medium freestone ripe peaches

3 tablespoons brandy

2 cups fresh red raspberries

Sugar

3 tablespoons kirsch

Combine the 1½ cups of sugar and water in a large saucepan. Bring to a boil, stirring until the sugar has dissolved. Add the vanilla bean and lemon peel — there must be no white pith on the peel. Simmer gently 5 minutes. Place the peaches in a large pan and cover with boiling water. Allow to sit ½ minute. Remove the peaches with a slotted spoon to a colander and slip off the skins. Cut in half and discard the seeds. Add peaches to the sugar mixture and simmer gently until peaches are tender, about 15 minutes. Turn the fruit over once during the cooking period. Remove from the burner and add the brandy; allow to cool. Wash the raspberries, drain and place in a small bowl. Sprinkle lightly with sugar and measure in the kirsch. Gently stir the berries with a wooden spoon. Cover with plastic wrap and refrigerate.

Presentation: According to the number of guests and the size of peaches, place one or two in a glass dessert bowl and top with raspberries. Repeat with remaining fruit. The dessert is lovely as described but if a topping is preferred use whipped cream with a touch of kirsch, vanilla ice cream or a custard sauce flavored with brandy. Serves 4 to 8.

Odds and Ends Or Facts About Foods

Oranges and their juice are a major source of Vitamin C in our American diet. The following contain at least as much C as an orange: one cup of strawberries, one sweet green pepper — red peppers possess even more — one kiwi fruit or one cup of cooked broccoli, cauliflower or brussel sprouts.

Plain yogurt may be used in place of sour cream, mayonnaise or a commercial dressing on baked potatoes, fruits, salads and in dips and tuna salad. If the flavor of mayonnaise is important, use half mayonnaise and half plain yogurt. Dripped yogurt (labne) can be used instead of cream cheese in cheese cake and in place of sour cream in cakes. Blend plain yogurt with fruit or juice to create a "smoothie" and try the Lebanese way of marinating chicken in yogurt before grilling.

Don't worry about indulging in sweet potatoes for they contain no more calories than white potatoes. Try a baked sweet potato just plain, very moist, or with a little butter, sweet and delicious, and supplying more potassium than a banana.

About nuts: Remember that cholesterol is found only in animal products. Nuts do contain fat with lots of protein but no cholesterol. The difficulty is that a handful of roasted peanuts contain as many calories as a piece of cake. Buy unsalted and non-roasted mixed nuts from a health food store or specialty shops. Roast in a 325° oven until just beginning to turn a golden color. Remove and serve unsalted—absolutely marvelous when warm.

Add nuts to your diet by combining with salads, in breads and pilafs. Some are wonderful with meats. When fresh chestnuts arrive, indulge, for they have fewer calories and less fat than other nuts. Buy a chestnut roaster and have fun on winter evenings when the fireplace is aglow or roast them in a 350° oven. Be certain to slice a slit in the end of each chestnut or they just might blow up!

Almonds contain as much calcium in one ounce as ¼ cup of milk.

Peanuts are actually a legume, not a nut. They impart wonderful nutrition to the soil in which they are grown, but sadly, that does not remove any of the fat.

Although fresh vegetables are preferred there has been much improvement in canning and freezing. With the latter, the vitamin content and other nutrients are still there for they are prepared immediately after harvesting. Microwaving vegetables quickly retains more vitamins than other cooking methods. To improve canned vegetables, place in a sieve and run cool water over to remove any excess salt. Never cook either the canned or frozen vegetables too long for more nutrients will be lost. When using canned, just bring to a boil, remove from burner and serve topped with butter or margarine. Sometimes the addition of dried herbs will improve the flavor.

CHOOSING AND BAKING BANANAS

When choosing bananas, what you see is what you get. A yellow banana with green tip is perfect for baking. An all yellow banana is ripe and ready to eat. As brown spots appear but the banana is firm, most of the starch has turned to sugar. The riper the banana, the sweeter. As long as the banana is firm, even though covered with brown spots, it will be good. When they become a bit soft, make muffins or bread. Don't worry about buying a green banana for they ripen fast. Avoid any that are quite soft and squishy.

> Baking in the Skin: This happens to be a favorite of ours. We have baked bananas occasionally instead of baked potatoes for they are a great accompaniment for grilled meats. For successful baking, the banana must have green ends. Choose bananas that have green tips; too ripe and they will split badly and much is lost. Brush the banana with oil (just as with a potato) and place on a baking sheet. Bake in a preheated 350° oven until the skin turns black, about 25 minutes. Sometimes the skin will split even though of the correct ripeness but only a few juices will run out which is no need for concern. Scoop the banana up with a spatula and place on a plate; they should be served immediately. Provide a sharp steak knife to cut the skin at one end and roll a section of the skin back. Then, dip in with a fork and enjoy the sweet and succulent fruit. Delightful, for neither butter nor sugar are necessary.

BUTTER WITH CANOLA OIL

A little boon for those concerned about cholesterol and calories and would love just a little flavor of butter on favorite foods. Place ¼ pound of butter in the small bowl of an electric mixer and allow to soften slightly. Begin beating and slowly add 6 ounces of canola Oil. Continue beating until the oil is well incorporated into the butter. The mixture will be quite liquid. Pour into a ramekin or attractive bowl and refrigerate until solid. Cover with plastic wrap. This combination of oil and butter will always be soft so it does spread easily over toast, hot rolls, biscuits and is excellent for flavoring of vegetables.

BLENDER HOLLANDAISE SAUCE

Several years ago a most elegant dinner given by a musical group in my home faced an emergency—someone had ruined the béarnaise sauce. I rushed to my files, extracted my recipe for Blender Hollandaise, and within minutes had a substitute sauce ready to serve.

1 cup unsalted butter

6 egg yolks

1/4 cup fresh lemon juice

1/4 teaspoon cayenne pepper

Heat the butter to boiling in a saucepan. Remove from the burner and let rest 5 minutes. Place the egg yolks, lemon juice and pepper in a blender or a food processor equipped with steel blade. With blender at high speed slowly pour in the butter. When finished, blend for 30 seconds or until thick. Transfer to the top of a double boiler and place over hot water (not boiling, for that was the problem in the first place) until ready to serve. Makes about 1½ cups.

MISSISSIPPI BARBECUE SAUCE

1/4 pound butter

1 medium onion, peeled and thinly sliced

1 large lemon cut in thin slices

1/3 cup white vinegar

1/2 cup water

1 tablespoon mustard

Worcestershire sauce to taste

1/2 cup ketchup

Combine the butter, onion, lemon, vinegar and water in a saucepan. Place on a moderate burner, stir well and simmer 20 minutes. Add the mustard, Worcestershire sauce to taste (one or two tablespoons), and the ketchup. Stir very well. Brush over chicken or pork ribs to be grilled outside. The recipe may easily be doubled. The amount given will be sufficient for 2 chickens, split or quartered.

FLAMBÉING

Warm choice of spirits in a small pan; do not allow to boil, only to warm, or all the alcohol will evaporate. Hold the saucepan over the food to be flamed and touch a lighted match to the fumes that arise pouring the flaming liquor over the contents, shaking the pan as it flames. Or pour a small amount of the warm liquor in a large spoon and touch with a lighted match pouring over the food with the remaining liquor. Shake the pan until the flame subsides. In either case, stand back, do not lean over to see if it is starting. Singed eyebrows will be the result! All this is completely safe when such precautions are observed. For a dramatic dessert in a chafing dish, spoon the brightly blazing sauce over the food and simultaneously shake the pan. Be certain to turn out the lights. Guests love the show.

ITALIAN PESTO

In the summer when the basil grows high, prepare pesto and freeze in refrigerator tray for winter. I keep several trays, well covered, and extract a cube or two for soup or to toss with pasta.

> 2 cups fresh basil, packed
> 1/4 cup fresh parsley, packed
> 3 cloves garlic, peeled and sliced
> 3 tablespoons pine nuts
> 1/2 cup olive oil, approximately
> 1/2 cup Parmesan cheese, freshly grated
> Grindings of black pepper

Combine the basil, parsley, garlic, pine nuts and 2 tablespoons of the oil in a food processor fitted with the steel blade. Process 1 minute, stop and scrape down the sides. Begin pulsing again and slowly add sufficient oil until the mixture is the consistency of mayonnaise. Add the Parmesan cheese and pepper. Scrape down the sides again and taste for seasoning. Whirl several seconds. Transfer to ice cube trays, cover well, label and freeze. When defrosting, if the pesto seems dry or stiff, add a small amount of warm water and beat until well mixed. The pesto, though, is ready to use immediately after preparation. Try boiling spaghetti for the family, serve in separate large salad plates and top each with two heaping tablespoons of fresh pesto—absolutely sublime!

MAYONNAISE IN A FOOD PROCESSOR

> 2 cups olive oil
> 4 tablespoons lemon juice
> 2 teaspoons Dijon mustard
> 2 large eggs
> Salt, if desired

In a food processor fitted with steel blade, combine 1/4 cup of the oil, lemon juice, mustard and eggs. Pulse several times to mix well. Continue pulsing and slowly pour in the oil. When all the oil has been added, continue to whirl for about 20 seconds until the mixture is the consistency desired for a good mayonnaise.

Note: A very satisfactory mayonnaise can be made with the same ingredients but substituting ½ cup of an egg substitute such as Egg Beater. The result will be quite thick but eliminates the cholesterol.

Epilogue

....

As this book goes to press, my eldest son, Nick, will be climbing Mt. McKinley. Peter and his wife, Annie have just returned from Eastern Europe and then Peter is off to Rome, Jerusalem, Jordan and the United Emirates and Michael is roaming the state of Colorado with his family. My eldest grandson, Charles, is working on his doctorate in Cambridge, England delving into RNA. Steve, the second grandson, is attending a six-weeks physics seminar in Chaminoix, France and will be joined by his brother, Charles, to enjoy technical ice climbing, then both will fly to Cambridge with Steven studying pure mathematics for a year before returning to Princeton to pursue his doctorate in theoretical physics. Sasha, my eldest granddaughter, is finishing her Senior year at Johns Hopkins and will then enter medical school but at present is enjoying a concentrated four-week Spanish course in Oaxaca, Mexico. Christi, number two granddaughter, flew to Nepal for an extended stay to absorb the culture of this mountainous country, then to India and ultimately to Kenya to teach and finally to Montana for an environmental study before entering the University of Pennsylvania. Heather, my youngest granddaughter, is absorbed in an independent study on nutrition, teaching fine needlepoint and taking an airbrush art class. John, an eighth grader, is strong on body development hopefully for football, and loves all the family menagerie of two dogs, tropical fish, a huge iguana, tropical birds, gold fish, toads and snails and such. Both have made many interesting trips and love trying exotic foods. Not long ago, I enjoyed a Smithsonian South American journey through the Magellan Straits, around Cape Horn, into the Pacific and finally to Santiago, Chile. Later I joined a group to tour Portugal, Tangiers, Morocco and southern Spain. Surely we shall all have exciting culinary and traveling adventures.

Index